INTELLECTUALS
AND POLITICS

KEY ISSUES IN SOCIOLOGICAL THEORY

Series Editors
JEFFREY C. ALEXANDER, *University of California, Los Angeles*
& **JONATHAN H. TURNER**, *University of California, Riverside*

This series of annual publications is designed to crystallize key issues in contemporary theoretical debate. Each year, the chair of the Theory Section of the American Sociological Association has the authority to organize a "conference within a conference" at the annual meeting. The intention is to provide a forum for intensive public discussion of an issue that has assumed overriding theoretical importance. After the miniconference, the chair assumes the role of volume editor and, subject to final approval by the series editors, prepares a volume based on the reworked conference papers.

We hope that this periodic focusing of theoretical energy will strengthen the "disciplinary matrix" upon which theoretical progress in every science depends. Theoretical consensus may be impossible, but disciplinary integration is not. Only if a solid infrastructure is provided can communication among different orientations be carried out in the kind of ongoing, continuous way that is so necessary for mutual understanding and scientifically constructive criticism.

Volumes in this series:

1. **Neofunctionalism**
   edited by *Jeffrey C. Alexander*

2. **The Marx-Weber Debate**
   edited by *Norbert Wiley*

3. **Theory Building in Sociology:**
   Assessing Theoretical Cumulation
   edited by *Jonathan H. Turner*

4. **Feminism and Sociological Theory**
   edited by *Ruth A. Wallace*

5. **Intellectuals and Politics:**
   Social Theory in a Changing World
   edited by *Charles C. Lemert*

INTELLECTUALS AND POLITICS

Social Theory in a Changing World

Edited by

CHARLES C. LEMERT

5

KEY ISSUES IN SOCIOLOGICAL THEORY

Series Editors: Jeffery C. Alexander,
University of California, Los Angeles
Jonathan H. Turner,
University of California, Riverside

SAGE PUBLICATIONS
The International Professional Publishers
Newbury Park   London   New Delhi

For information address:

SAGE Publications, Inc.
2455 Teller Road
Newbury Park, California 91320

SAGE Publications Ltd.
6 Bonhill Street
London EC2A 4PU
United Kingdom

SAGE Publications India Pvt. Ltd.
M-32 Market
Greater Kailash I
New Delhi 110 048 India

Printed in the United States of America

Library of Congress Cataloging-in-Publication Data

Intellectuals and politics : social theory in a changing world /
    edited by Charles Lemert.
        p. cm. — (Key issues in sociological theory ; 5)
    Most of the essays were originally presented at a colloquium
sponsored by the Theory Section of the American Sociological
Association in San Francisco on Aug. 13, 1989.
    ISBN 0-8039-3731-8 (c). — ISBN 0-8039-3732-6 (p)
    1. Intellectuals—Political activity—Congresses.
2. Intellectuals—Attitudes—Congresses. 3. Political culture-
-Congresses. 4. Political sociology—Congresses. I. Lemert,
Charles C. II. American Sociological Association. Theory Section.
III. Series.
HM213.I5455   1990
306.2—dc20   90-21368
                                                            CIP

FIRST PRINTING, 1991

Sage Production Editor: Judith L. Hunter

CONTENTS

INTRODUCTION

CHARLES C. LEMERT
Wesleyan University

MANY SUPPOSE THAT the world has changed. This supposition, so alluring today, is not without its troubles. If the world is changed, then in what does the change consist?

One would imagine, upon reading the news from East Central Europe, that the change of deepest moment is the collapse of the post-World War II political order. But Timothy Garton Ash observes that the demands of Civic Forum for a new Czechoslovakia founded upon an independent judiciary, free elections, a market economy, and the like boil down to little more than the dream of a "normal country in the center of Europe" (*The New York Review of Books,* January 18, 1990, p. 46). Dreams of normality fashioned out of the daily residue of the West's unfinished business are common to struggles throughout East Central Europe, as they are in the Baltic, Central America, and Asia. If, in the same spirit, revolutionary students in China take the Statue of Liberty as their emblem, we cannot, then, draw easy inference from these appearances of world change. The chapters by Craig Calhoun and Michael Kennedy in this volume explain the complicated but direct effect of very traditional Western values on revolutionary thinking in both China and Eastern Europe.

In the same report on Czechoslovakia, Ash reminds us that the 1988 protests against the riot police were memorable for the defiant chant, "The world sees you." One suspects there is truth in this observation. Chinese students in the United States faxing up-to-the-minute news of events in Tiananmen Square *back* into China in June 1989; many hundreds of international observers in Nicaragua on election night, among them Jimmy Carter; the international celebrity status of Lech Walesa, Nelson Mandela, Vàclav Havel—all these, and others, are signs of a worldly gaze of vast scope and acutely focused moral purpose. Yet, Martin Jay's discussion, in this volume, of the all too natural association of visual metaphors with modernizing political domination is fair caution against a naive reappropriation of the global village as explanation for world revolution.

It seems, therefore, improbable that what might yet be changed in the world is either its objective structures or its technical capability to project moral forces across national boundaries. Rather, if there is change of world magnitude, it is more likely an upheaval, deep and wide, in how people *think* the world.

It is, after all, very difficult today to possess a settled conviction about the state of world politics. Political opinions, even those voiced with conviction, seem less able to enforce, or even to hold, position against the resistance they encounter. At the moment, in the early 1990s, Presidents Gorbachev and Bush are apt metaphors for the state of thinking about the world. Inheritors both of world power, neither seems quite certain what to say about the events unfolding before him. Each resorts impulsively to threat of invasion, and its execution, in Lithuania and Panama. Yet, neither is able to put a persuasive spin on these moves. The surer voices are the calmer—those of Vàclav Havel, Lech Walesa, Fang Lizhi, Vytautis Landsbergis, Nelson Mandela. They are, perhaps, more certain to the degree they have done their thinking in local jails or otherwise under threat.

Though we cannot yet know the effects of a nationalist urge on these expressions of just but local concerns, one can consider this to be the change in the world: Those with global power deploy their authority in the absence of compelling ideas; while those with limited, or no, real authority revise grand, enlightenment ideas for the humblest of purposes—independent judiciaries, market economies, free elections. When these staples of democratic political theory are announced in sane, well-measured tones, one finds them shocking perhaps by virtue of being clean of the menaces by which in the late nineteenth and twentieth centuries they were used to justify the worst sorts of global ambition. Jeffrey Alexander's defense and elaboration of democratic ideas, and George Ross's description of the shift, in France, from grand and global ideas to a milder, familiar liberalism may be signs of the times. Normal uses of simple ideas may, at the moment, be exceptional. Normality arising from a shift in the balance of power between power itself and knowledge may not be so terrible after all.

Readers of this volume will have the advantage of seeing more clearly the shaped meanings of events of the moment. Yet, the authors contributing to this book's open-ended discussion of politics and intellectuals are well within their rights to frame their thoughts with current politics in near or, at least, shadowy background. Though each is an accomplished academic thinker, none is exception to the rule of contemporary social theory that its writers are, one or another way, influenced by the politics of the 1960s generation. All were at least close observers or, at near or remote engagement, actors in the political events to which they refer in their theories of intellectuals and ideas.

Dick Flacks and Ivan Szelenyi possess assured, and well-known, places in the recent histories of American and Hungarian politics, respectively. Roslyn Wallach Bologh, as her chapter makes clear, is one of numerous feminists who consider their academic and scholarly work in the last generation necessarily political. Alex Dupuy is both at home in the Caribbean region he analyzes and, today, thoroughly familiar with the struggles of those African American academics who, like feminists and others, must consider the university a political field. George Ross lived and worked in Paris close to the political left he discusses. Craig Calhoun was in Tiananmen Square as events unfolded in June 1989, and Michael Kennedy was frequently in Poland during the rise of Solidarity to power. Martin Jay's role in the interpretation and critique of critical theory and other politically intended traditions of social theory has made him a major voice in the politics of theory. No less, Jeffrey Alexander's sustained revision in numerous writings of the traditions of sociological theory owes no small debt to a personal commitment, shared by many others, to reconsider sociology in light of his experiences as a student radical in the late 1960s.

If it turns out to be true that what is changed about the world is how we think the world, then it is reasonable to believe that those contributing to this volume, and many like them, may no longer be considered "mere" intellectuals. I would not wish to press this point to extremes. Alex Dupuy's compelling demonstration of just how narrow the vision of First World intellectuals can be and Ivan Szelenyi's personal confession of the extreme difficulty even a participant has in predicting outcomes are sufficient cause for restraint. Yet, restraint can be its own excess.

There is warrant enough to consider the proposition that very real political events occurring from Wenceslas to Tiananmen squares bear some direct and important relation to changes in the last generation in social theories of the world by, even, academic intellectuals. Social theories are necessarily shaped by the experiences of theorists, most especially the experiences of their youth. The experience common to authors of social theory today is the politics of the 1960s, however refractory or to some (like Allan Bloom) repulsive those experiences were. Think simply of the vocabulary one must now learn— "decentering," "emancipation," "power/knowledge," "fractured identities," "deconstruction," "Afrocentrism," "difference," "the Other," and so on. Whatever one thinks of the terms and the ideas, it would be strange to ignore their affinity to a political history since the early 1960s in which the world has indeed been decentered first in Africa, then in Asia, then in the Europes and the Americas. It is indisputably a world in which difference and otherness, more than merely intellectual notions, are the daily experience of peoples no longer so deeply intimidated by old men in Beijing, Washington, and Moscow.

What is it about intellectuals themselves that they so often doubt that, between ideas and politics, causation can move in both directions? To be sure, social theorists have always recognized and defended the role of intellectuals in history. But it is surprising that, during a time in world history when ideas seem to be making a difference, academic intellectuals remain cautious. Even granting that skepticism is our proper professional attitude, one cannot help but wonder why academic intellectuals in the United States are reluctant to entertain the idea that the world is changing because thinking is changing. There is, even among those specifically invited to pose bold thoughts, a degree of tentativeness, or outright skepticism, in many of the chapters in this volume. There may be a good, if insufficient, historical reason.

Most of the chapters here were originally presented in a colloquium sponsored by the Theory Section of the American Sociological Association in San Francisco on August 13, 1989. Thus they were shaped to a degree in the days of hope for change in China. They now appear in writing after the changes in East Central Europe. They may be read in the midst of other changes. Important as these events are, it would be wrong not to consider also that, during this same period, the academy in the United States has become increasingly embroiled in a sometimes vicious debate over, precisely, the role of politics in college and university curricula. The specific issue of these debates, provoked first by Allan Bloom's book, *The Closing of the American Mind,* is the list of concepts and texts central to academic social theory. Bloom, any number of Washington bureaucrats, and increasing numbers of conservative faculty and students explicitly fear that the world is changing too much and that these ideas are the cause. They have, accordingly, launched a counterattack. Perhaps those who, at least theoretically, believe in the political power of ideas hesitate to proclaim the power of intellectuals because, many of them just old enough to remember McCarthyism, they see perhaps not the same thing but another kind of broad cultural revulsion against powerful ideas.

The contributors to this book and the ideas they express, whatever their cautions, are sure witness to the principle that social theory is beyond the academy because academics are among those intellectuals who are causing the world to think, and be thought, differently . . . and, thus, to change.

PART I

Social Theory and
Political Intellectuals

Chapter 1

MAKING HISTORY AND MAKING THEORY

Notes on How Intellectuals Seek Relevance

DICK FLACKS

University of California, Santa Barbara

1. THE DEVELOPMENT OF social theory is not necessarily best understood as happening in a self-contained framework or as arising simply out of desires to make "scientific" sense of the world. To make social theory is frequently to attempt to make history. Social theories are levers intellectuals use to influence power structures, to facilitate political outcomes, to enable groups interested in exercising control to improve their practice, to justify their ascendancy, to achieve their goals, or to advance their interests.

It is, however, too crass to assume that social theories mask intellectuals' efforts to gain power for themselves as individuals or as a class. Theories sometimes have such functions—but it may well be that theorists would rather think and talk than exercise institutional authority and that what most of us hope for most of the time is that our thinking and talking might actually help improve the world.

The problem, of course, is that we do not know how to get our words to make a difference simply by saying them. To teach and speak, to write and publish, does not guarantee that we have listeners—and the audiences we have may not be in a position to use ideas to accomplish the social change we advocate. Intellectuals seeking historical relevance inescapably must search for connection to those capable of exercising social power.

2. Two avenues of historical relevance seem to have typically been available to social theorists. One was to find connection with established power elites; alternatively, one might try to link to social forces seeking to replace or overthrow established power centers. Ever since sociology began as a self-conscious discipline, its practitioners have assumed that the purpose of the enterprise was to improve the capacity of elites to govern, to enhance the rationality of authority, and particularly to enable those in positions of power to understand the potential costs—to themselves and to the social order—of pursuing narrow self-interest and short-run advantage. For example, the more that markets and their logic determined action in society, the

more potential relevance there was in theoretical perspectives that called attention to the social costs of rationalization, industrialization, and desacralization. Sociologists from the beginning of their effort to create the discipline have sought to sensitize elites to the need for certain kinds of planning, tried to provide them with a rational basis for understanding the nonrational, and warned of the potential for social conflict and breakdown inherent in modernization.[1]

To a considerable extent, the development of sociology can be traced in terms of the degree to which the theoretical efforts of sociologists were (and were not) utilized in managing the state and other formal institutions. It was not until the post-World War II period that sociology came fully into its own as a state-sponsored enterprise in the United States. Those who went to graduate school in the 1940s and 1950s constitute the generation with the greatest optimism about how a professionally trained elite with access to the state would provide the means for sociology to achieve social relevance. When I took my first job in the mid-1960s, I was told, by one of the most prominent sociologists in my new department, that there was really only one political hope for sociologists and that was for us to position ourselves to advise the powerful. This, he said, was a highly moral enterprise because, without us, power would be exercised irrationally; with us, there was a chance for the rational exercise of authority. At the time, I thought this advice symptomatic of the man's own, rather unique, conservatism; later, I came to see that he was bluntly expressing postwar sociology's fundamental political aspiration.

Marx (1975, p. 257) provided a very different answer for the intellectuals' problem of historical relevance: "Philosophy cannot realize itself without the transcendence of the proletariat, and the proletariat cannot transcend itself without the realization of philosophy." Philosophy finds its historic relevance in the proletariat; human emancipation requires that the lightning of thought strike deeply into the virgin soil of the people. So wrote Marx at age 25. It is illusory to think that one can have historical effect simply by addressing one's fellow intellectuals in the self-isolating language of the merely theoretical. Moreover, if the goal of theory is human emancipation, how can it be fulfilled if intellectuals ally with elites and strengthen their capacity to rule?

Marx believed that workers, driven by necessity, would organize themselves in their collective interest and that, by participating actively in the working-class movement, intellectuals had a special role to play. Workers might find in their own experience the capacity to engage in local resistance and to win short-run amelioration of their conditions of life. What they would not spontaneously see was their shared historical mission to free humanity from domination altogether. Workers' own experience would not permit them to identify common bonds with workers of alien culture, language, and race, neither would it enable them to see an alternative social framework that superseded capitalism. The special role for intellectuals in the workers' movement was precisely to teach the necessity of transcending nationalism and overcoming the given structures of property relations—to teach the working class its potential as the social vehicle of universal emancipation. In the *Manifesto,* Marx defined communists as intellectuals who engaged in this kind of teaching. They might be drawn from the working class themselves or, more likely, from other classes—but their historical relevance and their capacity to grasp social truth depended on their readiness to merge their own fate with that of the proletariat.

Marx did not want the communists to form their own party; it was the workers and their indigenous leadership who would establish an organizational format capable of leading and speaking for the workers—and communist intellectuals ought to be participants in that party-building process. The mass working-class party would provide the specific institutional structure that would give the work of intellectuals historical meaning, direction, and influence.

Thus, when modern social theory was beginning to develop systematically, its creators charted two seemingly different pathways for making theory historically influential—to formulate a theoretical framework for rationalizing and professionalizing the practice of ruling elites or to construct a guide for the struggles of the organized proletariat.

3. In the 100 years since, efforts to follow these paths have had rather unexpected results, to say the least. By the turn of the century, some radicalized intellectuals were already impatient with workers' resistance to the historical mission offered them by theory. This impatience, spurred by the revolutionary situation in Russia, achieved its highest theoretical expression in Leninism. Among the ways that Lenin revised Marx was to insist that intellectuals not just merge into the workers' movement but become its professional (that is, full-time, fully self-conscious) vanguard. Communists in the Leninist mold were not simply to teach certain principles and contribute to a broad process of class development—they were equipped by virtue of their theory to take charge of the direction of that development. Lenin seemed to suggest that the very notion of an intellectual separate from full-time revolutionary activism was invalid. To make a difference, one must be a part of a collective that seeks to take the leadership of the movement and that aims to govern in the name of the working class.

In moments of revolutionary possibility, Lenin declared, leadership goes to those who are most selfless, least constrained by problems of personal livelihood, and most capable of seeing the big picture and articulating the boldest strategy. The intellectual as part of the revolutionary vanguard makes history directly, in action and not just words. In the aftermath of the Bolshevik

Revolution, Lenin's way posed a powerful practical and moral challenge to many intellectuals in many parts of the world.

Western European social democratic intellectuals, however, abjured Lenin's revolutionary totalism. Lenin's solution solves the problem of relevance for intellectuals by abolishing the intellectual in favor of a disciplined professional elite of a new type. European social democracy created instead a looser, mass-based party led by professional politicians. It was a structure in which socialist intellectuals could find audience, direction, and relevance. But the routinization and bureaucratization of social democracy resulted in a historic role for party intellectuals that, for many, did not seem fundamentally different from the state-oriented practice of more conservative colleagues. Indeed, to a very considerable extent, twentieth-century social theory has been shaped by the disillusionment of radical intellectuals with the emancipatory potential of the mass party. Michels early on compelled attention to the conservatism and bureaucratism of these parties. The rise of fascism, despite the apparent strength of German social democracy, raised deep questions about the effectiveness of the party form as an instrument of authentic change. The weakness of the social democratic model and the authoritarianism of the Leninist model greatly spurred the development of Critical Theory between the wars, as disillusioned German intellectuals tried to transcend the limitations of Marxist theory for comprehending their world and of socialist strategy as a means for changing it. Critical Theory contributed enormously to the theoretical development of sociology and social psychology—but its practitioners were not able to overcome their political impasse.[2]

In the United States, on the other hand, most politically minded intellectuals hoped that their theoretical and policy-oriented efforts would find increasing influence among the policy elite. The fluidity of the American polity, and the absence of working-class parties, led even socialist intellectuals to seek access to those in power.[3]

By the end of World War II, there was wide hope for a continuing development of the New Deal as a political coalition within the Democratic party and as a governing framework. State-sponsored reform would be designed and evaluated by social scientists. Academically based research would be supported by the public budget and would serve increasingly to identify social problems and test solutions. Trained practitioners of reform would flow out of the professional and graduate schools and into a growing public sector. The welfare state was to be a marriage of social science and social concern. The intellectual, the progressive politician, the labor leader, and enlightened civil servant—all were key elements in the leadership and professionalization of social reform.

Such visions got a big boost during the era of the New Frontier and the Great Society—indeed, it was in the 1960s that this scenario seemed to be really operative. Certain theoretical ideas about the causes of poverty and "social disorganization" were sources of major social programs that strongly affected politics and daily life in cities. Many of the features of the War on Poverty, of programs dealing with crime, and of educational reform were derived quite directly from theories developed by academically based sociologists.[4]

Social theory's moment in the sun turned out to be brief. War on Poverty programs had roots in an analysis that suggested that what the poor needed most were resources and space to organize politically (Reissman et al. 1964). Yet the same state that was willing to provide some sponsorship for a few self-organization experiments in American cities was devoting massive resources to suppressing such organization in the Third World. A Defense Department effort, Project Camelot, recruited scholars in an effort to "predict and influence politically significant . . . social change" in developing nations (Horowitz 1968, p. 289). The entire climate of the Vietnam era raised fundamental questions about the legitimacy of links between intellectuals and the state; the estrangement of American critical intellectuals and the American state that the war created seems, 20 years later, to be a continuing reality.

Such estrangement, however, is hardly total. Large numbers of liberal and left intellectuals would no doubt flock to Washington were an administration ready to show interest in their ideas in place. Indeed, in the last election campaign, the hunger for such an opportunity was evident in circles of politically minded intellectuals—perhaps most particularly among those who might be counted as members of the 1960s generation. The rage many felt toward Michael Dukakis seemed out of proportion to his flaws as a candidate; it expressed perhaps the deep disappointment that many felt in not having access to the national government that seemed, finally, to have opened with the passing of Ronald Reagan.

Thus, although the 1960s experience led to deep questioning about whether intellectuals should ally with the state and smashed the naive progressivism that dominated intellectuals' political discourse until that decade, there seems little doubt that a new wave of reformism in the national elite would sweep up large numbers of social scientists ready to swim in the tide of social change. Such a new wave is, however, proving quite elusive.

4. Something other than the weakness of Democratic party candidates seems to be blocking this sort of development. A deeper problem is that the size and character of the public sector required by statist theory appears increasingly incompatible with the fiscal and political consequences of corporate capitalism.

In the 1960s, the main line of development in the advanced industrial societies appeared to be corporatist. The state, operated by professional politicians, managers, and experts, would steer the national economy and ameliorate its political and social costs within a policy framework shaped by an ongoing dialogue among representatives of the major social sectors. In a postindustrial society, governed in this way, publicly financed enterprises (research and development, education, social service, collective goods production) would grow, employing a larger and larger fraction of the labor force. The strategic position of the private corporation and bank would be reduced, as knowledge and public planning became increasingly decisive.

Postindustrial theory helped explain a wide range of social and political happenings, including the student revolt, the state fiscal crisis, the transformations of politics then happening in the Western democracies, the apparent convergences between the West and the Soviet bloc, and much else. In addition to having considerable explanatory power, postindustrialism provided intellectuals with a promising theoretical foundation for their own political ascendancy. Indeed, the theory suggested that intellectuals would achieve historical relevance not by abandoning the study and the laboratory for political engagement but precisely by staying within the academy and doing the work that would increasingly be necessary for the society to operate. The university, not the private bank, would become the master institution in shaping the social future.

I think a case could be made that the reason the 1970s and 1980s have been so traumatic for so many liberal and leftish intellectuals has much to do with the way events have failed to follow the postindustrial scenario. The cause of our malaise is not Ronald Reagan or George Bush (or Margaret Thatcher); neither is it the surprising revitalization of free market ideology. These events—the political resurgence of the right—symptomize something even deeper. That is, they seem to belie the possibility, which undergirded much of the intellectual mood of the 1960s and early 1970s, that capitalist democracy might rather smoothly evolve into a corporatist state that would provide a framework for rational planning in the direction of social equality and balanced development—a framework in which intellectuals' work would be directly relevant to the social future.

Instead, for more than a decade, we've experienced systematic shrinkage of the public sector, constraining of the knowledge industry, deregulation of capital, increasing concentration of control in private boardrooms of transnational banks and corporations, and a movement away from social equality and planned development. The growth of the state, which in the 1960s was supposed to be essential for future economic growth, is now seen as a primary barrier to economic prosperity; planning that transcends the individual firm is thought to be inevitably irrational; and inequality is thought to be essential for guaranteeing appropriate economic motivation and work discipline. Intellectuals continue to have influence in politics—but the most influential have tended to be those ready to trash their own kind, to celebrate the market, and to justify authority (Blumenthal 1986).

It is not, moreover, that the wrong party is in power. Although conservative parties in power provide greater opportunities for conservative intellectuals, and leftish intellectuals are likely to be more visible when social democratic parties take over governments, the latter no longer seem able to change the course of their societies fundamentally, in large part because the capacities to steer now lie beyond the national states. Indeed, the national, mass party as a framework for achieving and maintaining hegemony seems obsolete. These same years when market principles and right-wing perspectives have been ascendant have also witnessed the crackup of the Communist party as the instrument of power in the Eastern bloc. But also, in these years, we have seen the decline of such hegemonic parties as Labor in Israel, the PRI in Mexico, the Liberal Democratic party of Japan, and the Democratic party in the United States. Regardless of ideology, once powerful national political organizations are decomposing. Perhaps the reason for this is simply that these parties, after decades of rule, have, coincidentally, used up their legitimacy and that no transnational pattern is reflected in their decline.

But I want to suggest something else. The decline of strong parties reflects the possibility that societies have become too complex and contradictory to be adequately represented within a single organizational format. The mass party, dominated by professional politicians, and capable of mobilizing the support, grudging or otherwise, of intellectuals, depended not only on a capacity to represent a majority but also on doing so as if that majority were homogeneous. Such parties worked not only by mobilizing but also by maintaining silence—especially the silence of those subordinated groups that lacked the capacity to be effective players in the party's core coalition. Such silence was, in many cases, engineered by the parties themselves—but the current breakdowns of party control have much to do with the newly found ability and determination of underrepresented groups to be heard.

Thus to continue to tie hopes for the historical relevance of one's intellectual work to established parties is to risk being in a position where one is defending the moribund, the indefensible, and the obsolete. Even a project aimed at party revitalization runs this risk because the very notion that a single organization can devise a program for society and that the needs and aspirations of the people can effectively be mediated through a bureaucratized, professionalized set of representatives must now be called into question.

5. The experience of the twentieth century has made it obvious that an alliance between intellectuals and power-oriented organizations is problematic. The logic of states and parties requires the subordination of truth to that

of organizational maintenance and growth. The organizationally mobilized intellectual is, by definition, not free to set his or her agenda of inquiry, to publish freely his or her knowledge and understanding, or to say fully what is in his or her mind. The organizationally linked intellectual is to at least some extent required to sacrifice the very freedom he or she most needs to fulfill the vocation of the intellectual.

Classical democratic theory presupposed an alternative—the idea of the public. In this perspective, the people themselves, or all those who wanted to, would constitute an arena for discourse about politics, would keep themselves reasonably informed, would hold public officials accountable. The press would be, by definition, the forum for such discourse and the source of such information—and the schools would serve as agencies for socializing persons to play their roles in the public.

The character of industrial capitalist democracy has made the vision of the public appear quaint. Political sociology is largely an effort to document the failure of this vision, an effort so successful that no one now maintains that any semblance of the theorized public exists, and very few seem to believe that a public, at least as defined in classical terms, can ever be realized.

C. Wright Mills was one of these few, but he was not optimistic. He did envision, in the midst of mass society, one hopeful possibility—namely, that the intellectuals might themselves constitute an autonomous public. Because their ranks had grown, and because they were positioned to spend time thinking about the larger picture, they ought to constitute themselves as the independent arena for political discourse. To do this, he argued, they have to steer clear of the circles of power—and recognize that the Marxian hope for a mass revolutionary historical vehicle was a nineteenth-century fantasy. Intellectuals could be a force in their own right, but to do so would entail breaking free of the boundaries of the merely academic and the narrowly professional. Indeed, the tragedy of modern academic sociology, as he described it, was precisely the ways it was constituted to avoid public relevance. Grand Theory and Abstracted Empiricism were little more than tokens for academic careerism. But a theory and an intellectual practice that enabled intellectuals to challenge the power elite—and that offered some possibility for ordinary men and women to connect their personal troubles to public issues—might offer a way out for potentially doomed modern society and its intellectuals.

Mills did not really have much hope that in the United States such a scenario might actually get going. He himself practiced a rugged individualism: "Each intellectual his own political party," he said.

The rise of the New Left in the 1960s, however, represented an effort to realize the Millsian vision of intellectuals self-organized as a counterweight to power. In Britain, the idea of a New Left was announced by a band of intellectuals (which included E. P. Thompson, Raymond Williams, and Stuart Hall) who had broken with the communist movement over Hungary but who were eager to sustain and build their radical politics. In the United States, the phrase "New Left" was, of course, taken over by SDS and other small groups of student intellectuals seeking to establish a political framework freed of the party identifications of the old left but fundamentally critical of the American and Soviet states. In early discussions, the young New Leftists thought of themselves as intellectuals but were strongly concerned about redefining the intellectuals' vocation. It was not enough to be academic; indeed, the New Left was impelled by a quest to transcend the boundaries of academic relevance. On the other hand, as the Port Huron Statement and other early New Left writings attest, there was a general recognition that academically based knowledge and the capacity for theory development were essential for effective politics. What was needed were ways to synthesize intellectual and activist roles, to bring the university into social relevance, or at least to define and defend ways for university-based students and faculty to link with social movements. The early New Leftists frequently expressed a vision of themselves as active participants in a coalition of social reform in the larger society and as the vanguard of university reform—both kinds of reconstruction being seen as needed and as mutually interpenetrating.[5]

One way to diagnose the limitations of the 1960s New Left is to emphasize the fact that this early self-understanding did not last. As the militancy and urgency of the black struggle intensified and the war in Vietnam escalated, a shift in moral perspective within SDS and the New Left generally occurred. To identify oneself as an intellectual was to take a social position that was both privileged and distanced from action. The heroic model for the New Left became that of the organizer—the one who was devoted full time to social change, who quit the campus and all other frameworks of middle-class comfort, who joined his or her fate with those most disadvantaged.

Once "intellectual" had been abandoned, New Leftists had an increasingly difficult time defining a shared identity. Refusing to identify themselves as intellectuals linked to the university, unwilling to take on a definite, established ideological label linked to an existing radical party, but, for the most part, unable to be effective as full-time organizers—committed New Leftists agonized endlessly over who they were. One solution—to conjure up a "new working class" based on education and based in the knowledge industry—seemed to project an identity that threatened to perpetuate the gap between privileged whites and oppressed Third World people. Indeed, the New Left ultimately split between those who wanted somehow to sustain an identity linked to a new class of intellectuals and those who sought total identification with Third World revolution.

The failure to evolve a shared identity resulted in the collapse of the organizational forms of the New Left by the end of the 1960s—a situation that has not, of course, been overcome in the two decades since. Yet, as members of the New Left generation looked out on their personal futures in the aftermath of the 1960s, large numbers opted for vocations in the university and the professions rather than efforts to try to sustain the full-time professional organizer role. Many experienced such moves as an abandonment of their earlier commitment, a form of retreat, a sign and a consequence of the decline of the movement. From the vantage point of the Millsian project, and the early New Left, however, the taking up of intellectual careers was not itself a betrayal, especially to the extent that many organized themselves in a variety of caucuses, networks, and intellectual circles aimed at challenging the status quo within their disciplines, professions, and institutions.

These efforts by left intellectuals and professionals in the early 1970s were sources of great ferment in a number of fields; a ferment that has helped reshape many disciplines and that continues to ramify through the academic curriculum and general intellectual discourse. As a result, issues of gender, race, and class have become central ones in intellectual analysis. Academic institutions are today more open, more democratic, more multicultural than they were 20 years ago. The intellectual left—including women and Third World faculty—has academic influence, some control over some resources, some weight in setting agendas and deciding policy. Compared with the situation when Mills was writing—30 years ago—there certainly is now a public, based in the universities and other social spaces controlled by the intellectual class, that fitfully serves an important critical function.

This situation is not adequate, however. The left-oriented intelligentsia, having won a niche in the cultural apparatus, seem, over the last decade, to have become less and less engaged in processes of social transformation or even reform. However overblown and unfair Russell Jacoby's diagnosis of the public role of left intellectuals may be, his essential argument seems inescapably valid—that is, most of our energy now is expended in theoretical discourse that is insulated within and driven by the logic of the academy. The need, urgently expressed in the 1960s and early 1970s, to connect intellectual work with everyday experience and with social movement seems to have been replaced by an urgent need to be recognized by fellow intellectuals. Moreover, the sense that politically engaged intellectuals might form and sustain their own community has faded as, more and more, we have become integrated into our disciplines, departments, and campus administrations. In effect, the intellectual left organized itself sufficiently to win some legitimacy, to gain a position in the institutional life of the society—but the price of this victory has been to accept the institutional logic of the academy, especially in terms of the styles of our writing and our work and the definition of our audiences and our social functions.

Still, such accommodations have been only partial. A sizable number of academics and professionals have continued struggling to connect their work and dedicate energy to change-oriented projects. Feminism remains a potent framework for defining the political identity of many intellectuals (male as well as female). The activist core of locally based peace, environmental, human rights, and social justice projects includes a high proportion of academics. And, despite Jacoby, at least a few intellectuals—especially within feminist and African American communities—have wide followings outside academia. The problem of the post-1960s generation, it seems to me, is that it has lost the sense of a shared project and vision—not that it has produced so few "stars" or that its members have become politically disaffiliated. A generation once possessed by a collective identity now finds itself dispersed into thousands of fragments.

6. Intellectuals seeking connection to potentials for social change thus have found available avenues for relevance to be dead ends. Both party and state require acceptance of the logics of domination, power, organizational aggrandizement. The academy and the professions require acceptance of the logics of disciplinary specialization, peer review, competitive achievement. The hope for a public as a sustaining framework for politically engaged intellectual work seems implausible, indeed chimerical.

One framework for possible relevance has, however, remained viable for many intellectuals of the left—and that is the framework provided by social movements. In the United States, which has never had the semblance of a mass party for social change, social movements have always been the primary basis for self-organization of workers and other subordinated groups and have for decades been the main vehicles by which left intellectuals have found political relevance. Social movements are supposed, according to Marxian scenarios, to be precursors for a party. It is the party that systematizes mass aspirations, that formalizes program, that develops and trains the professional leadership needed by masses—tasks that amorphous, voluntaristic, and particularistic social movements and their rather ephemeral organizational structures cannot adequately perform. The absence of such a party in the United States has been taken, by other American and European analysts, to signify the political backwardness of this country. This absence has been the stimulus for the vast literature on American "exceptionalism."

The emergence in Europe of "new" social movements that only weakly connect to established parties, and that depend on extraparliamentary strategies, compels reconsideration of the American exception. Today, European social thinkers argue that what is backward is an effort to retain the party as the representative vehicle of workers or as the repository of democratic hopes (see Laclau and Mouffee 1985).

Movements express difference; the "new" movements form and move precisely because of the existence of unrepresented groups and interests, because the parties cannot give authentic voice to contradictory interests within their potential electoral base and because the interests of party bureaucrats are fundamentally at odds with those of their mass constituencies. The rise of new movements, challenging preconceived notions of the shared interests of a homogeneous proletariat, compels a quest for new models of political action, new relations between intellectuals and the grass roots.

It seems obvious—it has seemed so since the 1960s—that university-based intellectuals searching for political connection must participate in social movements. In certain movement circumstances, such participation can be direct and unproblematic. There are, first of all, some movements whose social composition naturally includes university-based faculty and students—most particularly peace and environmental movements. Second, insofar as movements are concerned with complex technical matters, they are necessarily dependent on the expertise and legitimation provided by university-based participants. Third, feminist and minority intellectuals are drawn to movements whose actions may well have helped them gain entry into academic work; their problems have to do less with whether participation is possible than with how to define roles that make use of their training, skills, and position and how to overcome their marginality.

For intellectuals, the most problematic movements in which to find a ready place are class-based ones, especially labor movements. Professors and students are not workers—a cultural reality that no amount of conceptualizing about class location seems able to overcome. The kinds of leadership that formal intellectuals may be able to exercise in gender- and ethnically based movements are not imaginable in labor movements. Still, the example of Solidarity in Poland suggests a possibility for connection. There, dissident intellectuals organized material support for workers facing state repression; as a result, contacts were established that eventually enabled these intellectuals to create a framework for educating activists and for developing a shared political discourse. Somewhat similar processes seem to be going on in the Palestinian West Bank, where grass-roots self-organization, aided by those with professional training, has created a framework for autonomous health, education, and community development and other services. As in the Solidarity case, the interaction between intellectuals and grass-roots seems to be relatively unmediated by traditional party-type organizations.

In short, cultural and class differences that have in the past made for gulfs between intellectuals and the grass-roots in social movements now seem less fundamental. The intellectual awareness of those at the grass roots, created by schooling and mass media, today makes such contact much more possible. The needs of movements for the theoretical and technical skills of intellectuals is manifest to members concerned with practical achievement. Such needs derive not only from the technical character of public issues but also from the felt complexity of the polity and the social order—the need for help in social mapping and strategizing. The inevitable enveloping of the movement by mass media requires the development of rhetoric, style, and social analysis. In most cases, the forging of connections requires systematic effort, but there seems little in principle to prevent considerable numbers of university-based people from making the connections.

The trouble is that social movements are particularistic and relatively narrowly based. Because they can speak only for a fraction, they typically lack the social weight to achieve their most far-reaching goals; moreover, because they are outside the state, their strategies attempt to speak to power rather than exercise it. The political party was supposed to enable the possibility of coalition, common program, and centralized leadership, so that a popular majority could be formed in whose name power would be shifted.

If such a model has lost credibility, what can replace it? Nothing, some might argue. In a postmodern world, no unity can be expected; no common program can make sense; difference, diversity, fragmentation is all. Each social movement is an end in itself, because each is a necessary way of overcoming exclusion; the outcome: an inescapably fluid, constantly renegotiated pluralism of interests, expressions, identities.

A very attractive vista—because it seems at last to absolve us from the endlessly frustrating, and intellectually presumptuous, task of trying to define the direction of history. But accepting the apparent incoherence of social action, it seems to me, provides no way out of the spiral of inequality, egoism, and social irresponsibility. For the postmodern diagnosis seems to enshrine the market as the only viable model for managing difference. Counterposed to a social order organized as if it were a market is, however, the vision of democracy—that is, a social order organized through the free, continuous, shared discourse of members. Democratic models project the possibility of a common good and a degree of cultural synthesis. Moreover, in the real political world, coalitions are necessary—sectorally based social movements have to find themselves on some common ground (1) in order to gain sufficient social leverage to achieve needed change (as Jesse Jackson says, in the great social quilt, no group's patch is large enough to sustain self-sufficiency) and (2) in order to create the basis for democratic mutuality.

How can such common ground be found? How to envision social possibilities that go beyond individual rights and encompass collective goods and shared responsibilities? Here the author of the *Communist Manifesto* remains relevant: There is a social need for some people to take responsibility for seeing beyond the sectoral, the national, the immediate—and for teaching everyone else to see how their local experience is connected to the global. It seems that those most likely to see such interconnections are those whose livelihood is involved with ideas—with the theoretical—or who have the space and opportunity to engage in theoretical activity as a feature of their lives. University theorists spinning theories are by themselves incapable of providing the historically relevant material for making practical political sense.

If the party is an obsolete way of bringing such people together with political activists in the "real world," what other formats might be imagined? One vision is provided by Rudolf Bahro (1981), in his work *The Alternative in Eastern Europe*. Bahro here invents a new type of "communist organization" to fight against the official party. It would, he thinks, be formed as what he calls "the collective intellectual." Its membership would consist not just of university-based people or the formally educated but, instead, of

> all those who have a need to go beyond the pursuit of their immediate interests, having recognized that the barriers to their self-realization bear a social character . . . all thinking people are at least potentially intellectuals, and can acquire the ability to . . . [be] active experimenters and constructors. . . . Now that there are millions upon millions of intellectualized people [he imagines], not held back from solidarity by any constraining barriers of interest, and . . . themselves hungry for a more comprehensive social communication, it must . . . be possible to work out through discussion the necessary compromise of interests and carry it through primarily with the "gentle power of reason."

Bahro advocated, as a basis for organization of "emancipation" in Eastern Europe, the coming together of intellectuals and activists for systematic discussion, research, inquiry, policy formation, and strategy. He imagined that they would work as if they were in a university setting rather than in a party—that is, discuss, debate, discourse—but not require themselves to agree on a unified strategy or operate with an imposed discipline. "Free and convergent dialogue," "with the social facts . . . unreservedly taken into account and thought through"—this is, he says, the "royal road of social science," and it is this road, he believes, rather than the building up of power-oriented organization, that will actually be the way to develop an emancipatory movement. Instead of reaching for power, the task of the collective intellectual is to coordinate intellectual and moral efforts directed at a *cultural* revolution.[6]

How would such an organizational format operate? In large part, by using all of the techniques already familiar that promote collective intellectual/political work: periodicals, conferences, newsletters, retreats, computer links, manifestos, festivals, TV talk shows, and so on—but with the conscious aim of breaking the boundaries of both political and academic orthodoxy. The New Left started to build such a "collective intellectual"—a framework independent of party, state, and university, yet able to penetrate all of these, and able to bring together intellectuals and activists in a shared political enterprise. It is this project we have stopped doing, although many of us no doubt remain in networks that are traces of it.

If we were able to reconstitute an organized community of intellectuals and movement activists, what would be its immediate work? Some clues exist in the literature of academic sociology of recent years.

There is the suggestion of Alain Touraine (1988) for an action sociology: a bringing together of movement activists and social analysts for shared work of uncovering the "deepest meaning of the action." Instead of promulgating theory about such meaning at a distance, such meanings may best be uncovered through close-up processes of interrogation and dialogue between activists and engaged intellectuals. A primary aim of such dialogue would be to improve the capacity of movements to think strategically. Beyond resistance to threat and the expression of identity is the possibility that movements can consciously promote democratic transformation as a strategic goal. An action sociology would have the purpose of providing an arena within which such aims could be articulated and planned.

There is also the idea embedded in Bellah et al.'s (1985) *Habits of the Heart,* and in other recent writing, expressing the need to reconstruct public philosophy and arguing that such a reconstructive effort is a legitimate role for social scientists.[7] Such an effort, fundamentally necessary for the movements and for social theory, would be an attempt to formulate the material, social, cultural, and personal conditions for full democracy: What are the circumstances under which people might take full responsibility for the institutions and communities they inhabit? How can discourse replace power and profit as the basis for public decision? How can participatory models of governance work in various institutional settings? Is personal fulfillment best understood as the outcome of a privatized pursuit of personal interest or is such fulfillment the outcome of free opportunity for participation in a public life? How can public space be opened in places other than the university campus?

The future of social theory is connected then to the dynamics of social movements. Popular grass-roots movements have the potential of fostering a continuing process of societal democratization. But this potential is not inherent. It depends on the capacity of movement leaderships to theorize—

that is, to see possibilities for challenge, alliance, and expression that go beyond directly experienced (local, sectoral, particular, immediate) reality. Such a theory can grow out of the discovery of shared identity between movement activists and university-based intellectuals. A collective intellectual, developing in and as public space, is the social formation within which historically relevant social theory might be made.

NOTES

1. Compare Alvin Gouldner (1970, p. 91): "From its beginnings in nineteenth-century Positivism, sociology was a counterbalance to the requirements of an individualistic culture. It emphasized the importance of 'social' needs neglected by and required to resolve the tensions generated by a society that focused on individual utility."

2. See Martin Jay (1973) for an account of the development of Critical Theory.

3. One of the most instructive cases was that of Walter Lippmann, a bright young star of pre-World War I socialism, who became the outstanding establishment intellectual of his time (Steel, 1971).

4. For an examination of this development, see Horowitz (1968).

5. See Miller (1988) for a detailed description of the early intellectual perspectives of SDS.

6. The above argument condenses and quotes from Bahro (1981, chap. 12).

7. See also Sullivan (1986), Reich (1988), and Boyte and Riessman (1986).

REFERENCES

Bahro, Rudolph. 1981. *The Alternative in Eastern Europe*. London: Verso.

Bellah, Robert et al. 1985. *Habits of the Heart*. Berkeley: University of California Press.

Blumenthal, Sidney. 1986. *The Rise of the Counter-Establishment*. New York: New York Times Books.

Boyte, Harry and Frank Riessman, eds. 1986. *The New Populism*. Philadelphia: Temple University Press.

Gouldner, Alvin. 1970. *The Coming Crisis in Western Sociology*. New York: Basic Books.

Horowitz, Irving Louis. 1968. *Professing Sociology*. Chicago: Aldine.

Jay, Martin. 1973. *The Dialectical Imagination*. Boston: Little, Brown.

Laclau, Ernesto and Chantal Mouffe. 1985. *Hegemony and Socialist Strategy*. London: Verso.

Marx, Karl. 1975. "Critique of Hegel's Philosophy of Right." In *Early Writings* [of Karl Marx], edited by Quentin Hoare. New York: Vintage.

Miller, James. 1988. *Democracy Is in the Streets*. New York: Simon & Schuster.

Reich, Robert, ed. 1988. *The Power of Public Ideas*. Cambridge: Ballinger.

Riessman, Frank et al. 1964. *Mental Health of the Poor*. New York: Free Press.

Steel, Ronald, 1971. *Walter Lippmann and the American Century*. New York: Vintage.

Sullivan, William. 1986. *Reconstructing Public Philosophy*. Berkeley: University of California Press.

Touraine, Alain. 1988. *The Return of the Actor*. Minneapolis: University of Minnesota Press.

Chapter 2

THE THREE WAVES OF
NEW CLASS THEORIES
AND A POSTSCRIPT

IVAN SZELENYI
University of California, Los Angeles

BILL MARTIN
La Trobe University, Melbourne

WE DISTINGUISH THREE WAVES of New Class theories: the anarchist theories of the intellectual class of the late nineteenth and early twentieth centuries; the bureaucratic-technocratic class theories of the 1930s, 1940s, and 1950s; and the knowledge class theories of the 1970s. Each wave offers different insights, each wave captures in a fragmented manner different aspects, or dimensions, of a New Class formation.

From a textual analysis of New Class theories, we identified three such dimensions of class formation: agency, structural position, and consciousness. Although theorists in each wave do capture features in each dimension, they put particular emphasis on selected dimensions. Thus we found that the first wave of theories emphasizes agency, the second structural position, and the third consciousness.

Our key assumption is that a successful formation of a new class requires that all the three preconditions are present: there are agents who are ready to assume class power; a new structural position is created from which class power can be exercised; and, finally, the new agents with class aspiration do have the appropriate kind of consciousness, which is necessary to exercise class power from the new structural position. We believe that an analysis of these three dimensions of class formation could be applied to the study of any class. The making of the bourgeoisie or the modern proletariat also may be assessed this way, but such a distinction may be particularly pertinent for the understanding of the phenomenon we call New Class. After all, the new class, at least up to this historical moment, is a particularly unevenly formed class, its history is more a history of failures than of successes.

EDITOR'S NOTE: "Three Waves of New Class Theory," by Ivan Szelenyi and Bill Martin, is reprinted, in abridged form, by permission of Kluwer Academic Publishers from *Theory and Society* 17:645-67 (1988) with a new postscript by Ivan Szelenyi (1990).

THE ANARCHIST THEORIES OF THE
INTELLECTUAL CLASS (1870-1917)

The anarchists spotted early the latent scientism and elitism of the Marxian project of socialism. Bakunin's attack against Marx, during their collaboration in the First International, focused on the statist features of the Marxist conception of socialism. He argued that the complexity of the knowledge a government-run economy and society require will inevitably lead to rule by scholars and intellectuals.

W. Machajski, the Polish-Ukrainian anarchist, following the anarchist line of argument, suggested that there are two different visions of socialism: Workers expect socialism to be egalitarian, while intellectuals see the essence of socialism in state power (see Machajski 1937; Nomad 1937, 1959). Machajski believed that this intellectual vision of socialism is self-serving, intellectuals wanting to use the working-class movement to promote their own rise to power through the state bureaucracies. The society that will emerge would be as inegalitarian as capitalism is, except that here privilege based on private capital ownership will be replaced by privilege based on the monopoly of knowledge.

Thus both Bakunin and Machajski were skeptical regarding the role intellectuals would play in the socialist movement. To give primacy to the political over the economic in mass struggles, to underemphasize equality as a goal, and to concentrate on the nature of state power are ideologies that serve the power aspirations of the intellectuals but do not contribute to the emancipation of the manual workers.

The first wave of theorizing concentrates on the question of agency: Who are those agents who may attempt to form a new class? Why do intellectuals play such a prominent role in the working-class movement? Can one accept on faith that they are indeed altruistic, acting as the "mouthpieces" of the proletariat (as Marx and Engels suggested in *The Holy Family*) or is there a good enough reason to suspect that they may in the end serve their own particularistic interests, pursue their own power aspirations?

THE TECHNOCRATIC-BUREAUCRATIC CLASS THEORIES
(1930s, 1940s, and 1950s)

From the late 1930s onward, several theories have emerged claiming that a bureaucratic, a technocratic, or a managerial new dominant class is in the making or already in power in the Soviet Union, in Western capitalism, or in both systems. These theories are rather heterogeneous. The agents they think will become the core of the new class are quite different (from Stalinist bureaucrats to American managers); some theories insist that the New Class formation is only limited to the Soviet Union; others write about the evolution of a new dominant class under both capitalism and socialism. Still, the common feature of all these theories is the thesis that old claims for class power based on individual ownership of capital have been superseded and a *new structural position* has been created from which economic command can be exercised.

Although in the works of Veblen (1963) and Berle and Means (1932) such an analysis began to develop independently for Western societies alone, most of the bureaucratic class theories could be traced back to the work of Leon Trotsky (1974) and to the empirical analysis of the early Stalinist Soviet Union.

Trotsky himself was, of course, not a New Class theorist. He emphatically denied the class character of the bureaucracy and emphasized that the Soviet Union, even after the rise of the Stalinist bureaucracy, remained a workers' state (though a deformed one). Still, Trotsky powerfully documented the conflicts of interest between the ruling Stalinist bureaucracy and the working class during the 1930s in the Soviet Union and so opened up the theoretical space for bureaucratic class theories.

Indeed, the first comprehensive theories that described the Soviet Union as a society dominated by a bureaucratic class were developed by former Trotskyites who, particularly under the influence of the Stalin-Hitler pact, found it unacceptable to believe that the Soviet Union was a workers' state. Thus Trotsky's former disciples moved beyond their teacher by pointing out the class nature of the ruling Soviet bureaucracy and thus offering a more radical analysis of the character of the Soviet Union. Two versions of such post-Trotskyist bureaucratic class theories could be distinguished: (1) According to some (for instance, Tony Cliff 1979), the Soviet Union is state capitalist and capitalism was restored by the Stalinist bureaucracy; (2) others, under the influence of Bruno Rizzi (1985), claimed that the Soviet Union represents a fundamentally new social system, different from both capitalism and socialism, that rightfully should be called bureaucratic-collectivism (Shachtman 1962). Bureaucratic-collectivist societies are ruled by the state bureaucracy, constituted as the new dominant class. However, both the early state capitalism and the bureaucratic collectivism theories assumed that the class power of the bureaucracy is based in a new form of ownership. The bureaucrats collectively own the means of production.

These early theories of the Soviet Union as a new class society dominated by a collective ownership class—the bureaucracy—remained influential for some time. Elements of their impacts can be traced in theories emerging as late as the early 1970s. There are, however, three reformulations of these early bureaucratic class theories in the post-Stalinist epoch: (1) Djilas, and in the late 1960s, Kuron and Modzeleweski (quoted in Carlo 1974), accepted the idea of a new dominant bureaucratic class whose power is based on collective ownership, but they still regarded the Soviet-type societies as "communist" or "state monopoly socialist." (2) Maoists (and most lucid of all, Charles Bettelheim 1976) developed a new version of the state capitalism theory. The Maoists argued that the Soviet Union restored capitalism and became a new class society. But, unlike the post-Trotskyist theorists, they also believed that the agents who carried out this restoration were not Stalinist bureaucrats but enterprise managers. But in a crucial respect both Bettelheim and the post-Trotskyist bureaucratic class theorists are in agreement. They both identify the base of the class power of the managerial technocracy in its collective ownership of the means of production. (3) During the early 1970s, a new version of bureaucratic collectivism emerged in the works of Carlo (in his case, traces of the Maoist influence can be found) and, to some extent, in some writings of Castoriadis (Carlo 1974, pp. 2-86). Both Carlo and Castoriadis believe that the Soviet Union is obsessed with economic growth (Castoriadis 1978-79, pp. 212-248), and consequently it produced an economic system that is "production for production sake" (Carlo 1974, p. 55). Because production serves the interest of production rather than satisfaction of genuine social needs, the Soviet bureaucratic collectivism (Carlo) or total bureaucratic capitalism (Castoriadis), in the last analysis, serves bureaucratic class interests.

The idea that, in Soviet-type societies, individual private property withers away, and that the class power of the old bourgeoisie is replaced by the power of those who de facto control the means of production, influenced the thinking of those who analyzed the transformation of social structure in Western societies. Some of these Western "New Class theories" are spin-offs from Trotskyist analysis of the Soviet Union. James Burnham, a former Trotskyist, developed, in the early 1940s, the theory of "managerial society" (Burnham 1962), where he claims that the Russian Revolution replaced the bourgeoisie with managers as a dominant class. He also stated that the managerial revolution is a worldwide phenomenon. Fascist Japan and Germany too appear to be moving toward managerialism, as the United States did with the New Deal. Thus Burnham develops an East-West theory of the New Class that forecasts the evolution of a new dominant class for the Western world too.

During the 1930s, the idea of a technocratic-managerial transformation of modern capitalism had been emphasized by some with apologetical, others with critical, overtones. Berle and Means (1932) reported approvingly the advance of the managerial power in the United States. They claimed that capitalism is undergoing a major transformation, that private property is being dissolved and private owners are being replaced by managers in the position of economic power.[1]

Several theorists of the Frankfurt School, and even Habermas (1960) in his early writings, have an analogous, though critical, analysis of modern capitalism, fascism, and Stalinism. Some Frankfurt School authors (see, in particular, Marcuse 1978 and Pollock 1978) regard these societies as being technocratically deformed. They portrayed early capitalism as liberal-democratic and so they focus their criticism against advanced, technocratic capitalism. Technology intrudes increasingly on all spheres of life, even culture and politics. Fascism and Stalinism are extreme expressions of such a scientistic, technocratic development. The theorists of the Frankfurt School in such writings come close to a theory of postcapitalism, or state-capitalist society in which technocracy or the positivist scientists rule (though, in the last instance, none of the critical theorists accepts the New Class theory).

The second generation of New Class theorists concentrated their attention on the question of structural position. What kind of position do New Class agents have to occupy in the system of social reproduction to qualify as the new dominant class? Is there a new structural position in modern societies that replaces the position guaranteed under classical capitalism by private, individual ownership of capital? A few of the theorists argued that, in "postcapitalist" societies, incumbents of state bureaucratic positions perform functions similar to or equivalent to those performed by private owners under capitalism. The same argument has been made about the replacement of the position of the "owners" by "managers" or "technostructure" and "technocrats."

THE KNOWLEDGE CLASS THEORIES OF THE 1970s

During the 1970s, and for the first time, the political right (the neoconservatives) began to develop the own New Class theories (earlier theories were typically, though with a few exceptions, left-wing critiques of Marxist theory or Marxist-Leninist political practices). Their argument was that the left intelligentsia developed an "adversary culture"[2] that sought to undermine the value system of modern democratic society and establish the power of a modern "priesthood" composed of moralizing left intelligentsia (Schelsky 1974). The left intelligentsia, they contend, exercises undemocratic pressures through the media, or uses the welfare state, academia, or the combination of these institutions to create its own class domination (see Moynihan 1982).

Daniel Bell, in the *The Coming of Post-Industrial Society* (1976), develops a politically less charged but, in certain respects, similar argument.[3] In the works of Bell, the scientists are believed to play the fundamentally new role in postindustrial society. Scientific-theoretical knowledge, accordingly, becomes a major force of economic growth and social progress in the postindustrial epoch. Under such circumstances, there is room for a new, socially progressive knowledge class.[4]

Both Bell and the neoconservatives are knowledge class theorists. Like Bell, the neoconservatives point to the existence of a new quality of knowledge upon which rests the class aspiration of the intelligentsia. But, while for Bell this new quality is theoreticity, for the neoconservatives, it is simply destructive and subversive aspects of the new culture that the left intellectuals advocate.

Gouldner (1975-76) offered the most comprehensive knowledge class theory. Gouldner's research project on the New Class begins as a sociology of knowledge type of critique of Marxism and the role of the left revolutionary intellectuals. Gouldner (1974) spots certain features of Marxism—in particular, its "metaphoricality"—that make it suitable for the Marxist intellectuals to pursue self-interested goals while pretending to represent universalistic interests. Armed with this knowledge, the revolutionary intelligentsia can substitute itself for the proletariat and emerge from the revolution as a new dominant class. In his two major works on the subject, *The Dialectic of Ideology and Technology* (1976, pp. 9-13, 23-63, 195-294) and, of course, *The Future of Intellectuals and the Rise of the New Class* (1979), Gouldner develops a New Class theory encompassing the power aspirations not only of the Marxist revolutionary vanguards but also reflecting the increasing power of the technocrats/scientists. The key concept Gouldner develops is the notion of Culture of Critical Discourse, which captures the common feature, the common quality of knowledge, shared by Marxist radicals, professionals, the technical intelligentsia, and adversary or countercultural intellectuals. As the knowledge of the highly educated takes the form of a Culture of Critical Discourse, the cultural capital thus acquired enables them to "usurp" from the position of power both "old-line bureaucrats" of state socialism and private capitalists, owners of money capital.

Typically, knowledge class theories were reflections of the changing social relations in the West. But one of the authors of this chapter developed, in his book titled *The Intellectuals on the Road to Class Power* (Konrad and Szelenyi 1979), an analysis quite similar to that of Gouldner. It was argued there that the intelligentsia in Eastern Europe, by virtue of its monopoly over "teleological knowledge," formulates claims for class power, and in the post-Stalinist epoch there has indeed been a trend for the bureaucracy to open up, and join forces with the intelligentsia toward becoming a new dominant class.

TABLE 2.1 Insights These Theories Offer on Different Dimensions of the Formation of the New Class

Waves of New Class Theories	Agency	Structural Position	Type of Knowledge
Intellectual class	+++	+	+
Bureaucratic/technocratic class	+	+++	+
Knowledge class	+	+	+++

The last wave of New Class theories explores the changing nature of knowledge. They typically argue that a new type of knowledge (call it adversary culture, teleological knowledge, cultural capital, and so on) is gaining ground and the possessors of this knowledge are in a radically new relationship to domination. It is assumed that the possessors of this new type of knowledge can now make an autonomous bid for power.

Our main criticism of all existing New Class theories is that they are incomplete: They overemphasize one of the dimensions of the "New Class phenomenon," the process of the formation of the New Class. In Table 2.1 we assess, schematically, the different waves of New Class theories (more +s in the table mean more emphasis put on such a dimension by different theories).

The central task of theory building is to combine these fragmented insights into a coherent theory that combines all three dimensions.

POSTSCRIPT, 1990
(IVAN SZELENYI)[5]

The above text was written in 1986 and it was published in 1988. Meanwhile, the most dramatic events took place in Eastern Europe and the Soviet Union. I was invited by Charles Lemert to add a brief postscript and to reflect on the implications of these events for New Class theory.

We ended our book, *The Intellectuals on the Road to Class Power,* in 1979 with these sentences:

Paradoxically, no transcendent intellectual activity is thinkable in Eastern Europe so long as intellectuals do not formulate the immanence of the intelligentsia's evolution into a class. That, however, must wait for the abolition of the ruling elite's hegemony and the consolidation of the power of intellectual class as a whole. As to when that hypothetical third period of socialism will arrive, we can only say that when some East European publisher accepts this essay for publication it will be here, and not before. (Konrad and Szelenyi 1979, p. 252)[6]

November 1989, in the midst of crumbling walls and communist regimes, our book finally was published in Budapest by Gondolat, a government-owned publishing company. We owe answers to a few questions our readers may pose: (1) Is this an indication that intellectuals formed a new dominant class; does this support the claim we made in the above chapter, namely, that, "with the rise of Gorbachev to power, one could detect a revitalization of the New Class project"? (2) If the answer to this question is yes, it still has to be decided whether the newly won power of the intellectuals is a lasting phenomenon or whether it is just a brief era of transition. If it is likely to constitute a whole *epoch,* can it be called in any meaningful way "socialist"?

Of course, a proper examination of these questions would require more time and a little historical distance from current events. During the summer of 1989, Konrad and I discussed these issues at great length in Budapest. We thought we might eventually write a sequel on intellectuals and power. But, for the moment, all that I can do is to offer a few working hypotheses.

My answer to the *first question* is a qualified yes. The bureaucratic rank order collapsed all over in Eastern Europe and it is in shambles even in the USSR. This is consistent with the New Class theory we offered in *The Intellectuals on the Road to Class Power* in two ways.

First, intellectuals—or, to be more specific, what could be called the intellectualization of the bureaucracy—no doubt played a significant role in the rather unexpected collapse of communism, in the bloodless "velvet revolutions" against the bureaucracy, and the astonishing readiness of the ruling elite to dissolve itself and its organizations such as the Communist party. Certainly one of the reasons the bureaucracy demonstrated so little resistance can be attributed to the changing pattern of recruitment into the party and state bureaucracy over the last two decades. In Hungary, at least during the Kadarist consolidation, the party consciously tried to appeal to the highly educated and went out of its way to bring good young professionals into nomenclature positions, in particular into the party apparatus. Indeed, the overwhelming majority of the party apparatus under 40 in Hungary by the late 1980s were highly trained professionals. As these "communist yuppies" replaced the old-line bureaucrats, the ethos of the party apparatus changed. These young professional cadres, unlike those who were recruited from the working class and peasantry, did not depend exclusively on political bosses; their personal fates were not tied to the future of the party. They believed, because they had marketable skills, that, if their party jobs went, they could return to their professions and earn better salaries by working for large multinational corporations instead of the Communist party. This turned out to be a highly bourgeoisified party elite whose loyalties did not lie with communism. While some of the critics of *The Intellectuals on the Road to Class Power* ridiculed us for thinking party cadres could be intellectuals, our prediction about the intellectualization of the bureaucracy proved to be surprisingly accurate with the predicted devastating impacts on the bureaucratic rank order.

Second, there is a power vacuum today in Eastern Europe. The old elite collapsed and, in the absence of a domestic propertied bourgeoisie, the only serious contender for the role of the elite is the intelligentsia. A new political class is in formation. This emergent new elite is exclusively recruited from the intelligentsia. Its members are historians, economists, sociologists, jurists, and media professionals, and they all claim power, they all aspire for positions—such as members of parliament, government ministers, presidents, mayors—on the grounds of their expertise as professionals. If one wants to describe the power structure of Eastern Europe today (that is, early 1990), one can fairly confidently say it is characterized by power struggles between different fractions of the intelligentsia. In Hungary, the society silently, and quite apathetically, watches this struggle. The Polish working class looks at the new elite with increasing nervousness, if not hostility or disgust. The new elite freezes wages and boosts prices, tries to control strikes, and offers to sell the Lenin shipyard to Mrs. Johnson while promising her industrial peace. Undoubtedly, intellectuals today in Eastern Europe have more power than they ever had in their history. And what used to be conflict between "society and powers" is rapidly becoming a conflict between intellectual elites and the rest of the society.

My answer to the *second question* is this: I do not know. Intellectuals usually play a prominent, vanguard role in revolutionary social change, when one social formation collapses and a new one is emerging. But these vanguard intellectuals usually are unable to keep the power they grab during revolutions. As the new social order consolidates itself, intellectuals lose their power and surrender some of their political privileges to other classes or social categories, such as the propertied bourgeoisie or the bureaucracy (the former happened after the French, the latter after the Russian revolution). Will the intelligentsia be able to set a historic precedent this time by keeping its power? Can it constitute itself as a genuine new class, able to reproduce itself in the position of power? Or will it simply surrender its power to the new bourgeoisie? In other words (for those who subscribe to the Marxian theory that historical progress leads from capitalism to socialism), is the current revolution any more than a probably historically brief transition from socialism or communism to capitalism—in effect, is it a counterrevolution?

I think, at the current historic conjuncture, it is impossible to answer the second question. The social formation that currently exists in Eastern Europe is unquestionably *not a capitalist* formation. *Eastern Europe today is a socialist mixed economy* with a dominant statist sector, or state mode of production, which still employs full-time probably up to 85% to 90% of the labor force, and with a rapidly growing private sector. In terms of its economic institutions and social structure, therefore, contemporary Eastern Europe is almost exactly the third epoch of socialism Konrad and I predicted.

At the same time, there are indications of the total collapse of the statist sector. A significant fraction of the ruling intelligentsia by now wants to "go all the way." Liberalism is the major political ideology. Neoclassical economics are coupled with deep sympathies for the economic policies of Margaret Thatcher and Ronald Reagan, implying therewith an unrestrained shift toward reprivatization—the wholesale, unrestricted transformation of public property into private property. Reprivatization may mean nothing more than the transformation of public firms into private property of managers. According to Elemer Hankiss and Jadwiga Staniszkis, this is already happening both in Hungary and in Poland. Or it may mean the passing of Hungarian and Polish firms into the hands of foreigners for real or (more frequently) for token sums. This process of reprivatization to foreign capital took place in Hungary under the tutelage of Mr. Palmer, U.S. ambassador to Budapest. Mr. Palmer, in an interview granted to *The New York Times* in January 1990, talked about a "gold fever" in Hungary. He compared Budapest to a boomtown. A week later, he resigned from his ambassadorial position and announced that he had accepted a position as chief executive of an investment firm that funds Hungarian reprivatization. He knows what he is talking about.

This sudden, and somewhat unexpected, opening to capitalism offers new perspectives to East European intellectuals. I would not be surprised if the young Hungarian prime minister, a Harvard-trained economist who was known to be Mr. Palmer's tennis partner, would emerge eventually as a board member of one of the new "joint ventures." Nor would I worry about his professional and financial future after the anticipated electoral defeat of his party.

There is surely a New Class project unfolding in Eastern Europe, but it may not last very long. By the time the intelligentsia get a hold on power, it may slip away. Intellectuals may decide they are more interested either in well-paid positions with multinational corporations or in becoming private proprietors, a new bourgeoisie themselves—either by managing to receive rewards for their services from the foreign investors whom they help cut deals or by figuring out ways to transform their positions as managers into positions as proprietors of the formerly public firms.

Anyway, I just do not know now which way Eastern Europe may go. Does it have a chance to consolidate into a mixed economy? This would mean the preservation of a significant proportion of its state sector, with the unleashing of some private business. In this dual economy, a dual social structure may emerge: A social balance may be created between bureaucracy and a new bourgeoisie under supervision of a "super-master," the political class of the intelligentsia. But it is equally, or more, possible that Eastern Europe will let it go all the way to market capitalism. My liberal friends in Hungary enthusiastically believe this means "joining Europe." I hope they are right, but I fear they are wrong. Europe is a long way from Eastern Europe. This region never belonged to the West. During the last 40 years, it has been rapidly moving East. A leap from where these countries are now right into Western Europe impresses me as a courageous, but somewhat adventurous, move. If the leap falls short, the region may not land in Stockholm or Amsterdam (to which it aspires) but rather in Istanbul, in Seoul, or in Honduras, where Hungarians, Poles, or Rumanians may not feel all that comfortable.

The punch line of this postscript: Yes, intellectuals gained a lot of power, more than critics of New Class theories in general, or critics of *The Intellectuals on the Road to Class Power,* like to admit. But who knows if they can hold on to this power? They probably will not; and, as other vanguard intellectuals after the "big bang," they will pass their power on to some other historical agent. In this case, that new agent almost certainly can be none other than international capital.

NOTES

1. For a critique of this view, see Maurice Zeitlin (1974).

2. The term "adversary culture" was initially a concept of Lionel Trilling (1965).

3. Bell is certainly less critical and more sympathetic to the emergent New Class thesis than the theorists of the New Right are.

4. Veblen too had similar ideas about the future role of engineers, and Galbraith, following Veblen, developed a parallel analysis about "technostructure" (see Veblen 1963; Galbraith 1967, pp. 71-82, 97-108, 291-303).

5. This postscript was written by Ivan Szelenyi in Los Angeles in January 1990.

6. In the book, we distinguished two earlier periods of socialism: Stalinism, in which the bureaucratic rank has a power monopoly, and Brezhnevism, in which the bureaucracy begins to open up to the intelligentsia but retains a hegemonic position.

REFERENCES

Bell, Daniel. 1976. *The Coming of Post-Industrial Society.* New York: Basic Books.

Berle, Adolf A. and Gardner C. Means. 1932. *The Modern Corporation and Private Property.* New York: Macmillan.

Bettelheim, Charles. 1976. *Economic Calculations and Forms of Property.* London: Routledge & Kegan Paul.

Burnham, James. 1962. *The Managerial Revolution.* Bloomington: Indiana University Press.

Carlo, A. 1974. "The Socio-Economic Nature of the USSR." *Telos* 21(Fall).

Castoriadis, C. 1978-79. "The Social Regime in Russia." *Telos* 38(Winter).

Cliff, Tony. 1979. *State Capitalism in Russia.* London: Pluto.

Galbraith, John Kenneth. 1967. *The New Industrial State.* Boston: Houghton Mifflin.

Gouldner, Alvin. 1975-76. "Prologue to the Theory of Revolutionary Intellectuals." *Telos* 30 (Winter).

———. 1974. "The Metaphoricality of Marxism and the Context Free Grammar of Socialism." *Theory of Society* 4:387-414.

———. 1976. *The Dialectic of Ideology and Technology.* New York: Seabury.

———. 1979. *The Future of the Intellectuals and the Rise of the New Class.* New York: Seabury.

Habermas, Jürgen. 1970. *Toward a Rational Society.* Boston: Beacon.

Konrad, G. and I. Szelenyi. 1979. *The Intellectuals on the Road to Class Power.* New York: Harcourt Brace Jovanovich.

Machajski, W. 1937. *"Selections from His Writings."* In *The Making of Society,* edited by V. F. Calverton. New York: Modern Library.

Marcuse, H. 1978. "Some Implications of Modern Technology." In *The Essential Frankfurt School Reader,* edited by Andrew Arato. London: Basil Blackwell.

Moynihan, D. P. 1982. "Equalizing Education: In Whose Benefit?" *The Public Interest* (Fall).

Nomad, Max. 1937. "Masters, Old and New." In *The Making of Society,* edited by V. F. Calverton. New York: Modern Library.

———. 1959. *Aspects of Revolt.* New York: Bookman Associates.

Pollock, F. 1978. "State Capitalism: Its Possibilities and Limitations." In *The Essential Frankfurt School Reader,* edited by Andrew Arato. London: Basil Blackwell.

Rizzi, Bruno. 1985. *The Bureaucratization of the World.* London: Tavistock.

Schelsky, H. 1974. *Die Arbeit Tun die Anderen.* Koln: Oppladen.

Shachtman, M. 1962. *The Bureaucratic Revolution: The Rise of the Stalinist State.* New York: Donald.

Trilling, Lionel. 1965. *Beyond Culture.* New York.

Trotsky, Leon. 1974. *The Revolution Betrayed.* New York: Pathfinder.

Veblen, Thorstein. 1963. *Engineers and the Price System.* New York: Harcourt and Brace.

Zeitlin, Maurice. 1974. "Corporate Ownership and Control." *American Journal of Sociology* 79 (March): 1073-119.

Chapter 3

LEARNING FROM FEMINISM
Social Theory and Intellectual Vitality

ROSLYN WALLACH BOLOGH
*College of Staten Island and
the Graduate Center, City University of New York*

POLITICAL GROUNDS OF SOCIAL THEORY

Feminist theory owes its existence to the struggles of those who did not have as their goal the creation of theory.[1] That is, feminist theory is intimately tied to a political movement conceived as a struggle for liberation. This connection with the idea of liberation as carried forth by self-reflective, embodied human beings accounts for the meaningfulness and insightfulness of feminist theory as well as its creative, critical, and compelling nature.

It is my contention that critical social theory, best exemplified I believe by feminist theory, derives its value and power from a commitment to a notion of liberation and self-reflection. In the West, this commitment is also political, and it is political because it is sociological. That is, the bonds that constrain, constrict, and repress are formulated as social in nature (as opposed to natural or sacred) and changeable through political action understood in a broad sense, which I explain below.

I also contrast a broad version of social theory with a narrow version, often identified as sociological theory. The narrow version ascribes value to theory based on its predictive power. Thus, at the outset, I claim that social theory as a form of sociological self-reflection differs essentially from a form of theory (sociological theory in the narrow sense) that attempts to derive testable hypotheses in order to come up with lawlike generalizations. The aim of social theory in the broad sense that I intend is not so much to predict and thereby master an external reality; rather, the aim is to gain insight and understanding into, as well as a perspective on, one's own lived reality in order to affect (have an affect on) and change oneself and others who together not only share but shape and constitute that reality.

The change that is aimed for is, of course, one that is defined as liberating. "Liberation" can mean opening up a whole new reality, new possibilities; it can also mean naming one's privately experienced subjective discomfort and the conditions that produce it. Naming the discomfort and describing it makes it objective and public, something from which one can distance oneself and gain a perspective. From a mute personal experience, it becomes an instance of a social type or category of experience, something in principle experience-able by anybody, an experience defined by certain objective conditions. When those conditions are recognized as socially structured relations, the personal experience is recognized as political. These socially structured relations are, of course, culturally mediated. Hence feminism recognizes culture too as political.

It is my belief that sociology and the other disciplines can be reinvigorated by learning from feminism. The vitality of feminist theory comes from providing analytic insights that touch us in a way that is simultaneously personal and political, affecting us both as individuals and as members of a collectivity, implicating both self-change and social change.

The political movement of feminism has engendered an intellectual movement of critical significance. Feminist theory teaches us to see the gendered construction of "reality." It teaches us to appreciate "gender" as a category as fundamental as "social class" for the understanding of social life. Feminism "stands as the mark of desire for a new way to conduct human affairs, to think about the human being as an entity, as well as being the expression of a political will to achieve justice for women" (Braidotti 1986; pp. 58, 60). In these ways, feminism makes a vital contribution to critical social theory.

Not only is feminist theory grounded in a political movement, but feminist theory radically broadens and transforms the concept of politics to include the dynamics of power and domination and their effects on all aspects of social life, including personal relationships. Recent feminist theory expands even this notion of politics to include not just relationships of power and domination but relationships and dynamics of power, domination, and desire (Hartsock 1985; Young 1987; Benjamin 1988; Rubin 1975; MacKinnon 1988; Willis 1988). Looking at everyday life through the lens of this new expanded concept of politics generates new theorizing about the complex, political character of everyday life including the politics of desire as well as the desire of politics. Not only is there politics in desire, there is desire in politics.

According to feminist Jessica Benjamin, the fundamental desire underly-ing human life is the desire for recognition. Hegel, of course, had the same insight. She shows how this desire, which can only be realized as mutual recognition, comes to be split into mutually exclusive, gender-associated desires: a desire for rational mastery, domination, and control, on one side (the desire associated with politics and masculine struggles for power), and a desire to serve, to submit, to surrender, on the other side (the desire associated with love and feminine devotion). Mutuality becomes perverted into asymmetrical complementarity that resembles the complementarity of sadomasochism. Desire for recognition becomes perverted and politicized into desire for relations of domination and submission. These one-sided, perverted forms of the desire for recognition become gendered and eroticized.

The process by which this desire becomes split implicates the social relations and practices of child raising under particular historical patriarchal conditions of modernity. These conditions include the division between a masculine "rational" public, political sphere oriented to objective success as external goal attainment (what Weber calls instrumental rationality) and a feminine "nonrational" private, personal sphere oriented to subjective, internal feelings of well-being and nurturance (what I call aesthetic rationality).[2] As long as this aesthetic rationality is excluded from the public sphere and relegated to the private domestic sphere, we will continue to live in what I consider a patriarchal, repressive world, one that alienates us from our own feelings.

HISTORICALLY SPECIFIC FORMS OF LIFE AND SOCIAL THEORY

This exclusion of aesthetic rationality, grounded in a gendered division of labor, is not only a cultural matter, it is a profoundly structural one. The gendered division of labor in turn implicates a gendered and political mode of moral reasoning: a masculine political mode oriented to individual rights and a feminine personal mode oriented to caring (Gilligan 1982). Recent feminist research reveals the historically specific nature of the form of life that unself-consciously underlies these modes of moral reasoning. That is to say, recent feminist work offers a new understanding of the situatedness of moral reasoning and what counts as morality. The work of Smith and Valenze (1988) is a case in point. They provide an even more radical critique than Gilligan of dominant conceptions of morality. By focusing on working-class women's collective actions in nineteenth-century England, such as bread riots, their research implicitly presents an alternative to the model of moral individualism.

Smith and Valenze (1988, p. 295) claim that liberal "moral theory that places the individual self at the center denies the connections between individuals [Gilligan's point], and erases group history, whether it be the family, class, race, or nation, unless that history perpetuates the myth of individual agency." They conclude, "Within the bounds of liberal moral theory we cannot recognize the morality of working-class women in nineteenth-century England" (Smith and Valenze 1988, p. 298). Thus their work suggests that a seemingly apolitical, universalistic, gender-neutral conception of morality turns out to represent a politically repressive act of categorizing and theorizing from a politically repressive class position.

What Gilligan characterizes as a masculine mode of moral reasoning, based on the conception of an autonomous individual, is grounded in the social class relations of modern capitalist society. Gilligan's emphasis on a distinctively feminine mode of moral reasoning, to the extent that it too assumes individual moral reasoning as opposed to collective moral action, fails to challenge the roots of the masculine morality that she identifies for us. She fails to see how the masculine bias in moral reasoning is rooted in social class relations; hence uprooting or transforming masculine bias requires more than championing or adding "feminine" moral reasoning. It requires a radical transformation of social life.

Similarly, Carol Stack's work (1974) implicates both the class and the race bias in taken-for-granted assumptions regarding morality. Her ethnographic research on black women's networks of mutual support reveals a prevailing pattern of expectations that can be summed up in the saying, "What's mine is yours, and what's yours is mine," or what Smith and Valenze would consider a radical morality of mutuality. This means that each could expect the other to give up some possession just because the other liked it, wanted it, or needed it. With this ethic, relations of trust and mutual aid are established that enable people to survive under conditions of extremely limited resources. Stack's study of black women's kinship networks implicitly illuminates the extent to which middle-class morality is based on having enough money and resources not to be dependent on the help of friends and kin.[3]

Awareness of the historical, contextual character of morality moves us from a concern with individuals and their thinking and acting to a concern with forms of life and the kinds of thinking and acting that they generate, a move that can be compared with that from epistemology to ontology, from psychology to sociology, a recognition that knowing must be understood as practical activity (practical knowledge) or reflection on practical activity (theoretical or philosophical knowledge). As phenomenology argues, knowledge or consciousness cannot be divorced from the practical life world that gives it meaning.[4]

Individual actions are grounded in a form of life that generates not only the possibility of those actions but the moral interpretations attached to them. This tradition of feminist research on practical morality, instead of focusing on the moral nature of individual actions or individual reasoning, inquires into the moral possibilities and moral tensions generated by a given form of life. Feminist research and theory changes us from detached observers categorizing and evaluating the moral reasoning of others to thinkers and actors who are self-consciously aware of how our history, social relations, and practical life activities generate our respective ways of acting, feeling, and thinking, our conflicts and our tensions.

Drawing on the practical life activity of mothering, for example, Sara Ruddick recovers a distinct epistemological/ontological attitude she calls maternal thinking. A central feature of maternal work, she claims, is not murdering the baby or child. "Maternal thinking is profoundly marked by the complications involved in recognizing that such an impulse, *not acted upon, is fundamental to the whole project*" (Quilligan 1989, p. 15). The subtitle of Ruddick's book *Maternal Thinking* is *Toward a Politics of Peace*. Based on Ruddick's work, it becomes possible to claim (as does the reviewer: Quilligan 1989, p. 15) that

> maternal work is an excellent ground from which to theorize about peace, not because mothers are so adept at love in any soft, sentimental way, but because their work is so peculiarly embedded in potential violence that they have had to work out fuller repertoires of strategy for daily, active nonviolence than have disarmament experts who deal only with the abstract possibilities of war.

If we are going to create a different world order based on a non-violent way of relating to each other, maternal thinking may offer us some insights.

THE MAKING OF THE "OTHER"

Gender—like race, caste, and class—provides a marked identity that is simultaneously political and personal, affecting our personal biographies and our collective histories, our most intimate and private feelings and our most global and public deeds. For those in ruling positions, their race and gender may not seem to be defining or decisive features of their personal or public life; race and gender are marks of otherness, ways for identifying those others who are excluded and subordinated, whose voices do not have to be taken into account, whose voices can be silenced or disregarded.

The mark of gender, like that of race, creates an other: the silenced voice, the nonpresent other, the voice of difference that is simultaneously singular, "the other," and plural, "chaotic, disorganized, and anonymous." Those who remain unmarked, those who do the marking, are the unmarked markers who do not see themselves as fundamentally conditioned by the mark they impose on others. It is only in relation to the other—women, people of color, the working class, the colonized—that a singular, white male Western Eurocentric ruling class voice is identifiable. To collect people under a category assumes a reason for so doing, a practical activity and set of practical relations that make such categorizing intelligible and meaningful. These categories are, thereby, political designations.

Therefore, the act of reclaiming a political identity, of identifying oneself as a collective *subject,* brings about a redefining of the identity itself from its repressive designation—"woman"—to that which names an active empowered politicized people—"woman as feminist." However, the issue of a unitary subject is controversial. Outside the relationship of domination, woman as we know her does not exist. There is no essential content to the identity of "woman." The content varies by time and place. Moreover, because the world not only is divided between those deemed to be women (and, in many societies, men who do not make it into the community of warriors are deemed to be "women") and those deemed to be men but is further divided according to race, region, sexuality, religion, class, age, physical condition, and so forth, identity politics is fraught with contradictions and tensions as those in the feminist movement well know. The same contradictions and tensions are found in all nationalist movements.

The dissolution of collective identity begins almost as soon as the collectivity ceases to be a passive or unruly mass—a collectivity *in* itself—and achieves some success in acting on its own collective behalf—a collectivity *for* itself. As soon as the collectivity ceases to be a mere object of another's will or desire and becomes a subject with a will and desire of its own, differences within the collectivity, tensions between the individual and the collective, emerge and dissolve the idea of a single collective identity. The one shared identity the members of that collectivity have in common is the identity of being "other." This identity can unite the members in protest over their status and treatment as other. But once that protest results in the recognition of their subjectivity, a redefinition of identity, then the unitary nature of that subjectivity and that identity—woman—begins to dissolve. The dissolution of the unitary subject, a fixed identity, raises the issue of essentialism and postmodernism, nominalism and realism.[5]

FEMINISM AND POSTMODERNISM

We arrive here at the critique of traditional social science and the issues raised by feminism and postmodernism. The insights of postmodernism and those of feminism tend to converge; in fact, postmodernism, with its critique of master narratives and phallocentric logic, often draws on feminism and lends support to many of the claims of feminist theory, including the feminist critique of science and knowledge (see Harding 1986). Nevertheless, feminism and postmodernism tend to diverge as well as converge.

From a feminist perspective, Hartsock (1990) and others attribute the rise of postmodern theory to the struggles and movements of the second half of the twentieth century. Speaking as a participant in some of those struggles, she contends that "our various efforts to constitute ourselves as subjects (through struggles for colonial independence, racial and sexual liberation struggles and so on) were fundamental to creating the preconditions for the current questioning of universalist claims" (Hartsock 1990, p. 171). In like manner, Bordo (1990, p. 137) claims that the liberation movements of the 1960s and 1970s were "responsible for uncovering the pretensions and illusion of the ideals of epistemological objectivity, foundations, and neutral judgment. That uncovering first occurred, not in the course of philosophical conversation, but in political practice." These movements, she adds, not only claimed the "legitimacy of marginalized cultures, unheard voices, suppressed narratives, but also . . . expose[d] the perspectivity and partiality of the official accounts."

Nevertheless, Hartsock (1990, p. 163) wonders about postmodernism, "Why is it that just at the moment when so many of us who have been silenced begin to demand the right to name ourselves, to act as subjects rather than objects of history, that just then the concept of subjecthood becomes problematic?" Drawing on Memmi's (1967) analysis of the colonizer and the colonized, Hartsock uses the distinction between the colonizer who accepts, and the colonizer who refuses, to contrast modernist theorists and postmodernist theorists and to distinguish both of these from theorizing from the perspective of the colonized.

She is right to talk about the need to provide accounts not of *the* world but of our worlds, to demand recognition for the different worlds that we know that are not acknowledged in authoritative accounts. Hartsock identifies two fundamental intellectual tasks of theory: one of critique and the other of construction, the creation of alternatives. Unlike postmodernists who claim that we cannot speak in the name of some identity—woman—or construct new realities, but must only critique and deconstruct, feminists like Hartsock (1990), Zimmerman (1987), Rabine (1988), Bordo (1990), and others argue that we must reclaim our voice and our voices, that we must be willing to speak as women even while recognizing that there are differences that fragment and divide us as women, that there is no unitary subject or essentialist, universalistic identity called "woman."

THEORY AND THE RECONSTRUCTION OF REALITY

Feminist theory can help the task of constructing new kinds of social relations that are empowering by recovering and demanding recognition for the repressed dimensions of human life. Significantly, the activity of uncovering, revealing, and demanding recognition of that which is being repressed by a given discourse or form of life is simultaneously political and intellectual, practical and theoretical, empowering and illuminating. And this, precisely, represents feminism's most important contribution to social theory.

Yet, we must ask: Can our academic disciplines learn from feminism? Can they learn the importance of social theory as a form of self-discovery, of discovering one's own voice and one's own vision, by which I mean recovering an unacknowledged dimension of our social life and an unacknowledged possibility for reconstructing social life? Discovering one's voice and one's vision means liberating the repressed—emancipatory theorizing. It means naming aspects of experience or social life that are not recognized by an existing discourse, realities that are distorted or repressed by the current discourse. In other words, social theory, coming to terms with social life, means defining, describing, or naming our experience, our historical reality *for ourselves* rather than living within a definition imposed on us.

In naming our reality we comprehend it; we liberate our experience from a world and language community that denies or distorts it. Until it is named and expressed, the experience remains a mute suffering, an inarticulate experience, a vague discomfort, a feeling of confusion. A sense of not belonging, not being affirmed, a sense of being an outsider comes with not having a shared language for this seemingly subjective, personal experience. Naming this experience removes it from the personal, subjective, private realm of the individual while transforming it into a social and public reality.

In this sense, critical and emancipatory social theory can be understood as contributing to liberation from oppressive and repressive realities. We can understand repression not simply in the psychoanalytic sense but in the sociological and political sense as well and see how all three are related. The new categories constructed as a result of sociological deconstruction—that is, deconstruction that aims to uncover social relations of domination implicit in the very categories we use—enables us to see the world differently, to talk about relations and experiences differently, and to envision and reconstruct a new reality.

In calling for a sociology for women, Dorothy Smith (1979) challenges us to question the definitions of our reality, to redefine our situation for ourselves. This questioning of existing knowledge is theorizing that is simultaneously a form of political action. Theoretical action in this sense is also political action. As we attempt to reclaim and transform our realities, our relationships, and hence ourselves—a political impulse in the broad sense of "political"—we simultaneously reclaim and transform the language that defines and constrains our reality, our relationships, and ourselves. Hence the separation between theory and politics is overcome in this conception of emancipatory theorizing.

THE ACADEMY AS HOLDING ENVIRONMENT?

But, we must ask, does the academy in which so much social theory is done foster an environment in which we can get in touch with those aspects of ourselves and our world that are simultaneously created and denied by a given definition of reality? Can we, and our students, develop in the academy and in our disciplines terms that can name and illuminate experience in a way that helps to liberate us from an unarticulated sense of oppression? Do our disciplines encourage attempts to investigate and redefine social reality so as to acknowledge those aspects of our lives, our realities, our history that are denied, repressed, distorted by a given discourse or language? Does the academy see its goal as developing an emancipatory understanding of our multiple worlds and our multiple realities?

The term "emancipatory knowledge" excited a generation of social scientists, theorists, and graduate students.[6] But have the academy and the discipline embraced that idea as a goal? That some of the most creative and intellectually stimulating and rewarding theoretical work today occurs under different auspices such as feminist or cultural studies, both of which exist simultaneously outside and inside traditional disciplines, suggests that the traditional disciplines have failed to provide a home for those who desire to gain an emancipatory perspective on their world and their lives.

Emancipatory theorizing involves reflection on our experiences, "our" (tradition's) definitions, constructions, and representations of reality, "our" (tradition's) conceptual categories; a practice at which Marx, for example, excelled. Reflection on the very categories with which we perceive and define reality both requires that we become, and transforms us into, outsiders and insiders simultaneously. The challenge to a correspondence theory of truth—a theory that there is an objective language made up of categories that correspond to or mirror some objective external reality—gained some prominence in the social sciences about two decades ago with the interest in phenomenology, ethnomethodology, and ordinary language philosophy. Yet, the realization that our taken-for-granted knowledge involves unacknowledged assumptions and practices that need to be examined critically if we are to become self-conscious actors is not widely shared in the social sciences.[7]

Can the academy and the traditional disciplines provide a holding environment that can foster emancipatory theorizing—social theory in the broad sense? This is not simply a rhetorical question. Our world is going through a period of radical social change. The interests, perspectives, concerns that stimulated creative activity in the past are no longer compelling. Moreover, the academy is seeing more and more outsiders—women and nontraditional students. Are they/we encouraged to find a home within our disciplines? Are we providing the kind of environment that can foster a creative encounter with the social sciences and with the social world that the social sciences purport to understand, an encounter that can stimulate fruitful, creative, and insightful social theorizing in the form of social and societal self-reflection and critical inquiry?

Can we create within the academy the kind of holding environment for serious, intellectual work that a mother provides for her child at play? A "holding environment" refers to a social space that encourages and supports creativity and the capacity to be alone. Jessica Benjamin (1988), drawing on the work of D. W. Winnicott, elaborates on the notion of a holding environment and its importance for women. The presence of a maternal other, together with the freedom, space, and materials to explore and manipulate, constitutes a holding environment that Winnicott considered essential for creative play. A holding or facilitating environment enables one to explore a world for oneself and in the process discover one's own capacities. Such an environment affirms both self-discovery and creativity. Political, intellectual sociability, relations of mutual recognition with and among the dominated, excluded, repressed, or marginalized, provides the kind of holding environment that can promote critical reflection and insight, theorizing that is simultaneously personal and political.

In contrast with Winnicott's image, the academy and the disciplines are currently conceived as rational, instrumental apparatuses aimed at training, disciplining, and developing vocational specialists who will go out and conquer the world, specialists for whom the world is their data, a uniquely Western image in Weber's view. Feminists and deconstructionists will recognize the phallic and martial character of this imagery as well.

Can we create within the academy a more aesthetically sensitive, nurturant, and stimulating environment? Can we reconstruct the academy and the disciplines toward becoming an environment that nurtures self-reflection, self-understanding, and self-change, that encourages and supports inquiry into the discourses, desires, representations, and social relations that constitute the self and its reality, our multiple selves and our multiple realities? The self of sociological analysis is not a private being but a historical, cultural, and social being, a body that is inscribed with gender and class, the embodiment of particular cultures and traditions, multiple discourses, multiple realities, multiple desires, the embodiment of repressive knowledge. Can we in the academy promote theorizing that investigates and analyzes the repressiveness of our language, our taken-for-granted categories and realities, work that strives to recover the repressed dimensions of our lives and language, the repressed history of our social "reality" and social realities?

The academy is the institution, par excellence, that encourages self-reflection and questioning of reality. Nevertheless, like other dominant institutions, the practices of the academy and the disciplines undermine this liberating potential. Feminism, as a movement committed to liberation, challenges the institution's repressive practices and introduces alternative ones. I am referring to feminist practices that create a holding environment, the creation of "analytic space," the opportunity for intellectual, political sociability that fosters critical, self-reflective, creative work. It is what women's studies programs attempt to provide—for both faculty and students.

Susan Bordo (1990, p. 136) contends that the "*institutions* of knowledge/power that still dominate in our masculine public arena . . . now threaten . . . to harness and tame the visionary and critical energy of feminism as a movement of cultural resistance and transformation." She points out that "within the masculinist institutions we have entered, relational, holistic and nurturant attitudes continue to be marked as flabby, feminine and soft" (Bordo 1990, p. 148).

Feminists must re-create the institutions we have entered and that have in part created us as "women" *and* as feminists, including not least the academy. Feminists and *all those committed to emancipatory theorizing* must challenge the dominant, oppressive, and repressive cultures of these institutions by creating a space and culture, a holding environment, in which we can come to terms with our social realities and their representations. The ongoing process of creating a holding environment for ourselves and each other, a social, intellectual space for political, intellectual sociability, for reflecting on our given "realities," strengthens and empowers us to address and challenge the oppressive and repressive nature of those realities and the representations of those realities.

Can the academy and the disciplines, can we as professors and mentors, provide for our students, ourselves, and each other a holding environment for creative and re-creative intellectual reflection that we call social theory, the coming to terms anew with social reality? Can social theory and the social sciences regain their intellectual vitality by learning from feminism?

NOTES

1. I have borrowed this formulation from Nancy Hartsock's (1987) paper.

2. See Bologh (1990), Chapter 15, "The Female World: An Alternative Rationality," for an elaboration of the concept "aesthetic rationality."

3. Stack's argument is supported by the work of Stansell (1986). Stansell's research documents how working-class women in New York City between 1789 and 1860 were the guardians of the neighborhood, not the home (Murphy 1987). See also Kathy Peiss (1986) and Terry Haywoode (forthcoming).

4. See Bologh (1980, pp. 233-73) for a discussion and critique of Habermas and an analysis of the problem of consciousness in contemporary social theory.

5. See, for example, Linda Alcoff (1987, 1988), Bonnie Zimmerman (1987, p. 6), Leslie Wahl Rabine (1988), Joan W. Scott (1988), Mary Poovey (1988).

6. Habermas ([1968] 1971), *Knowledge and Human Interests,* developed the idea of emancipatory theory.

7. Stacey and Thorne (1985) make a similar argument in their piece, "The Missing Feminist Revolution in Sociology."

REFERENCES

Alcoff, Linda. 1987. "Justifying Feminist Social Science." *Hypatia* 2(3):107-27.

———. 1988. "Cultural Feminism Versus Post-Structuralism: The Identity Crisis in Feminist Theory." *Signs* 13(3):405-36.

Benhabib, Seyla and Drucilla Cornell. 1987. *Feminism as Critique.* Minneapolis: University of Minnesota Press.

Benjamin, Jessica. 1988. *The Bonds of Love.* New York: Pantheon.

Bologh, Roslyn Wallach. 1980. *Dialectical Phenomenology: Marx's Method.* London: Routledge & Kegan Paul.

———. 1990. *Love or Greatness: Max Weber and Masculine Thinking—A Feminist Inquiry.* New York: Unwin Hyman (Harper Collins).

Bordo, Susan. 1990. "Feminism, Postmodernism, and Gender-Scepticism." In *Feminism/Postmodernism,* edited by Linda Nicholson. London: Routledge.

Braidotti, Rosi. 1986. "Ethics Revisited: Women and/in Philosophy." In *Feminist Challenges: Social and Political Theory,* edited by Carole Pateman and Elizabeth Gross. Boston: Northeastern University Press.

Gilligan, Carol. 1982. *In a Different Voice.* Cambridge, MA: Harvard University Press.

Habermas, Jürgen. [1968] 1971. *Knowledge and Human Interests.* Boston: Beacon.

Harding, Sandra. 1986. *The Science Question in Feminism.* Ithaca, NY: Cornell University Press.

Hartsock, Nancy. 1985. *Money, Sex and Power.* Boston: Northeastern University Press.

———. 1987. "Rethinking Modernism: Minority vs. Majority Theories." Prepared for delivery at the meetings of the Western Political Science Association.

———. 1990. "Foucault on Power." Pp. 157-75 in *Feminism/Postmodernism,* edited by Linda J. Nicholson. London: Routledge.

Haywoode, Terry. Forthcoming. "Working Class Feminism." Ph.D. dissertation. New York: City University of New York.

MacKinnon, Catherine A. 1988. "Desire and Power: A Feminist Perspective" and "Discussion." Pp. 105-21 in *Marxism and the Interpretation of Culture,* edited by Cary Nelson and Lawrence Grossberg. Chicago: University of Chicago Press.

Memmi, Albert. 1967. *The Colonizer and the Colonized.* Boston: Beacon.

Murphy, Marjorie. 1987. "Learning to Breathe Free." *The Women's Review of Books* 4(7):15-16.

Nelson, Cary and Lawrence Grossberg, eds. 1988. *Marxism and the Interpretation of Culture.* Chicago: University of Chicago Press.

Nicholson, Linda, ed. 1990. *Feminism/Postmodernism.* London: Routledge.

Peiss, Kathy. 1986. *Cheap Amusements: Working Women and Leisure in Turn-of-the-Century New York.* Philadelphia: Temple University Press.

Poovey, Mary. 1988. "Feminism and Deconstruction." *Feminist Studies* 14(1):51-65.

Quilligan, Maureen. 1989. [Review of Sara Ruddick's *Maternal Thinking*]. *New York Times Book Review,* May 21, p. 15.

Rabine, Leslie Wahl. 1988. "A Feminist Politics of Non-Identity." *Feminist Studies* 14(1):11-31.

Rubin, Gayle. 1975. "The Traffic in Women: Notes on the 'Political Economy' of Sex." Pp. 157-210 in *Toward an Anthropology of Women,* edited by Rayna R. Reiter. New York: Monthly Review Press.

Ruddick, Sara. 1989. *Maternal Thinking: Toward a Politics of Peace.* Boston: Beacon.

Scott, Joan W. 1988. "Deconstructing Equality-Versus Difference: Or, the Uses of Poststructuralist Theory for Feminism." *Feminist Studies* 14(1):33-50.

Sherman, Julia A. and Evelyn Torton Beck, eds. 1979. *The Prism of Sex: Essays in the Sociology of Knowledge.* Madison: University of Wisconsin Press.

Smith, Dorothy E. 1979. "A Sociology for Women." In *The Prism of Sex,* edited by Julia A. Sherman and Evelyn Torton Beck. Madison: University of Wisconsin Press.

————. 1987. *The Everyday World as Problematic.* Boston: Northeastern University Press.

Smith, Ruth L. and D. M. Valenze. 1988. "Mutuality and Marginality: Liberal Moral Theory and Working Class Women in Nineteenth Century England." *Signs* 13(2):277-98.

Stacey, Judith and Barrie Thorne. 1985. "The Missing Feminist Revolution in Sociology." *Social Problems* 32(4):301-16.

Stack, Carol. 1974. *All Our Kin: Strategies for Survival in a Black Community.* New York: Harper & Row.

Stansell, Christine. 1986. *City of Women: Sex and Class in New York, 1789-1860.* New York: Knopf.

Willis, Ellen. 1988. "Discussion." Pp. 117-21 in *Marxism and the Interpretation of Culture,* edited by Cary Nelson and Lawrence Grossberg. Chicago: University of Chicago Press.

Young, Iris. 1987. "Impartiality and the Civic Public: Some Implications of Feminist Critiques of Moral and Political Theory." Pp. 57-76 in *Feminism as Critique,* edited by Seyla Benhabib and Drucilla Cornell. Minneapolis: University of Minnesota Press.

Zimmerman, Bonnie. 1987. "Disobedient Daughter." *Women's Review of Books* 4(7):5-6.

PART II

World Politics and Intellectuals

Chapter 4

FRENCH INTELLECTUALS FROM SARTRE TO SOFT IDEOLOGY

GEORGE ROSS
Brandeis University

OUR SUBJECT IS THE EVOLUTION OF relationships between French intellectuals and politics. We will focus, first of all, primarily on *left* intellectuals. Next, we will proceed by presenting rough narratives of *different* sets of left intellectual texts, including, but only as one such set, that of France's high cultural heroes, the *grands intellos*. We suspect that we will end up tracking the decline of ideas expressing strong impatience with the distribution of power in French society and profound Enlightenment optimism about the prospects for radical change. The deeper issue is how to explain such movements, which the chapter's second part will attempt.

DECONSTRUCTING CONTRADICTORY TEXTS

It is impossible to characterize an "underlying logic" of evolving relations between intellectuals and politics for any society. Just as there is a multiplicity of different kinds of intellectuals, there is a multiplicity of different such logics. In modern intellectual life, it is not only the Sartres and Foucaults who count. There are *many* intellectuals and "texts" that are important. Which should be discussed, then? Rather than trying to characterize one such text, then, what I would like to do here is to review three different sets to see what they have in common. Let us call them "mastersingers," "artisans," and "apprentices"—the grands intellos—the internationally acknowledged "greats," a fraction of professional social scientists, and those of successive "political generations" of young French left intellectuals.

Texts 1: The Mastersingers

The story of the "greats" of modern French social thought is so oft told that many, especially outside France, believe mistakenly that it is the *only* important text of modern French intellectual life. In it we read of ambitious men and women proposing grand theoretical schemes meant to endow the social world with meaning. Here the French have a grand tradition of pretension—in a number of senses. Intellos have aspired, perhaps since prior to the Enlightenment, but certainly since the Dreyfus Affair, to become accepted not only as "professionals" but also as thinkers proposing ideas to change the ways in which large numbers of people interpret the social and spiritual world.

The prelude to the modern battle of intellectual titans occurs in the years after World War II. The Vichy period destroyed the credibility of right-of-center thought. After Liberation in 1944, reformist and left-leaning *Socialisant* and *Marxisant* notions were dominant. The coming of the cold war after 1947 further narrowed debate to a battle of position between the ideas of the Communist party (PCF), such as they were, and left non- and anticommunist thought. Until well into the 1950s, the Communists were by far the most powerful political force of the left. This, in turn, despite the crudely instrumental nature of the PCF's "intellectual" positions, gave the Communists considerable power to define left intellectual debate.[1]

This came to a paroxysmic end in 1956. The PCF's unwillingness to undertake serious de-Stalinization, its failure to acknowledge Khrushchev's secret speech about Stalin's crimes, and its support of the Soviet invasion of Hungary dramatically undercut its power to compel intellectually. In a new environment of peaceful coexistence and economic growth, official Communist thought appeared more and more nakedly schematic and out of date, inadequate to the task of accounting for a rapidly changing French society.

Thus Marxism, which had briefly assumed immense importance in high left intellectual life, fell under seige. In this new context, none other than Sartre himself took up the tasks of revisionist reconstruction. The very model of the modern intellectual titan, Sartre, manipulating a huge store of intellectual capital accumulated by the success of existentialism, remained an overpowering presence (Ory and Sirinelli 1986). But it was neither the militant existentialist nor the cold war fellow traveler who stepped forward at this point. Instead, the great man offered the existentialo-Marxism of *Search for a Method* and, above all, *Critique de la raison dialectique*.

With Sartre in the lead, one major left intellectual vector for the next period, stretching well into the 1960s, was an attempt to revise reductionist, mechanical, and politically determined cold war Marxism toward greater causal complexity and epistemological openness. Important journals like *Arguments* and *Socialisme ou Barbarie* were founded by excommunists and other Marxisant thinkers. Their animators—Morin, Lefort, Lefebvre, Castoriadis, and so on—shared Sartre's basic concerns, if not his existentialist predilections (Biegalski 1970).

Despite Sartre's *patronage* and involvement, however, the quest for such an open-ended Marxism fell short. Sartre's public prominence remained very significant, but more as a celebrity and witness, ever eager to champion radical protests, than as a modernizer of Marxism. Intellectually, he failed to conquer. In a similar vein, most of the "lesser" post-1956 reformulators of Marxism, like the *Arguments* group, were quick to abandon the effort altogether.

As these attempts to reconstruct a new Marxism faded, a new "great," Claude Lévi-Strauss, armed with a new vision—structuralism—climbed to the top of the hill. Beginning the famous "linguistic turn" by analogizing from linguistics into anthropology, Lévi-Strauss and his followers sought deep, transhistorical constants in human experience, the buried structural "languages" common to most all social life. Structuralism, like Marxism, sought to decode social relationships and expose their basic logics. In contrast to Marxism, however, the logics uncovered by structuralism were so profound that they tended to make history disappear altogether. Perhaps more important, proponents of structuralism were quick to denounce what they considered to be the anachronistic historicism in Marxism's shorter-run focus on the connections between economic dynamics and social conflict. In its purest forms, in the master's own works, structuralism thus made Marxism look relative and ephemeral.[2] The structuralist movement thus "defeated" the old mechanical Marxism of the PCF. More important, it blocked the claims of post-1956 "independent" Marxism, of which Sartre's existentialo-Marxism was probably the most important variety, to institutionalize a more subtle Marxist-humanist vision of the world. In the battle to be intellectual king of the hill, then, Marxism was clearly on the defensive by the early 1960s.

As most chroniclers note, Marxism responded in the person of Louis Althusser, by adopting much of the conceptual vocabulary of structuralism and attempting to graft it onto the body of Marxism itself. While the patient was on the operating table, Althusser and his acolytes managed to create a "structuralist Marxism," which, while attacking the vogue of Marxist humanism and Stalinist economics, managed, in the words of Pierre Grémion (1985), to create a "history without a subject." By burying social causality in deep structures like "mode of production," the Althusserian turn undercut perhaps Marxism's greatest practical appeal, its purported capacity to lay bare the various motors of historical development and make them accessible to rational, progressive human action. The connection between the Althusserian reformulation of Marxism and real politics became ever more tenuous, therefore.

Having led to political, and intellectual, impasse, Althusserianism proved to be but a brief Parisian fad, in retreat by the mid-1970s. More modest efforts to adapt Marxism for political and social scientific use persisted through the 1970s, given political circumstances, as we will see, but the ultimate failure of the Althusserian enterprise meant the end of Marxism in the intellectual battle of left-leaning titans.

Pure structuralism was itself superseded in the 1970s by what Luc Ferry and Alain Renaut (1985) have labeled *La Pensée 68,* poststructuralist "anti-humanism." Michel Foucault, Jacques Lacan, and Jacques Derrida became the post-1968 kings of the left intellectual hill. All shared a profound rebelliousness, if each in his own differing way. More generally, all were united by a common rejection of Enlightenment thought with its historicist postulation of ever progressing rationality and understanding.

Foucault, a Nietzschean and perhaps the most important poststructuralist in explicitly political terms, explored the genealogies of various human meaning structures as almost serendipitous historical creations that blossomed into long-standing oppressive realities. History, for Foucault, produced underlying discourses that shaped and constrained social behavior, constituting power in the process but in a virtually random way. "Man" was dead, in the sense that Enlightenment "man," moving bravely forward progressive step by progressive step as an integral subject, was dissolved. Enlightenment humanism, including its Victorian subsidiary, Marxism, was demoted to parochial status. Oppressive power, to Foucault, could not be localized in explicit institutions and institutional complexes but had instead to be understood to reside in the discursive constructs within which such institutions and complexes operate.

Resistance to oppressive power was essential, Foucault implied, and indeed he practiced it himself. But the historically serendipitous genealogy of discursive structures and the relativized position of actors in these structures—the subject itself constantly changed in accordance with its positioning in different discursive constructs—meant that resisters could never be sure what their appropriate object was, what they should aim to change, and whether any set of specific actions would change things for better or worse.

The Freudian revisionism of Lacan was analogous, dissolving Freud's concept of the subject and undercutting Freud's projected rationalist, if tragic, trajectory of psychodynamics. Derrida, the Heideggerian, rigorously denounced the metaphysical cores both of humanism (with Sartre the main target) and of structuralism itself, proposing instead a hard-nosed deconstructionist hermeneutics in which the "subject" disappears. One could make analogous remarks about the nature of Lacan's and Derrida's rebelliousness to those made earlier about Foucault.

Taken together, all three—and we could include a number of other thinkers (Baudrillard, Lyotard, Guattari, plus the influential feminists Kristeva, Cixous, and Irigaray[3]—clearly struck responsive chords in post-

1968 debates. In the experience of many of the post-1968 generation, rebellious acts derived from rationalistic, Enlightenment-derived schemas for political action, including those of the traditional socialist left, might succeed in terms of their own logic, but this was quite unlikely. All of this cumulated into a conclusion that resonated with postmodern thought. Protest was necessary, given the oppressiveness of reality. Yet the diachronic setting of such protest would always be impenetrable and its outcome quite unclear.

Fate created a symbolic switchpoint at the beginning of the 1980s. In close proximity, a number of once and would-be kings died—Sartre, Aron, Lacan, Foucault—while there was the relative eclipse of certain others (Althusser, after the murder of his wife; even Derrida, despite his continuing American celebrity). Beyond this, beginning at the same point, the centrality of postmodernism and poststructuralism declined somewhat (except as an export product to the English-speaking world), wounded by ever more intense critical attack and changing political concerns. In fact, the post-1968 moment of rebellion had come to an end in ways that influenced the reception of different forms of thought. The 1980s became a time of hard-nosed economic and political reevaluations.

In the current period, predominant modes of thought in the left intellectual universe have thus changed rather dramatically. The characteristic mood of antistatism, apparent from the mid-1980s onward and contiguous with the policy failures of the left and movements of economic restructuring, has involved an assiduous resurrection of liberal political philosophy taking stage center from poststructuralism. If, in the new setting, one could no longer rely either upon Marxist guidelines to confer meaning on the social world or upon poststructuralist deconstruction to cast doubt on the very possibility of any such lasting meaning, then one had to philosophize in different ways about the state and society relationships.

Both state and society existed. Intellectuals in the 1980s seemed to realize that no foreseeable future change would abolish or dramatically alter the need for regulating relationships between them. The Marxist operation of reducing the separate dynamics of state and society to one set of causal variables and programming their reconciliation in a utopian, noncontradictory future was no longer on. The contradictions seemed, instead, to be permanent. Moreover, it could no longer be a question of positing the constantly shifting, unpredictable but nonetheless omniscient oppressiveness of *both* state and society in postmodern ways. The meaning of state-society relationships had to be reconstructed in the here and now.

A number of different intellectual quests converged on the final results. There was a massive reexamination of nineteenth-century French liberalism—Constant, Guizot, and, above all, Tocqueville (Rosanvallon 1985; Manent 1987). And then there was much direct translation from the

American, from 1950s and 1960s reflections on pluralism and from more recent liberal reflections on distributive justice, Rawls in particular. The underlying logic of this movement was to find a theoretical basis for a polity based on a democratic individualism where state power was limited and circumscribed, while avoiding the undesirable cul de sac of Anglo-Saxon atomistic utilitarianism. Left intellectuals in the later 1980s wanted America without Reagan and Adam Smith.

Quite as interesting as the dramatic shift in the theoretical biases of much of the left intelligentsia were the processes that underlay this shift. To be sure, there were semi-spectacular individual forays onto the battlefield like the Renaut and Ferry onslaught on poststructuralism in the interests of an individualistic reinterpretation of the movements of 1968 in *La Pensée 68*. Likewise, the more recent controversy, prompted by the Victor Farias book, about Heidegger's Nazi sympathies, which indirectly targeted French Heideggerians like Derrida, had significant debunking effects (Farias 1986).

In general, however, the "new individualism" achieved left intellectual preeminence without attachment to any monumental intellectual figure. Instead, it was the product of an accretion of middle-level individual contributions and the assiduous work of an important series of public intellectual institutions ranging through university colloquia and scholarly journals, elite reviews like *le Débat,* middle-brow weeklies like *Nouvel Observateur,* the efforts of key publishing houses (Editions du Seuil, Grasset), *Libération,* and the Fondation St. Simon. The left intellectuals' flight from Marxism and poststructuralism toward a Gallo-American individualistic political philosophy thus coincided with at least a momentary decline of the great man as left intellectual archetype.

Texts 2: The Artisans

French thought about state-society relationships, as in other societies, has also been carried on by "artisans," academic specialists working within their disciplines. The logic of production followed by such artisans has had its own rhythms. Here we only have space for limited impressions of the large amount of artisanal production and only those from some areas. Let us then glance at the cases of sociology, and peripherally history, with particular regard to one of the central issues for the intellectual discussion of state-society relations, that of the relationships between stratification and politics.

Academic specialties, in France as elsewhere, move forward through organized, but usually pluralistic, conflict between different schools of thought. French political sociology is no exception. It was really only in the 1960s that the discipline of sociology became a complex and varied enterprise with multiple outposts in CNRS (the *Centre National de le Recherche Scientifique*) research operations and expanding university faculties. As things gathered momentum after the Algerian War, many plants, if not 100 flowers, bloomed. Thus in the 1960s there developed a number of Socialisant sociological visions of state-society relations. Alain Touraine, but one example, worked toward a theoretical model in which class structuration and struggle were the key elements for understanding political behaviors and state actions in quite a Marxisant way, at least in the abstract. Pierre Bourdieu deployed a similar conceptual vocabulary in his earlier works on reproduction through education.[4]

Each of these *patrons* and his followers developed profoundly different specific approaches along with energetically pursued intellectual and institutional rivalries. And each developed visions that were profoundly different from orthodox Marxisms, PCF or other. But the basic perception of a society structured unequally into classes determining political behaviors and state action through conflict persisted. Moreover, around such *grands patrons* there existed a swarm of Marxisant sociology—often quite tied to the debates of political groups like the *Parti Socialiste Unifié* (PSU)—which shared similar basic premises. From such quarters came, for example, the important contributions of Serge Mallet (1963, 1964), Pierre Belleville (1963), André Gorz (1964), and others. Important left journals like *Les Temps Modernes* and *France Observateur* were willing vehicles for such ideas.

In the 1960s, there was, therefore, little parallel between the widespread development of Marxisant state-society reflections in sociology and the rise of mastersinger structuralism. May 1968 and its aftermath only intensified these different artisanal dynamics. There was no dramatic shift analogous to that from structuralism to poststructuralism for the sociologists. Instead, neo- and "post-" Marxist visions of state-society relations flowered.[5] Touraine and his équipe, for example, agressively pursued their efforts to elaborate and disseminate their "revisionist" class conflict view in which May 1968, and its aftermath "proved" that the relationships characteristic of "industrial societies" were beginning to give way in France to those of "postindustrial" societies (Touraine 1968, 1969). Production-based conflicts over an economistic "historicity" were being transcended by "new social movements" and class conflicts over the "programming" of society by new technocratic elites. The form of traditional Marxisant arguments—arguing from the structural, class characteristics of social stratification to politics— was thereby maintained better to argue against the traditional political *content* of such arguments, in particular against the more classical propositions of the PCF. The Bourdieu boutique likewise expanded its production on reproduction, with arguments that proceeded from class conflict to various types of behaviors, via the Bourdivin conceptual toolbox of cultural capital, habitat, "field," cultural investment, and so on. Bourdieu's actual conclusions were redolent of the Frankfurt School's pessimism about the eternalization of domination, but the neo-Marxist flavor of the argument was what counted.[6]

Thus far we have been talking about the stars of the artisanal world. Alongside the accelerated productivity of the various established sociological *boîtes,* there was also great expansion in the numbers of stratification-based Marxisant contributions from other, less strictly academic, sources. As the 1970s—and the renaissance of the French left—progressed, the effects of "official" intellectualization coming from within the various left parties provided important inputs into left intellectual debates. The elaborations of State Monopoly capitalism theory from the PCF's *Section Economique* and PS (*Parti Socialiste*) discussions about *le Front de Classe* (see Ross 1978, 1987a) were important contributions, for example. Later Eurocommunist and Euroleft reflections (like those of Nicos Poulantzas and Christine Buci-Glucksmann) were significant. Even *autogestionnaire* political sociology in much of the 1970s, whether associated with the PSU or the CFDT, tended to follow a neo-Marxist outline, rejecting, of course, statist correlations in the interests of decentralized class actions.

The situation changed dramatically beginning in the later 1970s. First of all, there was a rapid deflation of artisanal confidence in neo-Marxist stratification-based models of politics. By the mid-1980s, Marxism and its concepts had disappeared from the word processors and bookshelves of French social scientists. Only Bourdieu persisted along such lines. In more influential recent works, issues pertaining to social stratification and politics—Luc Boltanski's *Cadres,* for example—one finds a newly phenomenologized sense of the social construction of groups rather than reference to underlying social structures.

More generally, left political sociology has ceased being "left" in the older French sense of the term. But no single coherent alternative has yet come to replace the "old" class analytical orthodoxy; instead, a pluralism of outlooks coexists. Still, there has also been a rise in new reflection about nineteenth-century French liberal republican political culture and its social bases that parallels the rise of similar concerns in general social theory. Tocqueville, often retranslated from the American, has replaced Marx. Underlying this, confidence in the state's capacity to reorient social behaviors, to coordinate the economy in more just and equitable ways, to regenerate civic virtue, and so on seems to have disappeared. Much theoretical and methodological attention has turned toward individuals and their calculations—aided and abetted by evidence from opinion polls and election studies that showed a rise in individual, as opposed to class, orientations—and to the textures of nonpolitical associative life. The increasing intellectual prominence of economists and economic ideas has prodded the artisans in similar directions.

The story thus far is striking. Until the later 1970s, the clash of master-singers and the debate among the artisan sociologists proceeded according to quite different logics. Basic, rough-and-ready Marxisant notions survived and thrived in political sociology while poststructuralism came to dominate among the grands intellos. By the 1980s, however, the mastersingers' and artisans' trajectories, if quite remarkably different, did seem to reach analogous conclusions. The end of the poststructuralist vogue and the rise of "political philosophy" in the 1980s mastersinger debate does share certain common concerns with much recent political sociology. Both debates are profoundly skeptical about theoretical perspectives that posit the scientific comprehensibility of the social world. Each has become immeasurably more modest even if, France being France, they may have become *dramatically* more modest.

It is worth mentioning what is perhaps the most striking example of left intellectual artisan activities in recent years, even if it falls outside the realm of sociology. The bicentennial of the French Revolution was celebrated in 1989. As the event approached, it was quite natural that historians' debates about the revolution should percolate out of specialist discussion into the public domain. The ways in which this happened were nonetheless extraordinary.

For decades prior to the 1980s, the "social" approach to understanding the revolution had dominated among professionals, following Jaurès, Mathiez, and Soboul. This Marxisant approach stressed the conflictual interactions of social classes around economic concerns and contended that the events of 1789-94 were the core of "bourgeois revolution." In the 1980s, this all began to change, and a new orthodoxy emerged from a social movement of historians led by Francois Furet.

This new orthodoxy contended that the older social approach had profoundly misunderstood what the revolution was about and hence focused on the wrong issues. What was at stake in and around 1789 was not class conflict and bourgeois revolution but ideological combat over political institutions and doctrines. The "revisionists" asserted, moreover, that one could find the beginnings of the great twentieth-century struggles between liberal democracy and totalitarianism in the Great Revolution. The initial period of the revolution presented arguments for the rule of law, republicanism, and constitutional representation, while with the later years—with Marat, Robespierre, and Saint Just—came the first modern totalitarian innovations, intolerance and terror.

As the bicentennial celebration approached, advocates of the new orthodoxy seized the public platform to argue their positions. The politics of the later twentieth century in France and the world showed that the revolution was finally over, they claimed. Everyone except a few extremists agreed that a democratic republic that institutionalized the rule of law and the rights of man while socializing citizens to tolerate difference was the logical culmination of 1789 and that it had been achieved in France. Moreover, everyone agreed, they continued, that the Marxist-Leninist and totalitarian vision of further revolution was abhorrent and had failed. The real lesson of the Great Revolution was that great evil could come from the intellectualization of utopian social goals and subsequent efforts, often also promoted by intellectuals, to remodel actual social arrangements to conform to these goals.

One could elaborate these arguments, but their content is less interesting than their provenance. A group of left intellectual artisans—rapidly moving to the right, it should be noted—were able to use their professional preeminence to enter general debate thanks to the 200th anniversary of the revolution. Their effort to convert the public to their particular view of what had happened in the eighteenth century was largely successful. Moreover, in arguing intellectually about the precise contours of a long-ago set of events, the Furetistes and their allies were also attempting to shape political debates in the France of 1989. Finally, and perhaps most important, with the Furetistes we yet again see an intellectual operation that leads in the direction of renewing with nineteenth-century liberal debates in political philosophy.

Texts 3: Apprentices

Any given period in the history of intellectual life can be examined as a succession of political generations.[8] A "generation," in this sense, is a cohort formed by a profoundly important set of political events that set its intellectual compass and shaped its subsequent biography. The generational ideas that are usually referred to when the concept is used are "practical political" rather than formalized professional intellectual productions (even if the two may be relatable). There are any number of conceptual problems remaining to be resolved in the notion. Nonetheless, used in a rough-and-ready way, the idea of generation may provide us with yet another set of texts to illuminate the paths of modern French intellectuals.

As the all-important turn to the 1960s occurred, there were three "elder" generations in place. Resistance-Liberation groups, though divided on many things, were united by a propensity to see the social world in terms of classes, nationalism, and Jacobin statism (Ross 1987b). The "Mendesists," perhaps the first important post-Liberation left generation, were pragmatic, technocratic "modernists" who believed in a mixed economy pointed in an American consumerist direction, regulated and humanized by Keynesian welfare state techniques. They rejected the ideological rigidities and transformative pretentions of the official left, the conservatism of the right, and the statism of both in the interests of what Mendès-France himself called the *République Moderne* (Sirinelli 1985). The third "ancestor" generation contained the post-1956 *deçus* of PCF Marxism. Here there was cacophony from the start, if initially from a roughly similar neo-Marxist score. This group worked first to erect a non-PCF and less schematic Marxism in ways that made a real dent in the already dented hegemony of communism over intellectuals and legitimated thenceforth the existence of an independent Marxism in France.

The post-1956 Marxist revisionists and the Mendesists innovated in essential ways by dissociating themselves from the partisan orthodoxies that surrounded them. The generation of younger intellectuals formed by the last years of the Algerian War followed this lead almost with a vengeance—establishing what turned out to be a longer-run pattern of divorce between rebellious young members of the intelligentsia and the official left. French socialism, flat on its back and largely complicit with repression in Algeria, provided only the weakest flicker of protest leadership while the PCF, eager to protect de Gaulle and the prospects of a postwar alliance of the left, behaved in a moderate and circumspect way. Student and intellectual rejection of the war was, therefore, much more strident and militant than the official left wanted to see.[9]

The Algerian War generation of left intellectuals was a segmented one. Each segment, however, came to a committed rejection of the PCF's theories and practices. The most Marxisant segments of the generation sought a different "vanguard" than the PCF and a different, more muscular, Marxism, sometimes Trotskyism (as in the trajectories of Alain Krivine and Henri Weber) and sometimes, prodded by identification with the FLN, romantic involvement with Third World revolutionary movements. Finally, youth protest against the Algerian War was an essential moment in the development of the left Catholicism whose role would be so important in 1960s and 1970s France.

The Algerian War and May 1968 generations were intimately connected. May 1968 had its own complex causes and logics, of course. The protest movement, sparked in large part by the day-to-day ineptitude of university administrations, Gaullist ministerial staffs, and the police, had quickly to improvise structures and organizations practically out of nowhere. The politically proven cadre of the Algerian War generation was available for such tasks. This juxtaposition of generations explains the May movement's exceedingly strange combination of extreme libertarianism, even anarchism, and Marxist sloganizing. "Imagination" was brought briefly to power, amidst some chaos, to the words of the *Internationale*. But those who coached the crowds in the words to Citoyen Pottier's very French poem, if they could not agree among themselves *which* International was being referred to, were united about the one that was not. The Marxism of May, such as it was, was an anti-PCF Marxism.[10]

The complex consequences of this strange blending marked the May generation, which, in turn, was to make a profound impression on the politics of the 1970s and 1980s. The renaissance of *gauchisme* in its Maoist and Trotskyist forms was only one important outcome. The plethora of "new social movements" of the post-1968 era—the new feminism, regionalism, ecology, and so on, not to speak of the PSU and the left Catholic trade unionism of the CFDT—was another, quite different one. Finally, parts of the post-May generation also opted for "straight" left politics, either in the PCF or in the new PS as it came into being. And, of course, there was a "new culture" side to much of the May generation, whatever specific trajectory one discusses—excepting, perhaps, the *gauchistes,* an important shared conviction that social life, including sexual life, ought to be more relaxed or at least different from what it had been before.

The subsequent biographies of important segments of the May 1968 generation are very important to an understanding of contemporary intellectual politics. The Maoist part of the gauchiste segment has been reviewed recently in detail by Hamon and Rotman in *Génération.* The passionate *encadrement* of Maoists and others like them in quasi-cult grouplets could not be sustained in an ever more indifferent environment. The feelings of self-deception and personal waste that followed contributed to the creation of an important community of apostates. The so-called "new philosophy" was one manifestation of this apostasy. From nearly hysterical confidence in miracle solutions to France's problems—whether proletarian revolution or *autogestion*—there first emerged anger that the world was refractory to such utopian visions and then fury at the "straight" left, which, in the 1970s, was capitalizing on French discontents using traditional political programs and methods. By the mid-1970s, the underlying intellectual direction that had emerged was that the politics of the "old" left, embodied in *Union de la Gauche,* were both out of date and dangerous.

The separation of important segments of the maturing *soixante huitard* generation from official left politics was thus reconfirmed even as the justifications for this separation changed dramatically. The new perspectives that began to take root involved a strong rejection of global social thinking plus strong antistatism. Convictions grew that decentralized and democratic, often nonpolitical, movements below central state level were the real bearers of progressive change in France—in the jargon that was to come, "civil society" was the locus of social creativity, not parties and not civil servants. Here the ex-gauchistes rejoined other, more *autogestionnaire,* segments of the 1968 generation. From this it was but a few short steps, or years, to the modest politics of 1980s modernism—à la Michel Rocard, for example, or Jean Daniel and Jacques Julliard.

We must be careful here. The pattern of divorce between politicized generations of young intellectuals and the official left that appeared around Algeria was indeed reproduced after 1968. But the fallout from 1968 was more complex than this. Gauchiste apostates and politically disoriented autogestionnaires were not the only important parts of the 1968 generation. A large group of soixante huitards found their ways toward the two major parties of the left by the mid-1970s. In retrospect, the coming of Union de la Gauche was quite as important an event for the 1968 generation as the publication of *La Barbarie au visage humain*. By the early 1970s, the reformulating Socialist party offered young intellectual militants new openings to do left politics within an open and rapidly changing political organization that might, in the medium term, confer large career rewards. Large numbers of the 1968 and Left Unity generations also joined the PCF, motivated by a desire to combine militancy, passion, and career similar to that of their PS *frères-ennemis*. The complex processes and battles around the "Eurocommunization" of the party from 1973 to 1979 preponderantly involved intellectuals who were, to varying degrees, the bearers of propositions about inner-party reform involving greater internal democracy, attenuation of ties to the Soviet Union and the Soviet model, autogestion of a certain kind (decentralized movements for change), and changes in the PCF's theoretical mapping of the social world.

The fate of the 1960s and 1970s left intellectuals who aligned themselves with the various socialist *courants* was interesting. To the degree to which the PS became a sophisticated machine to manufacture political careers, they tended to fight out their various fractional battles inside the party. Prior to 1981, when the party finally came to power, such struggles could be justified in terms of their influence on the course of future left governments, even though in fact they were often as much struggles between elite cliques as anything else. After 1981, the entire PS, including intellectuals of all generations and all fractional stripes, fell hostage to the experience of left power. And when, after 1982-83, François Mitterrand and parts of his government decided that the time had come to abandon the voluntaristic politics of Union de la Gauche in favor of "accepting the mixed economy" and "modernizing" France, PS intellectuals were obliged to follow.[11]

Those parts of the post-1968 and Left Unity generations that entered the PCF brought dimensions of the 1968 experience with them and changed the party almost as much as they were changed by the party: up to 1978-79, that is. The PCF's dramatic shift at this point involved nothing less than the surgical removal of these intellectual generations from French communism altogether.[12] It was rare, subsequently, for the ex-communists who emerged from this horrendous massacre to follow ex-gauchistes and autogestionnaires toward apostasy. Rather, they became political orphans, people with ideas, often very good ideas, with no institutional place to express them.

One gets quite a different picture of intellectual movements and the forces behind them when one chooses the prism of political generations of intellectuals rather than those of the "mastersingers" and "artisans" discussed earlier. On this level, things are very complex. Still, once again, there is at least an *analogous* evolution in intellectual visions of state-society relationships. By the earlier 1980s, a "certain leftism," Marxisant or Socialisant, statist, and hypervoluntarist about the uses of political power to change economy and society in a radical way, had disappeared. It has been replaced in different ways, of course, but there are common themes placing much greater weight on the importance of creativity and innovation in the social sphere together with much greater skepticism about the capacities of the state to promote social change. And, almost as significantly, the "market" has been rediscovered as a part of this creative social world and not as an appendage of politics to be manipulated by the state.

CAUSES: INTELLECTUAL SPACES AND
POLITICAL DISCOURSES

From our three "texts," one sees a very large variation in left intellectual trajectories. However different they have been, there is a rather striking parallelism by the later 1980s. It would be wrong to claim that *intellos de gauche* have discarded their distinctive post-Dreyfusard role as universalistic beacon of political enlightenment for the less cerebral masses. But the actual content of this enlightenment, often in the past an injunction to radical change, has become decidedly less radical. Documenting this is easier than explaining it, however. I must try to make a sociological argument about the changes in the French left intelligentsia that have been discerned, while always remembering the reductionist dangers in so doing. On one level, this is because of the clear distinction that must be maintained between the actual operations of thought creation by intellectuals and the social structures within which thinkers create. And in our period, roughly between the end of the Algerian War and 1990, there have indeed been major changes in the underlying contexts for intellectual work in France. Let us now turn to two sets of such contexts, the changing "space" or social geography in which the French intelligentsia has lived and the changing "universe of political discourse" in France.[13]

The Changing Social Space of French Intellectuals

We reject one simpleminded approach to this puzzle, that of generic "modernization theory," from the outset. The real problem with the "modernization" paradigm, and modernization theories more generally, is that there are *many* modernizations and *many* modernities. The trajectory of French intellectuals is obviously different than those of intellectuals in other modern societies. This assertion draws us toward more detailed scrutiny of the spaces in which *French* intellectuals lived and how these spaces changed. And here there is much to say.

First of all, recent decades in France involved a massification of education, caused by the postwar demographic boom and policy choices leading to major increases in access to secondary and higher education.[14] The traditional Parisian left intellectual prior, say, to 1960, was the center of a relatively small world, few in numbers, often recruited from a narrow social base and a small circle of elite schools and reasonably well connected with provincial "troops" with similar backgrounds and values. By the later 1960s, this world had changed out of all recognition. There were still important elite networks and cliques, to be sure. But there were also thousands of intellectuals who did not partake of them at all spread over France. Because of this massification, by the late 1970s, the members of France's vastly enlarged corps of teaching and research functionaries could maintain few illusions. There might still be "mastersingers," but the bulk of French intellectuals could not aspire to be or know one.

Massification, connected with the coming of a more "postindustrial" occupational structure, meant that there was an even vaster increase in the numbers of people in occupations where "processing" and credentialing by higher education occurred. Thus a very large "quasi-intellectual" public came to exist in the new middle strata.[15] Intellectuals, strictly speaking, thereby became part of a much larger population of roughly similar people with similar cultural predilections.

In this context, it was not surprising that the structures of a wide range of institutions pertinent to intellectuals changed, in ways that in turn impinged on important intellectual concerns. The chaotic and unplanned ways in which rising numbers flowed into educational and research institutions created major tensions and strains and multiple discontents, for example. The turmoils of universities and research institutes over the years, May 1968 being only the largest, are the best known instances of these problems. Although this long history is marked by outbursts in which the institutional issues of intellectuals became, in one way or another, high politics, often clothed in leftish rhetoric, it has also no doubt enhanced the degree to which intellectual institutional movement and action became "corporatist" over time, with intellectuals acting to protect their own situation. To be sure, these same intellectuals voted massively for the left, but less out of any utopian concerns than because of a "pressure group" belief that the left would be more lavish with budgetary credits and more favorable to their corporatist demands.

The existence of a vastly increased number of academic and research intellectuals has also tended to foster more professional and "American" structures of intellectual association and peer evaluation. For individuals setting out on new careers in a progressively more fragmented world of knowledge and with much less of the universalistic esprit de corps than older intellectual elite status had conferred, the changing system has tended to establish new gatekeepers over cultural creations. Although such things vary greatly from discipline to discipline, it is no doubt true that intellectuals immersed in the problem-solving task presented by a highly specialized and fragmented academic area, often connected directly to an international dialogue, are somewhat less likely to conceive of their own intellectual work as a universalistic prescription for French society. "Professionalizing" intellectuals and researchers were not any less likely to lean electorally leftward than their predecessors. What was likely to change were intellectual identities and hence the place of politics in these identities. For the new professionals, especially those in the social sciences with a "political" vocation, worldviews would become less general and more narrow, following the logic of the intellectual division of labor.

The massification of "intellectualized" publics attendant upon increases in those practicing intellectual occupations and in those whose nonintellectual occupations presupposed extensive schooling also created a new and much more variegated "market" for cultural products. The new middle strata, a population of "intellectual workers," sought many of their cultural *and* political cues from the printed word. Media products tailored to such demands emerged in response. Dailies like *le Monde* and *Libération* and weekly newsmagazines in France not only "informed" but also "socialized" their readers—that is, within limits, tried to tell them what to think. The correlation between the political lines promoted by these particular organs and the political conclusions reached by the intelligentsia in the 1980s, which we earlier summarized, is striking. We will return to this later.

There are a number of other "spatial" arguments about changing intellectual politics. Régis Debray (1980, 1981) and others make much of what they call "mediacracy" and its effect on intellectual outlooks. A generic version of this argument might go as follows. Television, which becomes a major public fact only in our period, the massification of a new middle-strata reading public (plus increases in literacy in other groups), and the consequent concentration of publishing together reconfigure the cultural products industry. In consequence, the field of incentives within which many intellectuals operated is restructured. Television enhanced rapid turnover in intellectual modes and a shortening of historical perspective. In this setting, mass publishing controlled by a few large houses sought quick "coups" that could be widely advertised and rapidly sold. Becoming a "famous French intellectual" (Michele Lamont's phrase) in this context involved "flexibilization," to borrow a barbaric word from the economists. Aspirants had to write very quickly on very contemporary subjects in ways that would be accessible to wide audiences. Those who succeeded often had to work in a somewhat ephemeral world of current events and be prepared to change swiftly. The rewards for becoming this new kind of intellectual were very great, the argument went, thus many were tempted into careers that involved networking from, say, an academic point of departure into regular writing for a newsweekly like *Nouvel Obs* and into affiliations with important Parisian publishing houses. Patient dissemination of large intellectualized political doctrines over time—in the ways done by left intellectuals in the past—became immensely more difficult.

The analytical point of this argument is not that this new publishing-television complex is to be damned (although this is Debray's point) but that it contributes to changes in the nature of intellectual politics and, probably, to change in the political proclivities of important publics. Intellectuals, including left ones, who desire wide recognition may embark upon such "mediacratic" trajectories. To the degree to which their public work has political relevance, its shape will be constrained by the nature and demands of the publishing-television complex. The political "causes" and visions contained in the subsequent products, even if left leaning, will not be those of traditional left forces.

It is not easy to synthesize these different points. In our period, we are faced with a set of complex, crosscutting, and sometimes contradictory forces acting on the "space" of various kinds of French intellectuals. The increasing numbers of practicing intellectuals of all kinds—academic, research, scientific, journalistic, artistic—have definitely involved a growing fragmentation of identities and an increasingly complex professional division of labor, perhaps promoting some retreat from the kinds of global, universalistic, and somewhat messianic self-assigned missions held by many earlier intellectuals, especially of the left. Vastly greater numbers, professionalization, and continuous institutional turbulence may also have increased "corporatistic" senses in many intellectuals, senses that are not incompatible with left political views but that may undercut utopian and voluntaristic perspectives about radical social transformation. Third, the emergence of a commercially significant educated new middle-strata public created new market segments for media and publications. Because of marketing skill, "elective affinities," and political intelligence, the left-of-center parts of this segment have been largely filled with important new institutions disseminating political cues to the new audience in very effective ways. Finally, the "mediacratic" complex of publishing and television institutions has changed messages and changed incentive structures for those intellectuals who continue to seek public political notoriety.

Do we have here some causes for the parallel changes in intellectual political passions that we noted in our earlier three texts? Perhaps, but there is no compelling logic in them that "explains" the changing intellectual politics that our three different "texts" showed.

Intellectuals in France's Official Political Space

Intellectuals do not create political ideas either for private pleasure or in response to their own changing social structural positions. Political ideas are produced to influence a world that is dominated by those who actually "do" politics. The primary occupants of this world are political organizations and institutions. Mapping the evolution of relationships between these organizations and left intellectuals may tell us a great deal, then.

Our story really begins in the Algerian War years when the tenuous cold war moment of PCF intellectual hegemony came to an end. There were numerous causes, but the party's coalition-seeking moderation on the Algerian issue was the immediate one that alienated radical student and intellectual antiwar activists. At the same time, the socialists, with their deep complicity in colonial welfare (one important left Catholic claims that, to his generation, the SFIO represented a *socialisme expéditionnaire*)[16] and their sordid domestic political record, had little to offer intellectuals either.

The Algerian conflict produced a strong student and intellectual antiwar movement. There existed little official left space for intellectuals thus mobilized to occupy and influence, however. Neither official left parties nor labor unions had strategies that welcomed collaboration with this new intellectual rebelliousness. The result was divorce between much of the left intelligentsia and official left organizations. Much of the drama of ensuing decades was to involve unsuccessful efforts by official organizations to end this divorce by seducing the new intelligentsia, which was beginning to emerge from France's expanding and changing educational system.

The growing political "independence" of left intellectuals in the 1960s was not a unified phenomenon. The "high" intellectuality of the post-Algerian period involved the rise of structuralism, on the one hand, and attempts by non-PCF Marxists to regenerate a workable intellectual Marxism on the other, as we have seen. The "artisans," in the meantime, were busily using categories borrowed from Socialisant political catalogues to describe the modernizing—and occupationally postindustrializing—France that official left political reflection proved unable to confront. Among younger intellectual generations, there was a variety of "Third Worldisms" in the 1960s air, given the decolonizing, national liberation, nation-building events of the time.

Because the PCF remained, in 1962, by far the most powerful force on the official left, the opportunity to respond to the emergence of independent intellectual leftism fell first to it. The major failures of the 1960s were thus accumulated by a PCF that was unable to see anything in the rise of independent left intellectual reflection and activism beyond anticommunism and the agitation of annoying petit bourgeois class enemies. PCF behaviors involved a self-fulfilling prophecy. By 1968, the party's shortsightedness had encouraged the formation of a broad and determined network of anticommunist leftist young leaders. Then, when this generation assumed important roles in the May-June 1968 movements, the party treated them in exactly the same way it had earlier treated the Algerian War protesters, as pesky agents of reaction. Alienation from the PCF among large parts of the post-1968 generations followed. Here the story is clear. The PCF and its appendant organizations failed to perceive the importance of the changes in France's social map and adapt their theoretical and programmatic ideas to appeal to the burgeoning new middle strata.

The new intelligentsia, growing apace, clearly began a "left turn" around 1968. Given the PCF's failures, the reconstituting PS was in the most promising position to gather in its political support and intellectual assistance. The rebuilding of the PS as a federation of jockeying factions was an important move, because it allowed parts of the post-1968 generation of leaders of the intelligentsia an open door to try to promote their own views within the new party. To the degree to which this worked, the PS placed itself in a position to acquire the political allegiance and influence the political attitudes of the left intelligentsia. During the 1970s, however, the PS faced a contradiction between its coalitional setting and the social alliance needs to which it had to respond. Opting for Union de la Gauche involved "dealing" with the PCF better to subordinate and weaken French communism. We now know how successful this choice turned out to be. But Union de la Gauche meant compromising with the PCF on program and ideology.[17] This meant a general PS outlook in the 1970s governed by the spirit of the 1972 Common Program, a statist, *dirigiste* platform of reforms. The appeal of such politics to many intellectuals was limited.

By the mid-1970s, indices of growing electoral success for the official left and Union de la Gauche were clear. Moreover, this reconfiguration of official left politics did appeal to some of the "independent" left intelligentsia. Inside the PS, there were struggles over ideas and power to be had: Even those who disagreed with the logic of Common Program proposals could have their say, and there were promising political careers to be built. The PCF also opened itself to change, inviting left intellectuals to hasten such change and assume roles that also promised careers.

This incorporation of intellectuals into the official left was but partial, however. There were strong intellectual currents that found the left's chosen Common Program strategy unpalatable. One rather large cluster of left intellectuals, with connections to the labor movement through the CFDT, roots in the PSU, and important university and publishing ties, advocated what one might call autogestionnaire politics, stressing decentralized democratic social creativity embedded in a vague antistatist, antitraditional social democratic and, of course, anticommunist feeling.[18] Autogestionnaire segments of the intelligentsia supported the left electorally. The problem was that they did not recognize their own political ideas and outlooks in the official political ideas of the left in the 1970s.[19]

PS strategists, François Mitterrand in particular, quickly recognized the problem and moved to include major parts of the organized autogestionnaire forces into the PS at the autumn 1974 *Assises du Socialisme*. In consequence, the PS made solemn declarations about its commitment to autogestion. But the operation did not convince the groups in question because Mitterrand immediately used the PS's new autogestionnaires for his own purposes in the party's complicated internal politics without really modifying the basic statist and Jacobin line of the party. The opportunity was missed, then. Autogestionnaire parts of the post-1968 left intellectual generation were never effectively integrated into the politics of the official left.

By the later 1970s, the consequences were evident. A clear movement of ideological opposition to official left politics had crystallized around a "second left." What was most interesting about this movement, beyond the actual political maneuvers in which it engaged, which are beyond our scope, was its evolution into the 1980s. Responding to the coming of economic crisis after 1974 and the wave of anti-Sovietism that swept much of the French intelligentsia in the later 1970s, the second left moved considerably from its original post-1968 politics. Autogestion was gradually decoupled from radicalism, in particular from the goal of transcending capitalism. Deradicalized, autogestion became an appeal to destatize the left, to promote solutions to various social problems through decentralized bargaining, to revitalize "civil society," and to recognize the utility, as a decentralized mechanism, of the market. Tocqueville supplanted Proudhon and Rosa Luxemburg while Alfred Marshall replaced the young Marx.

This evolution was accomplished, in part, through the symbiotic fusion of the autogestionnaires with another, largely pre-1968, left intellectual generation. Mendesism, by the 1970s, had become a variety of centrist modernism that stressed economic and ideological "realism." Not "socialist" in any conventional ways, it explicitly rejected notions about the transcendance of capitalism as utopian. It recognized the centrality of the market and the importance of innovative management while, through its stress on the "mixed economy," it also acknowledged the market's limits and the important role that remained for state intervention. Above all, it stressed the need for conscious and continual efforts, informed by scientific knowledge, to modernize France. Mendesism, therefore, rejected the lyrical, transformative, and exaggeratedly statist rhetoric of the left Common Program and the strategic inclusion of the PCF into legitimate left politics that the Common Program implied.

What was interesting about modern Mendesism was, in part, its skillful use of new political technologies. This use, however, was predicated on complex new political realities. As we have earlier remarked, the numbers and life-styles of the new intellectual middle strata had changed in ways that challenged traditional left parties and other organizations. Put another way, the coalitional and social alliance logics that official left organizations faced pulled them in different directions. The actual politics chosen by these parties for the 1970s made room for the seduction and incorporation of a number of the left intellectual currents that had emerged in the 1960s and 1970s, but not for all of them. Large parts of the new middle strata, if still left leaning in *electoral* terms, were thus distanced from official lines and developed a sense of themselves as autonomous political and social actors.

This situation "opened" parts of the new middle strata to political influences coming from outside the official left. For such groups, *militantisme* and older types of "engagement" gave way to a more synthetic cultural adhesion that political parties were either unable or unwilling to provide. Media entrepreneurs were quick to perceive the opportunities in this new setting. *Nouvel Observateur,* a Mendesiste weekly by the 1970s, is the most interesting case. In the 1970s, *Nouvel Obs* practically became a quasi party. Disseminating trendy cultural material plus a shrewd combination of "second left" ideas, the journal explicitly tried to undermine the prevailing political discourses of the official left, targeting the political perspectives of the new "massified" intelligentsia with the message (Pinto 1984). *Nouvel Obs* was not alone, either. Concentrated efforts in the same direction by publishing houses—like Editions du Seuil—intensified the effects. Moreover, by the end of the 1970s, *Libération,* an important daily newspaper, had come to play an analogous role as quasi party for the "new culture" segments of the post-1968 left intelligentsia.

By the later 1970s, new dialogues between parts of the left intelligentsia and such commercially oriented quasi parties had been solidified. The explosion of anti-Sovietism among French intellectuals occurred largely in such dialogues. Furor around Solzhenitsyn in 1974-1975, the *Republica* affair in Portugal in 1975, and, more generally, the breast-beating, anti-Enlightenment, apostasy of the "new philosophy" representing the collective mea culpas of the post-1968 gauchiste generation passed through them. The trials and tribulations of Union de la Gauche in 1977-1978 provided new material about the evils of statism and the inherently manipulative nature of official left ideas and apparatuses (here, of course, the PCF was the prime target, but the PS was not exempt) as did the frightening internal crisis of the PCF after 1978 that saw the Communists lose most of their intellectuals and turn back toward the kind of strategic fundamentalism that would seal off the PCF from the intelligentsia permanently.

By 1981, when the official left finally came to power determined to implement its long-standing program, an important impasse had thus been reached. Much of the intelligentsia, and many important intellectuals, had voted to make this political success happen. At the same time, however, substantial parts of the left intelligentsia felt profoundly alienated from the official politics of this successful left.

The story did not end here. The experience of the left in power after 1981 was disastrous for the remaining credibility of "old left" programmatic and theoretical ideas. The Common Program's statism and radical Jacobin reformism could not survive the economic and political failures of 1982-83. In response, the PS changed its policies dramatically while the PCF accelerated its sectarian tangent toward further decline. For the PS, "breaking with capitalism" gave way to a much more cautious posture. The left's political failures and about-faces necessitated a changed ideological identity. The PS in particular needed to find a new package of political ideas to match its new policies. One major consequence was that the dominant political discourse left of center in France was completely transformed. What the PS and François Mitterrand seized upon in these critical years was a combination of international "econospeak," the collected wisdom of the progressive but neoliberalizing "realist" economics pundits the world over, plus the ideological politics of the *deuxième gauche*. The PS, in other words, tried to repair its damaged political position by adopting the vocabularies of the new middle-strata groups that had earlier found the Common Program so repellent. The prevalent left neo-Tocquevillean intellectual climate of the second half of the 1980s was in part consequence, in part the cause, of this.

PROVISIONAL CONCLUSIONS

The purposes here have been relatively modest. First, I tried to deconstruct three different left French intellectual "texts" to uncover central developmental themes about state-society relationships. Then I speculated on certain causes of the dynamics that were uncovered. Here, there are interesting conclusions to report. The unfolding trend in mastersinger texts is unmistakably clear. Socialism, Marxism, and virtually all other post-enlightenment, largely nineteenth-century, visions of dramatic human liberation through political struggle have vanished. Symbolically, the concept of revolution has completely disappeared. Ultimately, a modest, largely imported, and gentle liberalism assumed pride of place. The sequencing of developments in political sociology was very different. Most notably, during the period in the 1970s when poststructuralist thought assumed preeminence, political sociology persisted in its reference to stratification-based Socialisant models of state-politics-society relationships. Nonetheless, by the mid-1980s, the center of gravity in left political sociology had also shifted toward a modest liberal revisionism as well. The movement of left intellectual generations, our third text, is too complex to summarize in detail. Suffice it to say that its developmental logics have been, in recent decades, yet again different from those of our other two texts; yet, by the later 1980s, they also had moved into a "soft" liberal orbit.

The literature on French intellectuals almost always postulates the crystallization of a specific French intellectual "type" in the Dreyfus affair. This type sees a particularly unmediated relationship between the creation of ideas as an intellectual vocation and doing politics. The intello thinks and writes about the structures and dynamics of the world in universal terms, understands this process as one that is destined to enlighten the less informed, and then feels compelled to intervene in the political world to transform these ideas into social reality. Despite substantial changes in their social settings, French intellectuals still *do* politics in relatively unmediated and quite distinctive ways. Compared with earlier periods, however, what seems to have happened is that they now do so in the interests of unusually humble and modest political ideas.

The real puzzle lies in explaining *why* this has occurred. The various indices of changes in the specific life and work situations of French intellectuals do not seem to provide any strong determinations for the intellectual events that we see—indeed, the different indices would seem to cut in very different ways. The major overdetermining factor that we did discover was, not surprisingly, the changing relationships of left intellectuals and official left politics. In a society that has given its intellectuals a uniquely direct political voice, the interaction between this voice and the organizational field of left politics has been very important, in contrast to societies where intellectuals are largely "ghettoized" in specifically academic settings or are otherwised neutralized politically. Here we saw something truly extraordinary happening. For complex reasons having to do with very real contradictions between coalitional demands and changing social alliance problematics, the official left was unable to include important fragments of the left intelligentsia into its ideological orbit in a viable way during a moment of great social change.

What happened was extraordinary. The different strains of official left politics in the two decades after the end of the Algerian War never really made satisfactory connections with the desires and goals of important parts of the new intelligentsia that emerged in France in these same years. These ideas had come, by the later 1970s, to live a thriving parallel existence in the more general evolving universe of left intellectualism in France, even if they did not impinge decisively on the evolution of official left politics until the 1980s. When they did move into a position of quasi orthodoxy, this occurred following the abject failure in 1982-83 of left policies. Policy failure meant ideological and intellectual failure for the official left. It was thus absolutely necessary for the official left to undertake an ideological conversion experience to avoid political bankruptcy. In consequence, the PS borrowed as much as it could from the storehouse of "second left" ideological and intellectual material that had accumulated outside the corridors of official left power prior to the early 1980s. In all this, left French intellectuals came to play a very important reorienting role in the ideological sphere of French left politics. By this point, however, the ideas of these intellectuals had evolved away from the corrosive radicalism both of poststructuralism and of autogestionnaire thought into the "soft" liberal revisionism that now dominates both the left political and intellectual scene. Thus, by the end of the 1980s, both the left intellectual scene and the left ideological scene had been completely transformed. Marxism was dead. Traditional social democracy was dead. Classes and workers had been removed from discourse. Tocqueville was very much alive. A new individualism had emerged triumphant.

NOTES

1. Jeannine Verdès-Leroux (1983) conveys a good sense of what PCF intellectualism was like in this period.

2. See Lévi-Strauss (1966), *The Savage Mind,* Chapter 9.

3. The so-called (usually by Anglo-Saxons) "French feminists" like the three mentioned and others (Antoinette Fouque and Catherine Clement, for example) present us with an interesting subplot. The French women's movement emerged from the student rebellion of the 1960s in much the same way as the new feminism exploded in other societies. The fate of the French women's movement proved very different from those of new feminist movements in Anglo-Saxon societies, however. At the precise movement when French feminism began to define itself—in an atmosphere of sectarian disputation, it should be said—in the early 1970s, the official French left, which had been out of power for decades, reconfigured its programs and approaches and began to gather the steam that eventually brought it to power in 1981. The effect of this on the women's movement was extraordinarily debilitating. Both the socialists and the communists, the major components of the official left, were concerned with maximizing their

support and, to do so, were eager to co-opt the energies of various post-1968 rebellious currents, including feminism. Moreover, both had a long history of what one might call "socialist feminism," of raising women's issues in the context of a broader "class" appeal and program. The new women's movement in France—like virtually all of the other 1970s "new social movements" in the French context—had, therefore, to choose strategically between independence, which promised the efflorescence of newer approaches, and integration into the official left, which promised a certain amount of political effectiveness at the price of accepting "socialist feminism." The consequence of this situation was to divide and severely weaken the autonomous women's movement in France. Different fractions of the movement made different choices, but the "vacuum cleaner" effect of the official left parties was considerable. Those segments of the movement that remained outside the orbit of the official left (and the unions, which were also important players), themselves rapidly divided into small competing groups. The ultimate result of this complicated process was that important postmodern feminist thinkers like those we have mentioned acquired only the most limited audience in France—they never became "titans" in our sense of the word. On the other hand, they have become extremely important figures in the academic and other debates of Anglo-Saxon, and particularly North American, feminism. The best source we know on this subplot is Jane Jenson (1989).

4. See, for example, Touraine (1973) and Bourdieu and Passeron (1964).

5. Aronian, Crozierian, and other liberal perspectives survived. Each wrote his treatise on 1968, for example, which conformed to his earlier theories. See Aron (1968) and Crozier (1969).

6. See Pierre Bourdieu (1985), *Homo Academicus,* published much later but initially put together in the aftermath of May 1968.

7. Raymond Boudon's work is the leading source of this in French sociology (see, for example, Boudon 1985).

8. See *Les Cahiers de l'Institut d'Histoire du Temps Présent,* No. 16, November 1987. The IHTP *Bulletin Trimestriel,* No. 31 of March 1988, provides an extensive bibliography on "generations."

9. See Hervé Hamon and Patrick Rotman's (1979) excellent *Les Porteurs de Valise* for a thorough overview of this.

10. It was also frenetic in its search for a new, more viable and militant "vanguard" for the *damnés de la terre,* whether Trotskyism, Maoism, role modeling on *El Che,* or whatever agencies Herbert Marcuse may have had in mind.

11. The history of all this is recounted analytically in Geroge Ross, Stanley Hoffman, and Sylvia Malzacher (1987); but compare with Ross and Jenson (1988).

12. We have talked about dimensions of this massacre in George Ross and Jane Jenson (1985) *The View From Inside: A French Communist Cell in Crisis.*

13. This term is lovingly borrowed from Jane Jenson.

14. The numbers are astounding. In the 1930s, 1 in 500 students obtained the *baccalauréat,* a figure that had become 1 in 8 by 1960 and 1 in 4 by 1979. There were 737,000 secondary school students in 1946; there are 6 million today. The number of university students grew geometrically—150,000 in 1955, 510,000 in 1967, 750,000 in 1974, 861,000 in 1985. In 1936, there were 9,000 secondary school teachers—the shock troops of intellectual networks, left and right—today there are 290,000. There were 1,200 university teachers in 1946, 8,000 in 1959, 31,000 in 1969, and 41,000 in 1985 (and these numbers do not include the large numbers of CNRS researchers). There were 2,500 educational buildings opened between 1965 and 1975, or, in Henri Weber's calculations, one for every school day. These numbers are gleaned from Antoine Prost (1982) and Desire Calderon (1984).

15. Liberal professionals and *cadres supérieurs* grew from 2.9% to 7.7% of the active labor force between 1954 and 1982, for example; *cadres moyens,* from 5.8% to 13.8%; and *employés,* a mixed bag, to be sure, from 10.8% to 19.9% (numbers are from J. and G. Brémond (1985).

16. The term is Michel Winock's (1978).

17. We have discussed these issues at greater length in George Ross and Jane Jenson (1989), "The Tragedy of the French Left."

18. Pierre Rosanvallon's (1976) writings provide a bellwether for this very large segment of the intelligentsia.

19. For a solid, if biased, overview of major parts of this autogestionnaire movement, see Hervè Hamon and Patrick Rotman, *La Deuxieme Gauche* (1982).

REFERENCES

Aron, Raymond. 1968. *La Révolution introuvable*. Paris: Julliard.

Belleville, Pierre, 1963. *Une Nouvelle Classe Ouvrière*. Paris: Julliard.

Benton, T. 1984. *The Rise and Fall of Structural Marxism*. London: Macmillan.

Biegalski, Christian, ed. 1970. *Arguments/3, Les Intellectuels, la pensée antricipatrice*. Paris: Gallimard.

Boltanski, Luc. 1988. *Cadres*. Cambridge: Cambridge University Press.

Boudon, Raymond. 1985. *L'Ideologie*. Paris: Fayard.

Bourdieu, Pierre. 1985. *Homo academicus*. Paris: Minuit.

Bourdieu, Pierre and Jean-Claude Passeron. 1964. *Les Héritiers*. Paris: Minuit.

Brèmond, J. et G. 1985. *L'Economie Française*. Paris: Hatier.

Calderon, Desirè. 1984. "Enquête sur les intellectuels." *Révolution* (February).

Crozier, Michel. 1969. *La Société Bloquée*. Paris: Seuil.

Debray, Règis. 1980. *Le Scribe*. Paris: Grasset.

———. 1981. *Teachers, Writers, Celebrities: The Intellectuals of Modern France*. London: Verso.

Farias, Victor. 1986. *Heidegger et le Nazisme*. Paris: Gallimard.

Ferry, Luc and Alain Renaut. 1985. *La Pensée 68: Essai sur l'antihumanisme contemporain*. Paris: Seuil.

Gorz, Andrè. 1964. *Stratégie Ouvrière et Neo-capitalisme*. Paris: Seuil.

Hamon, Hervè and Patrick Rotman. 1979. *Les Porteurs de Valise*. Paris: Albin Michel.

———. 1982. *La Deuxieme Gauche*. Paris: Ramsay.

Jenson, Jane. 1989. "Ce n'est pas un hasard: The Varieties of French Feminism." In *Contemporary France 3*, edited by Jolyon Howarth and George Ross.

Lèvi-Strauss, Claude. 1966. *The Savage Mind*. Chicago: University of Chicago Press.

Mallet, Serge. 1963. *La Nouvelle Classe Ourvière*. Paris: Seuil.

———. 1964. *Le Gaullisme et la gauche*. Paris: Seuil.

Mament, Pierre. 1987. *Histoire Intellectuelle du libéralisme*. Paris: Calmann-Levy.

Ory, Pascal and Jean-Francois Sirinelli. 1986. *Les Intellectuels en France, de l'affaire Dreyfus à nos jours*. Paris: Armand Colin.

Pinto, Louis. 1984. *L'Intelligence en action: "Le Nouvel Observateur."* Paris: Anne-Marie Metaillie.

Prost, Antoine. 1982. *L'Ecole et la famille dans une société en mutation*. Paris: Nouvelle Librairie de France.

Rosanvallon, Pierre. 1985. *Le Moment Guizot*. Paris: Gallimard.

———. 1987. *L'Age de l'autogestion*. Paris: Seuil.

Ross, George. 1978. "French Marxists and the New Middle Classes." *Theory and Society* (Winter).

————. 1987a. "Destroyed by the Dialectic: Politics, the Decline of Marxism and the New Middle Strata in France." *Theory and Society* (Fall).

————. 1987b. "Adieu vieilles idées: The Rise and Fall of Resistance-Liberation Left Discourse." In *Contempory France,* edited by Jolyon Howorth and George Ross. London: Frances Pinter.

Ross, George and Jane Jenson. 1985. *The View from Inside: A French Communist Cell in Crisis.* Berkeley: University of California Press.

————. 1988. "The Tragedy of the French Left." *New Left Review* 171 (October).

————. 1989. "The Tragedy of the French Left." In *The Future of the European Left,* edited by Patrick Camiller. London: Verso.

Ross, George, Stanley Hoffman, and Sylvia Malzacher, eds. 1987. *The Mitterrand Experiment.* New York: Oxford University Press.

Sirinelli, Jean-François. 1985. "Les intellectuels et Pierre Mendès France." In *Pierre Mendès France et le Mendésisme,* by Jean-Francois Sirinelli. Paris: Fayard.

Touraine, Alain. 1968a. *Le Mouvement de Mai ou le communisme utopique.* Paris: Seuil.

————. 1968b. *La Societe post-industrielle.* Paris: Denoel.

————. 1973. *Production de la Société.* Paris: Seuil.

Verdés-Leroux, Jeannine. 1983. *Au Service du Parti.* Paris: Fayard-Minuit.

Winock, Michel. 1978. *La République se meurt.* Paris: Seuil.

Chapter 5

POLITICAL INTELLECTUALS IN THE THIRD WORLD
The Caribbean Case

ALEX DUPUY
Wesleyan University

DURING THE 1970s, barely a decade after most of the English-speaking island-nations of the Caribbean gained their formal independence from Great Britain,[1] there emerged a wave of mass movements protesting against the widening socioeconomic gaps between the small elites comprised of European or Middle Eastern expatriates and/or individuals of Afro-Caribbean/European/Middle Eastern/Chinese/East Indian origins, and the predominantly Afro-Caribbean and East Indian working classes. At the leadership of these movements were groups of intellectuals largely based at the various campuses of the University of the West Indies. These intellectuals, who composed the New World Group, not only were calling for the creation of a more just and equal society but were also demanding a restructuring of the unequal relationship between the Caribbean economies and the advanced capitalist economies that they saw as the root cause of the continued underdevelopment and poverty of the region. Although, in most of the island economies, the indigenous elites in control of the state followed procapitalist and pro-Western policies, in others, like Jamaica and Grenada, political parties led by Western-educated professionals and intellectuals, like Michael Manley and Maurice Bishop, came to power and sought to establish a democratic socialist or a noncapitalist model of development as an alternative to the dependent capitalist model bequeathed to the region by centuries of colonialism.

The assumption of state power by political parties led by credentialed intellectuals and professionals signaled the emergence of a new social class in the Caribbean alongside the old propertied class comprised mostly of expatriates from Western Europe and the even smaller representatives of the foreign corporations. The main concern of this chapter is to assess the emergence of this new class in the Caribbean in light of the debate that

AUTHOR'S NOTE: I would like to thank Jerome Karabel, David Swartz, and Barry Truchil for their comments and suggestions on earlier drafts of this chapter.

originated in the advanced countries on the nature and class location of the intelligentsia—lawyers, medical doctors, professional politicians, corporate managers, notaries, and so on—and intellectuals—scholars, scientists, artists, teachers, journalists and so on, that is, those who engage in the "production of ideas and the manipulation of cultural symbols" (Gagnon 1987, pp. 5-6). The debate of the "new class" in the advanced countries paid little attention to the counterparts of this class in the underdeveloped countries of the "Third World."[2] The debate thus ignores whether the hypotheses it generated on the characteristics of the new class are applicable to Third World realities or whether they need to be modified. This chapter argues that new conceptualizations and hypotheses are needed to explain the Caribbean experience.

The chapter makes three related arguments. First, contrary to the views of some of the main proponents of New Class theory in the advanced countries, I argue that the credentialed in that class remain subordinated to the propertied bourgeoisie—that is, those who own or control capital and the means of production. Second, and in contrast to the advanced countries, the credentialed class becomes the dominant fraction of the dominant class in Third World countries like those of the Caribbean. This is so not because they possess "cultural capital" but because they control the state and constitute themselves as a managerial bourgeoisie. And, third, though the managerial bourgeoisie in control of the state is the dominant fraction of the dominant class in the postcolonial Caribbean, it remains technologically and economically subordinated to and dependent on foreign capital and hence on the international corporate bourgeoisie based in the advanced countries.

CULTURAL CAPITAL AND THE
NEW BOURGEOISIE

For several decades now, many theorists have argued that, in the twentieth century, industrial society has been transformed into "postindustrial" society, that there has been a correlative transformation of the class structure of postindustrial society that no longer corresponds to the dual class structure of the industrial period, and that the old propertied bourgeoisie has been disempowered by the rise of a "new class" of professional managers and intelligentsia. I do not intend here to review that whole debate. Rather, I want to focus on the arguments advanced by those who consider the emergence of this "new class" in the context of a theory of class domination and exploitation in contrast to those who see postindustrial society as representing the disappearance or attenuation of these social relations.[3] I will limit my discussion to those I consider to be among the strongest proponents of the competing perspectives on the new managerial and professional class before developing my own argument in a later section of the chapter.

Alvin Gouldner (1979) may not have been the first to advance the view that the professional intelligentsia and intellectuals, as possessors of cultural capital, represent a new cultural bourgeoisie that competes with the traditional moneyed bourgeoisie for dominance in contemporary or postindustrial society. But Gouldner grounds his conception of the new cultural bourgeoisie in a general theory of class domination and sees the new class in terms of its contradictory relations to other classes. For Gouldner, the new cultural bourgeoisie exists in a state of tension, and even antagonism, with the old business and propertied bourgeoisie, which it seeks to replace. The primary cause of the tension and conflict between the old and new bourgeoisies stems from the different ethos governing these two classes, with the old bourgeoisie presented as concerned primarily with the accumulation of money-capital and the new cultural bourgeoisie, though also motivated by material interests, mostly concerned with the advancement of technology and the creation of a productive and rationally administered welfare state. Thus, for Gouldner, the new class of intellectuals seeks to replace the traditional moneyed bourgeoisie as the dominant class by claiming to be the new "universal class" in whose hands the future of society lies. It is, therefore, both revolutionary and elitist, thereby making it a "flawed" universal class (Gouldner 1979, pp. 19-20, 85).

The old and new classes, therefore, are engaged in a struggle to control the processes of production and administration, a struggle that expresses the conflict "between the class which has legal ownership of the mode of production and the class whose technical knowledge increasingly gives it effective possession of the mode of production " (Gouldner 1979, pp. 12, 16-17). Thus, at the same time that the new class seeks to illegitimatize and ultimately displace the old class, thereby making it a revolutionary class, it aims to impose its own domination and a new elitist hierarchy based on the possession of cultural capital (Gouldner 1979, pp. 17-18, 53, 61, 85).

What is missing from the argument, or, more precisely, what is underemphasized, is the relationship of this new knowledge class to the subordinate, working classes. Gouldner stresses that the new class has no interest in abolishing the wage system and that it aims to appropriate a greater share of the social surplus while simultaneously expanding the welfare state. But it is not at all clear that the relationship between the new cultural bourgeoisie and the working class is as exploitative as it was with the old bourgeoisie. Indeed, Gouldner even talks of the new class entering into an alliance with the working class against the old bourgeoisie while wanting to control and dominate the working class (Gouldner 1979, pp. 19-21).

It is in this context that Frank Parkin's contribution to the debate on the new class must be considered.[4] Parkin not only agrees with Gouldner that cultural capital is another form of property but takes the argument further by locating that form of capital in the context of the exploitation of the subordinated or excluded classes by the dominant or exclusionary classes. Cultural capital, just as property ownership, represents but another means of exercising social closure whereby those who possess credentials are granted legal—that is, state-enforced—control over key positions in the division of labor and their rewards (Parkin 1979, p. 48).

As a form of exclusionary closure, credentialism is a strategy used by the nonpropertied fractions of the dominant class to secure positions of power and privilege at the expense of the noncredentialed, subordinated classes. The relationship between the credentialed and the noncredentialed is not based on the appropriation of a surplus by the former from the latter, as in the case of property owners versus nonproperty owners. That relationship is nonetheless exclusionary and exploitative because power is used in a downward direction to create a subordinate and less privileged social group or to prevent that group from having access to the positions and rewards yielded by credentialism. In this case, credentialism is not unlike other strategies of exclusion practiced not only by dominant against subordinate classes but also by fractions of subordinate classes against other fractions. For Parkin, then, "exploitation" is defined as "the nexus between classes or other collectivities that stand in a relationship of dominance and subordination, on whatever social basis" (Parkin 1979, p. 46). What makes those who possess credentials part of the dominant class in contrast to those who use other strategies of closure, such as those of trade unions or racist and sexist discrimination, is that the credentialed groups succeeded in winning legal protection from the state (Parkin 1979, p. 58).

For Parkin, then, economic and cultural capital are forms of capital used by members of the dominant class to extract benefits and privileges from their positions by excluding members of the lower classes from these positions. He has, therefore, reversed the order of the relations between the cultural bourgeoisie and the old propertied bourgeoisie. Whereas, for Gouldner, credentialism represented a struggle waged by an emergent new class against the traditional propertied bourgeoisie, for Parkin, credentialism is a struggle directed against members of the lower classes through exclusion. Unlike Gouldner, then, Parkin does not see the credentialed class as aiming to supplant the old bourgeoisie to establish itself as the dominant class; it is, rather, concerned with preventing its usurpation by the lay public. As a constituent element of the dominant class, then, the interests of the credentialed fraction converge with those of the propertied fraction to preserve their respective exclusionary monopolies (Parkin 1979, p. 58; Bourdieu 1984, p. 125).

AN ALTERNATIVE APPROACH TO THE
NEW CLASS

Despite the important differences between Gouldner and Parkin, they make a compelling case for reconsidering the criterion of property ownership in the strict sense—of ownership of money-capital and/or fixed capital—as the only determinant of membership in the dominant or ruling class. Yet, as I will argue, by introducing the concept of cultural capital as another determinant of membership in the dominant class, these theorists make it difficult to distinguish between the social relations of exploitation and domination based on the ownership or control of capital, on the one hand, and those based on the possession of credentials or specialized skills, on the other. The social group based on the possession of credentials or skills—the *nonmanagerial* professional and technical intelligentsia and intellectuals— ought to be placed in the broad category of the "new middle class"[5] and distinguished from those who have control over assets, such as top corporate or state managers, who belong in the dominant or bourgeois class. Such a perspective avoids homogenizing social groups whose members do not all share the same structural positions with regard to property ownership or nonownership, or to market opportunities, and hence do not have the same power to dominate and exploit those subordinate to them. The argument I propose draws from the respective contributions of Raymond Murphy (1988) and Erik Olin Wright (1985).

Conceiving of class as structured relations of domination, exclusion, and exploitation, Murphy and Wright make it possible to understand the many ways in which social groups struggle to monopolize privileged and advantaged positions in capitalist society, such as those based on property ownership, credentials, ethnicity, race, and gender. The strategies of exclusion, viewed in this way, are analytically richer than a conception of class based strictly on property relations because they facilitate a fuller understanding of both the composition and alliances of groups engaged in these struggles and the constraints and limits on their actions (Murphy 1988, pp. 48-50, 98-101; Wright 1985, pp. 73-77).

Nonetheless, in this view, legal title to private property is the principal form of closure in capitalism because it constitutes the principle of organization of the society, determines the structure of positions, and confers upon its owners a relative monopoly on the accumulation of capital and the concentration of resources by excluding nonowners from such opportunities. The possession of credentials, on the other hand, is a derivative form of closure, because, even though it differs from property laws per se, it patterns itself after such laws of exclusion. What makes credentialism a derivative form of exclusion is that the owners of companies have the legal right to determine the requirements for entry into positions within the companies to conform to the owners's "assumptions concerning competence for positions and careers." Credentialism, moreover, represents a set of rules that confer claims to socially valued skills that enable their possessors to monopolize certain opportunities and privileges not available to the noncredentialed (Murphy 1988, pp. 71-72).

What holds for credentialed groups also holds for corporate managers, those whom Wright refers to as having organization assets. Whatever may motivate corporate managers, they can realize their interests insofar as they maximize the profitability of their firms, and hence they are likely to pursue strategies that are compatible with the interests of the owners. Similarly, state managers, who one might think have a power base that is more independent of capital than the managers of private corporations, are not likely to follow anticapitalist strategies because "state revenues depend upon privately generated profits, [and] the state is systematically constrained to act in a way that supports the profitability of capital and thus capitalist exploitation" (Wright 1985, p. 90)

For Murphy and Wright, the "new middle classes" do not necessarily seek to displace the propertied class, as claimed by Gouldner, but they are nonetheless in an "uneasy relationship"—Murphy's term—or in a "contradictory location"—Wright's term—vis-à-vis the propertied class. Because the propertied class is the dominant class in capitalism, and hence excludes the organization asset and skill/credential asset groups, the latter enter into conflict with the propertied class to "usurp its exclusive power and advantages." On the other hand, because they have "effective control" of organizations and/or possess skill assets, they oppose the interests of workers (Wright 1985, p. 87; Murphy 1988, pp. 78-79). Murphy's and Wright's perspectives make it possible to explain how social groups who have control over organizations or credentials create intermediate classes that are simultaneously subordinate to, and hence exploited by, the propertied classes, but who in turn dominate and exploit groups subordinate to them.

Thus a distinction must be made between those non-property owners who appropriate a surplus on the basis of a direct class relation of domination/exploitation and those who appropriate a surplus on the basis of their special skills or credentials through market exchanges. Those whose exploitation of others is based on their control, but not ownership, of organization assets, then, properly belong in the dominant class, even though their position is "derived" from or is in a "central contradictory location" with the propertied bourgeoisie. Thus these managerial groups may be considered as part of a "new corporate bourgeoisie" that shares the interests of the old propertied class even if it remains subordinate to it. The new corporate bourgeoisie, then, may be thought of as the subordinate fraction of the dominant class, to paraphrase Bourdieu's classification of the "cultural capitalists" (Bourdieu 1984, pp. 114-120).

This new middle class benefits from its privileged position in capitalist society and, for the most part, defends the existing system through its ideology of professionalism. Some members of this class serve as what Gramsci calls the "organic intellectuals" of the dominant class. According to Gramsci, every social group that comes into existence

> on the original terrain of an essential function in the world of economic production, creates, together with itself, organically, one or more strata of intellectuals which give it homogeneity and an awareness of its own function not only in the economic but also in the social and political fields. (Gramsci 1971, p. 5)

The organic intellectuals include the "specialists in political economy, the organizers of a new culture, of a new legal system, etc." (Gramsci 1971, p. 5). And though they are not members of the bourgeoisie, they are recruited by the bourgeoisie as "specialized employees" to whom the bourgeoisie delegates the responsibility of "organizing the general system of relationships external to the business itself" (Gramsci 1971, p. 6). Thus it is not the "intrinsic nature of intellectual activities" that determines who are the intellectuals and what position they occupy in society. Rather, it is "the ensemble of the system in which these activities (and therefore the intellectual groups who personify them) have their place within the general complex of social relations" (Gramsci 1971, p. 8).

But, because the new class of professional and technical intelligentsia and intellectuals engages in what Gouldner (1979, pp. 28-29) calls the "culture of critical discourse," its members are capable of generating criticisms of the inequities of capitalism and propose more "universalistic" alternatives, partly because their possession of valuable skills and credentials renders them more independent from the capitalist class proper. These groups, and to some extent state managers, can conceive of a social order where private property in the means of production is either abolished or restricted significantly to no longer constitute the principal form of exclusion but where they would retain and perhaps augment their value to society.

My argument, therefore, is that, *in the context of the advanced capitalist societies,* the professional and technical intelligentsia and intellectuals are members of a "new middle class" subordinated to capital and not part of a new "cultural bourgeoisie." While some members of the professional intelligentsia and intellectual class become part of the organic intellectuals of the bourgeoisie, and hence identify and defend its interests, others are capable of adopting more critical stances and exerting a greater degree of independence, largely because they possess the specialized skills and occupy positions in the social division of labor that do not make them directly dependent on the bourgeoisie for their existence.

STATE POWER AND THE MANAGERIAL
BOURGEOISIE IN THE CARIBBEAN

The preceding discussion has focused on the characteristics and location of the "new class" in the class structure of the advanced capitalist societies. Consideration will now be given to its emergence in the Caribbean, as part of the underdeveloped "Third World," to see how and in what ways it differs from its homologue in the advanced countries. I argue that, if in the advanced countries the "corporate bourgeoisie" represents the subordinate fraction of the dominant class, in Third World countries, like those of the Caribbean, the "new managerial bourgeoisie" becomes the *dominant fraction* of the local bourgeoisie but *in the context of its subordination to the international corporate bourgeoisie.* This is because of the relative weakness of the propertied bourgeoisie as a class in Third World societies in general and in the Caribbean in particular, the dominance of foreign capital, and the expanded role of the state in the postcolonial era. Henceforth, the term "corporate bourgeoisie" will be used to designate the bourgeoisie in the advanced capitalist countries, and the term "managerial bourgeoisie" will refer to the "new bourgeoisie" in the Caribbean that has its basis in the control over state or branch plant multinational corporate assets rather than in the private ownership of property. These terms are taken from Sklar (1987), who first used them to distinguish between the two fractions of the international bourgeoisie, as we will see.

I further argue that, *in the context of the Caribbean societies* and in contrast to the core capitalist economies, the professional and technical intelligentsia and the intellectuals are members of the dominant class largely because of the tight connection between these strata and the managerial bourgeoisie. Put differently, it is from the ranks of the professional intelligentsia and the intellectuals that the members of the managerial bourgeoisie are recruited. The managerial bourgeoisie emerged in the Caribbean when the previously excluded brown and black educated elites took control of the state apparatuses at the time of independence and entered into a new set of dependent relations with foreign multinational capital. Thus it is control of state power that transformed the members of the new middle class into a managerial bourgeoisie in the Caribbean and not their mere possession of credentials or "cultural capital."

The emergence of the managerial bourgeoisie is not peculiar to the Caribbean but is a widespread phenomenon throughout the postcolonial Third World. As Sklar (1987) and Becker (1987a, 1987b) argue, the managerial bourgeoisie in the Third World is part of the "organizational revolution" caused by the development and internationalization of multinational capital. Rather than developing capitalism "on their own," emerging national bourgeoisies in the underdeveloped or former colonial countries tend to adopt and adapt themselves to the advanced "organizational capitalism" of the postwar era in the management of business corporations and the state. As with the corporate bourgeoisie of the advanced countries, the managerial bourgeoisie in the Third World espouses the managerial ideology of professionalism and technocratic elitism (Becker 1987a, p. 90).

The Third World managerial bourgeoisie has its basis in the management of the state enterprises and agencies as well as the subsidiaries of multinational corporations (MNCs) operating in those countries, either as branch plants or through partnerships with state or local capital. Thus the degree and range of control over capital and assets by the managerial bourgeoisie is usually larger than that of the private bourgeoisies in most of the newly industrializing countries of the Third World. This fact reverses the relationship between the propertied and managerial bourgeoisies, making the latter "the ruling stratum of the national bourgeoisie." Because of its links with and dependence on multinational capital, the Third World managerial bourgeoisie becomes a "junior partner" to the propertied and corporate bourgeoisies in the central capitalist countries. This process of transnational class formation, then, creates an international bourgeoisie comprised of a dominant corporate bourgeoisie in the advanced countries and a subordinate managerial bourgeoisie in the Third World. Likewise, the working classes of the capitalist world confront a well-organized and formidable international social force, that is, the corporate bourgeoisie in the advanced countries and the managerial bourgeoisie in the less developed countries (Sklar 1987, pp. 30-32).

I contend, however, that the relationship of the managerial bourgeoisie to the corporate bourgeoisie is contradictory and may compel the former to struggle to alter its relationship with the corporate bourgeoisie. On the one hand, the corporate bourgeoisies of the center countries want to preserve the conditions that facilitate the accumulation of capital by their multinational subsidiaries operating in the Third World. On the other hand, the Third World states, confronted with the demands of their creditors for debt repayment, the demands of the poor and working classes for better living conditions, and the desire by their national bourgeoisies to exercise greater control over their national economies, may struggle to exert greater control over the MNC subsidiaries and the wealth they produce. In other words, the managerial bourgeoisie in the Third World attempts to usurp the power and dominance of the corporate bourgeoisie.

For all the interests they share in common, however, the Third World managerial bourgeoisies remain *dependent* on the corporate bourgeoisies of the center countries. Rather than expressing an inevitable condition of existence, the term "dependency" is here used to mean the nature of the relations between countries and between the ruling classes in the dominant and the subordinate countries. "Dependency" expresses the dynamics of relations entered into by social classes with unequal economic and political power on the world scale. Or, as Torres-Rivas puts it, dependency is "precisely that articulation of forces in which foreign interests appear to define themselves as a domestic factor at the economic and political level" (Torres-Rivas 1989, p. 113). Dependent relations, therefore, are not given or permanent once established but can be reinforced, reformed, or overcome. With the exception of a few Third World countries, the root cause of the dependent relations between the managerial and the corporate bourgeoisies continues to be the absence of a substantial home market for the expanded and integrated accumulation of capital in the Third World. This is due to the lack of a technology and capital goods sector and hence the lack of linkages between that sector, the agricultural and raw materials sectors, and the consumer goods sector. Consequently, the Third World countries with these characteristics must depend on their ties with the advanced countries to obtain most of their technology and capital equipment, their consumer goods, and sometimes most of their foods in exchange for the goods they export, usually natural resources and some manufactured goods, in the form of assembly manufactures (Munck 1984, p. 34).

It is the negative consequences of these dependent relations for the Third World—unequal terms of trade, balance of payments deficits, International Monetary Fund (IMF)-imposed austerity measures, and so on—that led to the resurgence of economic and political nationalism in the Third World and that gave rise to the movement for a New International Economic Order and the Non-Aligned Movement. Though by no means representing a unified bloc with an agreed upon agenda, the common denominator of this twin movement is the demand for better terms of trade between developed and underdeveloped countries, greater equality in relations among states, more regulation of the activities of the MNCs in the Third World, and greater control over their resources by the Third World countries (Girvan 1976, pp. 7-8).

To be sure, the corporate bourgeoisies in the advanced countries and the MNCs they control have responded—though not in all cases and not without often bitter conflicts—to the economic nationalism of Third World states by making some concessions to the managerial bourgeoisies while co-opting them. By relinquishing ownership of formerly foreign-owned assets, especially in the natural resource industries, the MNCs now force the Third World states to assume the risks of investments and of market fluctuations and to regulate the labor force employed in those industries. At the same time, the MNCs retain control over the technology, many other inputs used by and the servicing of these industries, and the markets for their products. Nonetheless, as Girvan concludes,

> these developments imply the emergence of new and stronger linkages with the capitalist centers. But this model of dependent industrialization corresponds to the class interests of the local state bureaucracy, since, in conjunction with state participation in the resources industry, it creates substantial new opportunities for employment of high-level technical, professional, and administrative cadres. (Girvan 1976, p. 7)

INTELLECTUALS AND THE MANAGERIAL BOURGEOISIE

The foregoing discussion makes it possible to focus specifically on the emergence of the managerial bourgeoisie in the Caribbean and its relationship with the intelligentsia and the intellectuals. The process of formation of the Caribbean managerial bourgeoisie began in the post-World War I era but became consolidated after the gaining of independence by the former English colonies during the 1960s and early 1970s. It was after World War I, but particularly after 1935, that the movements for national independence emerged throughout the English colonies. The leadership of these movements were members of the petty bourgeoisie, the professional groups, and other, educated intermediate strata. But is was the urban workers, the unemployed, and the peasants who put pressure on middle-class leaders to engage the colonial administration, which grudgingly granted reforms (Lewis 1968, p. 108; Thomas 1988, p. 71).

The uprisings of the 1930s throughout the English colonies proved a major turning point in the struggle for national independence. It was at that time that clear nationalist and anticolonial sentiments crystallized into a social movement that claimed widespread mass support. The anticolonial struggles first began as a movement for self-government before being transformed into a demand for outright independence. Socially and politically, the nationalist struggles challenged the racist premises of colonial rule to demand the removal of the social, political, and economic obstacles that excluded the black and brown majority from the opportunity structures of colonial society (Henry 1983, pp. 106-7).

The radical and even revolutionary potential of the mass movement, however, was channeled into institutions, such as trade unions, political parties, cultural and literary clubs, and cooperative societies, that could express the aspirations of the colonized but be safely controlled by the emerging middle-class groups. The middle class, which had been nurtured by the colonial administration through preferential, though limited, access to education and the professions, had grown to resent its racist exclusion from the major economic and political opportunities of colonial society. It regarded independence as the vehicle by which it would become the logical heirs of the levers of power by replacing the colonial administrators. As such, the middle-class elements were not predisposed toward a revolutionary overthrow of the colonial order that would empower the poor working and peasant classes (Thomas 1988, p. 72; Lewis 1968, p. 396).

The single most important characteristic of the postindependence period in the Caribbean, then, is the emergence of the state sector (including the government) controlled by the indigenous middle class, that is, the professional intelligentsia and intellectuals. The postcolonial Caribbean state derives its significance from its interventionist role in mediating the conflicting interests among local private capital, foreign capital, and the working and peasant classes. In addition, the postcolonial state expanded its economic role through its public sector enterprises, both in the form of service industries—such as in communication, public transport, health, education, and sanitation—and in those sectors where formerly foreign-owned enterprises were nationalized or entered into joint ventures with the state. The extension of the state's service and productive capacities made it the most important economic actor in the Caribbean next to the subsidiaries of the MNCs. It also provided increasing opportunities for the previously racially excluded social groups to experience unprecedented upward social and economic mobility. Thus the control of the state apparatuses by those in the Caribbean new middle class served as the primary basis for their transformation into a managerial bourgeoisie.

The expansion of technical and university education, such as the creation of the University of the West Indies with campuses in several island-nations, opened up hitherto unavailable opportunities for members of different classes, but primarily the middle class, to acquire different types of educational credentials and skills. Such credentials, along with membership in the major political parties led by the middle class, became the basis for entry into the top administrative and technical positions in the various state and quasi-governmental agencies. They also opened up positions in private enterprises as well as the pursuit of professional careers in education and in the private sector (e.g., in the media and as dentists, medical doctors, lawyers, engineers, and primary, secondary, and university teachers). The Caribbean professional and technical intelligentsia also occupied managerial positions in the foreign sector, which remained dominated by subsidiaries of MNCs in the tourist, banking, mining, and refining industries. During the 1960s and 1970s, new foreign investments in the form of manufacturing assembly industries proliferated in the region, often in joint venture with local entrepreneurs or through the hiring of local managers.

Unlike the corporate bourgeoisie and the professional and technical intelligentsia that emerged because of the changes in the economic structures of the advanced capitalist societies, the Caribbean managerial bourgeoisie and professional and technical intelligentsia came into being as a result of the capture of state power by the indigenous middle class, who displaced the former colonial rulers after independence.

This fluidity does not mean that there are no conflicts between these two fractions of the dominant class and between the dominant class and the intelligentsia, especially over the internal regulation of the economy, foreign exchange/foreign debt policies, and IMF-imposed austerity measures (Thomas 1988, p. 192). But, given the close connection between the intelligentsia and intellectuals and the managerial bourgeoisie, the former, as members of the latter, play a direct role in the formation of policies, both within the political parties to which they belong and for the government itself when their party is in power. The intellectuals, in effect, function as the organic intellectuals of the managerial bourgeoisie. Indeed, as we will see below, the failure of the development strategies formulated by the intelligentsia and adopted by the managerial bourgeoisie in the postindependence era has led to their rejection by a critical and even radical faction among the intellectuals and the managerial bourgeoisie in search of alternatives to underdeveloped capitalism. The attempt at "democratic socialism" in Jamaica under the prime ministership of Michael Manley from 1972 to 1980, and the "Non-Capitalist Path" adopted by the New JEWEL Movement under the leadership of Maurice Bishop in Grenada from 1979 to 1983, are expressions of the emergent radicalism among sectors of the Caribbean managerial bourgeoisie and intellectuals.

The Caribbean managerial bourgeoisie has attempted to transcend its respective national boundaries to become a regional managerial bourgeoisie. It created an intraregional institution, the Caribbean Community and Common Market, or CARICOM (in 1973), which replaced the former Caribbean Free Trade Association, or CARIFTA (created in 1968), with the objective of integrating and coordinating the economic and foreign policies of the individual member states. As Thomas aptly summarizes the *raison d'être* of

CARICOM, it is to consolidate regionally the capitalist structures and market relations established in each individual nation-state. This is to be done by liberalizing intraregional trade and facilitating transportation and communication to create a uniform regional market for both the "emerging local bourgeoisies and their TNC [transnational corporation] counterparts to exploit" (Thomas 1988, p. 319). Thus, because of the central position occupied by the postcolonial Caribbean state in the local and regional economies, the managerial bourgeoisie in control of it becomes the dominant fraction of the local bourgeoisie, without, for that matter, threatening the latter's privileges. Inasmuch as the managerial bourgeoisie is the dominant fraction of the dominant class in the Caribbean, it remains subordinated to the international bourgeoisie in general and to those sectors of the corporate bourgeoisie whose MNCs dominate in the Caribbean in particular.

The Caribbean managerial bourgeoisie, therefore, is a *dependent* bourgeoisie. Those relations of dependency are contradictory because they are unequal. That is, the presence of foreign capital in the Caribbean is conditioned on continued access to resources and to the profits produced from its operations. The ultimate weapon possessed by foreign capital to compel compliance with its interests is the threat of withdrawal from the region or individual countries, a threat that is backed by the full weight of the state in the core countries. The Caribbean economies, on the other hand, do not derive equal benefits from their relationship with foreign capital. On the contrary, insofar as more wealth is taken out of the Caribbean than remains, it loses more than it gains from that relationship. At the end of 1986, the combined balance of payments deficit for CARICOM member countries stood at about U.S. \$9,000 million. This represents over U.S. \$1,800 per capita (Thomas 1988, p. 326). Yet the costs of the alternative are greater in the short run, as the bitter experiences of those who have attempted to "opt out" of the international capitalist system can testify.

The Caribbean economies are dependent, first, because they lack the necessary sectors of production that traditionally have laid the basis for the expanded accumulation of capital. Most important, the Caribbean economies do not have the capacity to produce their own technology and capital goods. Therefore, they must import them. This means, among other things, that, by not producing its own technology, the Caribbean cannot engage in the research and development that is essential for technological innovation. The Caribbean intelligentsia, therefore, is not in a position to create alternative technologies that correspond to the needs of the island economies.

Given the economic and political realities under which the Caribbean exists, and the class interests of the managerial bourgeoisie, it is not at all surprising to find that it pursued policies that reinforced foreign capital's dominance in the region.[6] Thus the managerial bourgeoisie is not prepared to confront a future when, based on the production of synthetic substitutes for the natural resources the Caribbean currently supplies, the MNCs may no longer need access to those resources. Having no capital goods sector further means that the Caribbean cannot produce its own mass consumer goods by integrating those two sectors. Not having the ability to produce its own capital and consumer goods, the Caribbean economies must continue to rely on the export of a single commodity or a number of limited goods to the markets of the advanced industrial countries to earn enough foreign currency to pay for the needed imports and repay the foreign debt accrued in the process (Payne 1984, pp. 9-10; Girvan 1976, p. 6).

The Caribbean, then, continues to be structurally underdeveloped. Foreign capital still dominates the economies of the region. And, politically, the Caribbean exists in the context of the hegemony of the United States, whose policies are geared to keep the economies of the region open to foreign capital and to the principles of the market. These factors combined to generate a growing polarization between the wealthy minority and the poverty of the majority. And it is this fact more than any other that can explain the divisions that emerged not only among Caribbean intellectuals but also within the ranks of the managerial bourgeoisie in terms of possible alternatives to dependent capitalism.

The struggle for an alternative to underdevelopment occurred within the academy, in the halls of parliament, and in the streets of Caribbean cities and towns. It was among radicalized circles of intellectuals based in the various campuses of the University of the West Indies who formed the New World Group that the break with the traditional theories of modernization and their substitution with more critical dependency theories, including variants of Marxist theories, occurred (see Payne 1984). These oppositional theories not only criticized but also offered alternative explanations and solutions specifically suited to Caribbean conditions and needs.

The radical theories and the alternative strategies they suggested were never fully adopted or implemented by any state in the region. But some of them were incorporated in the policies of the People's National Party (PNP) in Jamaica from 1972 to 1980 when it opted for a "democratic socialist" alternative, and in those of the People's Revolutionary Government (PRG) in Grenada from 1979 to 1983 when it declared itself in favor of a "third path" between capitalism and socialism. Thus it could be said that the intellectuals who developed these views, and who supported them and became influential in those regimes, constituted the organic intellectuals of the emerging progressive managerial bourgeoisie, in contrast to those intellectuals who allied themselves with and served the predominant procapitalist factions.

The stated objectives of these progressive regimes may be summarized as follows. They sought to reduce as much as possible the dependence of their economies on foreign capital, to create a mixed economy with the state assuming control of the "commanding heights" of the economy through selective nationalization of foreign assets and public utilities, to broaden political democracy and work participation in decision making, and to pursue an independent foreign policy of nonalignment and solidarity with other Third World countries, including socialist countries like Cuba.

My purpose here is not to assess the merits or demerits of these experiments. Rather, I only want to point out that the adoption of this socioeconomic model represented a break from within the ranks of the managerial bourgeoisie, which up to that point had pursued strictly procapitalist policies that accorded with the interests of multinational capital. Neither the Manley regime nor the Bishop regime was opposed to foreign investments, but both sought to control certain vital sectors of their economies to regulate them better and derive greater benefits from such investments. And neither attempted to expropriate their respective local propertied bourgeoisie.

Nonetheless, both foreign capital and the local propertied bourgeoisies reacted strongly against these regimes. The perception, justified in part by the rhetoric and actions of the two governments, that they were "socialist" and "anti-imperialist"—read anti-U.S.—drove foreign and local capital, and sectors of the middle class, into a hostile opposition. The ensuing "strike of capital"—that is, the withholding of investments that is the ultimate trump card of capital—combined with the bellicose policies of the United States and the punitive measures of the IMF toward these regimes fostered popular discontent and divisions within the ranks of the ruling parties themselves. Consequently, neither regime could survive this multilevel onslaught. The Manley government suffered an electoral defeat at the polls in 1980 (even though it received 41% of the vote, mostly from the working class, the peasants, and the poor), and the PRG was overthrown by a U.S. invasion in 1983 after Bishop had been assassinated following a *coup d'ètat* led by a more radical faction.[7]

From the standpoint of the perspective of this chapter, however, the option of the progressive sectors of the managerial bourgeoisie and their organic intellectuals for a "socialist" alternative was a manifestation of the fundamental contradiction between the interests of foreign capital and those of the managerial bourgeoisie that sought to exercise greater control over the local economies. To achieve this goal and pursue its redistributive policies, the progressive managerial bourgeoisie had to move to the left. To gain popular support, it mobilized and allied itself with the working and peasant classes while appearing not to be threatening the interests of the local propertied bourgeoisie. The model of the mixed economy, therefore, seemed to meet both objectives. For, if successful, it would have reduced the (direct) power and influence of foreign capital, enhanced further that of the managerial bourgeoisie vis-á-vis the local propertied bourgeoisie, and rallied mass support with the expansion of the welfare state and increased popular participation in decision making.

The mixed economy model of socialism, therefore, seems to be the ideal socioeconomic system for the managerial bourgeoisie and its organic intellectuals in the Caribbean. It also conforms to Gouldner's vision of the "flawed universal class." As we have seen, implementation of the democratic socialist policies would have strengthened and legitimized the rule of the managerial bourgeoisie by presenting it as the defender of the "national interests." But it would also have maintained a class society, albeit one with reduced levels of inequality and with greater popular participation. As Gouldner also suggested, this alternative was sought in the underdeveloped Caribbean and not in the core capitalist countries because it is in underdeveloped types of economies that capitalism tends not to bear fruits, so to speak, and, therefore, becomes illegitimatized.

The successful implementation of this model would have lessened the direct control over the resources of the countries concerned by the multinational corporations. But it would not have necessarily meant that their interests could not have continued to be served profitably by the "socialist" managerial bourgeoisie, for the reasons alluded to earlier. The international corporate bourgeoisie, however, did not share that view. Given the powerful political and economic resources at its disposal, the international corporate bourgeoisie simply compelled the left-leaning managerial bourgeoisie in Jamaica and Grenada to conform to its dictates.

CONCLUSION

We can now see the extent to which the perspectives of Gouldner and Parkin, and those of Wright and Murphy, are extracted from the experiences of the advanced capitalist countries and have very little to say about the class structures of Third World societies like those of the Caribbean. The emergence of the new managerial bourgeoisie in the Caribbean was not due to the possession of credentials or corporate assets by its members but more directly to their capture of state power after independence.

The new state managerial class became the dominant fraction of the Caribbean bourgeoisie, but it remained subordinated to foreign capital and the corporate bourgeoisie in the advanced countries. Thus, though state power, and not cultural capital, was the *sine qua non* for the emergence of a new bourgeoisie in the Caribbean, the Caribbean's subordination to international capital is also the basis for the relative powerlessness and subordination of the Caribbean bourgeoisie vis-á-vis the corporate bourgeoisie. Capital, therefore, in its most immediate form of ownership or control of corporate property, remains the dominant and determinant force in the world economy because of its power to command and allocate resources on a global scale.

By ignoring the uneven development of capitalism on a world scale, therefore, the theories of cultural capital developed in the advanced countries ignore the limits of their postulates. Put differently, theories that assume the universality of conditions or developments in the advanced countries cannot accommodate counterfactual evidence from the Third World. They either must be modified or discarded altogether.

NOTES

1. I focus on the 13 former British colonies (Antigua-Barbuda, the Bahamas, Barbados, Belize, Dominica, Grenada, Guyana, Jamaica, St. Kitts-Nevis, St. Lucia, St. Vincent, Trinidad-Tobago, and Montserrat) for two reasons. First, they gained their independence during the 1960s and early 1970s. Second, all, except Montserrat, belong to the Caribbean Community and Common Market (CARICOM) and have very close political, cultural, and economic ties to one another. Thus their common postindependence history and their relations with one another make it possible to treat them as a unit and in a manner not possible for the other island-nations that have very different linguistic, cultural, colonial, and postcolonial legacies.

2. I use the term "Third World" to refer to those groups of countries in Asia, Africa, and Latin America who at one time or another since the sixteenth century were colonized by a Western European power and today exhibit the characteristic structures of underdevelopment. The term is not used to suggest homogeneity of cultures or social structures or unchanging economic position vis-á-vis the "advanced," "developed," or "core" capitalist countries.

3. Among the more well-known proponents of this thesis are Adolf Berle and Gardiner C. Means (1932), Talcott Parsons and Neil Smelser (1957), Ralf Dahrendorf (1959), John Kenneth Galbraith (1967), and Daniel Bell (1973).

4. Parkin (1979) and Pierre Bourdieu (1984) offer similar perspectives on the nature and role of cultural capital in advanced capitalism. I will only deal with Parkin's views in this chapter.

5. As is well known, Poulantzas was among those Marxist theorists in the 1970s who advanced the thesis of a "new petty bourgeoisie" that comprised not only credentialed wage earners but also other categories of "nonproductive" workers like those employed in banks, service industries, government, schools, and commerce. This category of "new petty bourgeoisie" did not represent a distinct class but was seen as simply a new fraction of the traditional petty bourgeoisie. Thus its existence did not require a modification of the dual class structure of capitalism (see Poulantzas 1973, 1975).

6. These policies, referred to as "industrialization by invitation," were based on a *selective* (mis)application of the model of development proposed by the St. Lucian-born economist W. Arthur Lewis as well as on the practical experience of Puerto Rico during the 1940s and 1950s. Basically, the strategy of "industrialization by invitation" sought to promote development

by offering incentives to investors, including tax exemptions; by building infrastructures and providing service to industries, even if this meant that the government had to borrow money to pay their costs; and by protecting local manufacturers through tariff barriers and import restrictions. The result of these policies was to allow foreign capital to penetrate and control more deeply the national economies of the region. For a fuller, but critical, assessment of Lewis's views, see Thomas (1988, pp. 76-78) and Dupy (forthcoming).

7. For an in-depth analysis of Jamaica under Manley and the PNP during that period, see Kaufman (1985) and Stephens and Stephens (1986). For Grenada, see Lewis (1987) and Mandle (1985). For a succinct analysis of both, see Thomas (1988, pp. 210-250).

REFERENCES

Becker, David G. 1987a. "Development, Democracy, and Dependency in Latin America: A Postimperialist View." Pp. 41-62 in *Postimperialism: International Capitalism and Development in the Late Twentieth Century,* edited by David G. Becker et al. Boulder, CO: Lynne Rienner.

———. 1987b. " 'Bonanza Development' and the 'New Bourgeoisie': Peru Under Military Rule." Pp. 63-105 in *Postimperalism: International Capitalism and Development in the Late Twentieth Century*, edited by David G. Becker et al. Boulder, CO: Lynne Rienner.

Becker, David G., Jeff Frieden, Sayre P. Schatz, and Richard L. Sklar. 1987. *Postimperialism: International Capitalism and Development in the Late Twentieth Century.* Boulder, CO: Lynne Rienner.

Bell, Daniel. 1973. *The Coming of Post-Industrial Society.* New York: Basic Books.

Berle, Adolf, Jr., and Gardiner C. Means. 1932. *The Modern Corporation and Private Property.* New York: Macmillian.

Bourdieu, Pierre. 1984. *Distinction: A Social Critique of the Judgment of Taste,* translated by Richard Nice. Cambridge, MA: Harvard University Press.

Dahrendorf, Ralf. 1959. *Class and Class Conflict in Industrial Society.* Stanford, CA: Stanford University Press.

Dupuy, Alex. Forthcoming. "Export Manufactures and Underdevelopment in Haiti: A Reassessment of the Perspective of W. Arthur Lewis." In *The Social and Economic Thought of Arthur Lewis,* edited by Ralph Premdas and Ralph Henry. Mona, Jamaica: Institute of Social and Economic Research.

Gagnon, Alain G. 1987a. "The Role of Intellectuals in Liberal Democracies: Political Influence and Social Involvement." Pp. 3-16 in *Intellectuals in Liberal Democracies,* edited by Alain Gagnon. New York: Praeger.

Galbraith, John K. 1967. *The New Industrial State.* New York: Signet.

Girvan, Norman. 1976. *Corporate Imperialism: Conflict and Expropriation.* New York: M. E. Sharpe.

Gouldner, Alvin W. 1979. *The Future of the Intellectuals and the Rise of the New Class.* New York: Oxford University Press.

Gramsci, Antonio. 1971. *Selections from the Prison Notebooks,* translated by Quintin Hoare and Geoffrey Nowell Smith. London: Lawrence and Wishart; New York: International Publishers.

Henry, Paget. 1983. "Decolonization and Cultural Underdevelopment in the Commonwealth Caribbean." Pp. 95-120 in *The Newer Caribbean: Decolonization, Democracy, and Development,* edited by Paget Henry and Carl Stone. Philadelphia: Institute for the Study of Human Issues.

Henry, Paget and Carol Stone, eds. 1983. *The Newer Caribbean: Decolonization, Democracy, and Development.* Philadelphia: Institute for the Study of Human Issues.

Kaufman, Michael. 1985. *Jamaica Under Manley: Dilemmas of Socialism and Democracy.* London: Zed.

Lewis, Gordon K. 1968. *The Growth of the Modern West Indies.* New York: Monthly Review Press.

———. 1987. *Grenada: The Jewel Dispossessed.* Baltimore: Johns Hopkins University Press.

Mandle, Jay R. 1982. *Patterns of Caribbean Development.* New York: Gordon and Breach.

———. 1985. *Big Revolution, Small Country: The Rise and Fall of the Grenada Revolution.* Lanham, MD: North-South.

Munck, Ronaldo. 1984. *Politics and Dependency in the Third World.* London: Zed.

Murphy, Raymond. 1988. *Social Closure: The Theory of Monopolization and Exclusion.* Oxford: Oxford University Press.

Parkin, Frank. 1979. *Marxism and Class Theory: A Bourgeois Critique.* New York: Columbia University Press.

Parsons, Talcott and Neil Smelser. 1957. *Economy and Society.* London: Routledge & Kegan Paul.

Payne, Anthony. 1984. "Dependency Theory and the Commonwealth Caribbean." Pp. 1-17 in *Dependency and the Challenge: The Political Economy of the Commonwealth Caribbean,* edited by Anthony Payne and Paul Sutton. Manchester: Manchester University Press.

Poulantzas, Nicos. 1973. "Social Classes." *New Left Review* 78(March/April):10-35.

———. 1975. *Classes in Contemporary Capitalism.* New York: Humanities Press.

Sklar, Richard L. 1987. "Postimperialism: A Class Analysis of Multinational Corporate Expansion." Pp. 19-40 in *Postimperialism: International Capitalism and Development in the Late Twentieth Century.* Boulder, CO: Lynne Rienner.

Stevens, Evelyn Huber and John D. Stephens. 1986. *Democratic Socialism in Jamaica: The Political Movement and Social Transformation in Dependent Capitalism.* Princeton, NJ: Princeton University Press.

Thomas, Clive Y. 1988. *The Poor and the Powerless: Economic Policy and Change in the Caribbean.* New York: Monthly Review Press.

Torres-Rivas, Edelberto. 1989. *Repression and Resistance: The Struggle for Democracy in Central America.* Boulder, CO: Westview.

Walker, Pat, ed. 1979. *Between Labor and Capital.* Boston: South End.

Wright, Erik Olin. 1985. *Classes.* London: Verso.

Chapter 6

EASTERN EUROPE'S LESSONS FOR CRITICAL INTELLECTUALS

MICHAEL D. KENNEDY
University of Michigan

> If the hope of the world lies in human consciousness, then it is obvious that intellectuals cannot go on forever avoiding their share of responsibility for the world, hiding their distaste for politics under the alleged need to be independent. (Havel, 1990)

IN EASTERN EUROPE, the political engagement of intellectuals has been the rule rather than the exception. Before the reign of communist parties, they were often the spokespersons for nations and the leaders of governments. Under the rule of communist parties, intellectuals were also prominent but initially as an anachronism. Their inclination toward self-definition was discouraged in favor of political incorporation or narrow specialization. This moved some intellectuals to a variety of opposition politics based on national traditions or Marxism's revision, but it was not until the articulation by intellectuals of an ideology of civil society and human rights that an alternative for Eastern Europe was realized. Although this intellectual contribution by itself did not cause the revolutions of 1989, intellectuals have been restored to authority in the wake of these transformations, and this framework of civil society has guided their new political practices. But the authority of intellectuals is limited, for new structures of dependency ultimately restrict their capacity for action. Alternative structures and practices might, however, facilitate the emergence of an alternative intellectual politics that is not so visible currently.

Any analysis of intellectuals and politics in Eastern Europe is likely to be immediately outdated by events, but the foundations for future intellectual politics in Eastern Europe have been established by a peculiar evolution of

AUTHOR'S NOTE: I am indebted to the Working Group in Social Theory at the Center for Psychosocial Studies in Chicago for discussions that have contributed significantly to this chapter. Thanks are also due Roman Szporluk, David McQuaid, Geoff Eley, and Craig Calhoun for comments on previous versions of this text.

intellectuals in East European communism, from anachronism to opposition to authority. Nonetheless, the events taking place in the early 1990s can serve as a frame of reference for the broader history of intellectuals in Eastern Europe and thus for its unique contributions to our understanding of critical intellectuality—or that inclination and capacity to understand personal situations as reflections of the public condition and the recognition that such a condition is constituted through potentially transformed power relations.

EASTERN EUROPE, NATIONALISM, AND INTELLECTUALS[1]

The weakness of the East European bourgeoisie in the emergent capitalist world system is well known and is important to the history of intellectuals in the area. In the late sixteenth century, the region was incorporated as a periphery of the capitalist world system (Wallerstein, 1976). The power of an agrarian aristocracy was augmented, a second serfdom introduced, and the development of a capitalist class structure distorted. Ethnicity also shaped these relationships made in production. Politically dominant nationalities formed class cultures in their own languages and practices, reinforcing the barriers of class experienced by subordinate populations (Gella 1989).

The East European periphery began to decline as the core turned its attention more to its colonies across the ocean. The consequences of economic decline in Eastern Europe were, however, mitigated by the region's imperial politics. By the end of the eighteenth century, Eastern Europe was dominated by the great powers in the Austrian, Prussian, Russian, and Ottoman empires, who used their imperial apparatuses to shape the development of some peripheralized areas (Kennedy and Smith 1989; Spechler 1989). In turn, this development facilitated the growth of nationalist ideologies. Children of the privileged obtained higher educations in national centers marked by imperial constraints, but these centers also educated their students in the politics of nationalism, especially when official curricula were supplemented by lessons in underground "flying universities" (Gella 1989).

The politics of nationalism dominated Polish discourse from the time of the Partitions in the end of the eighteenth century but became more generally prominent in Eastern Europe after the revolutions of 1848. Intellectuals in turn dominated these politics. Not only did they often provide leadership in political struggles, but, perhaps even more significantly, intellectuals helped to fashion politically conscious nations out of ethnic groups by constructing national histories and sensibilities. The romantic verse of Polish-Lithuanian Adam Mickiewicz and the reconstructed history of the Czech nation by Frantisek Palacky, to name but two of the most obvious, contributed more to nationalist politics than letters could in virtually any other part of the world. But the significance of intellectuals was not the only thing distinctive.

The politics of East Europe intellectuals in this period was fundamentally different from that of intellectuals in the metropolitan countries. In the latter, intellectuals would construct opposition programs based on securing space free from the state, as in England, or distributing power among actors to limit absolutist power, as in France. By contrast, East Europeans would construct programs that would discuss how state power could be won to empower their oppressed nations (Bauman 1987). In many senses, then, the East European intellectual of the nineteenth and early twentieth centuries would have found much in common with the anti-imperialist intellectual in the colonized periphery of the latter twentieth century (Szporluk 1988).

Although there has always been a great deal of variation in the politics of East European intellectuals, some variety of nationalism has figured prominently in most of their political projects. For the suppressed "historic nations," to use terminology favored by Marx and Engels, nationalism was most obvious. But even among the nonhistoric nations, those whose peoples were not privy to previous kingdoms or states, as Slovaks were not, nationalism became increasingly central. Polish Jewish intellectuals too found assimilation more difficult, which in turn increased the appeal of their own nationalism in the years before World War I (Hertz [1961] 1988). But it was in the states formed after the 1919 Versailles Settlement that intellectuals were transformed into figures with more than moral or charismatic authority.

The highly educated frequently returned from abroad to help construct the new nation-state. The premiere example of this was the first president of interwar Czechoslovakia, Thomas Masaryk (1850-1937), a philosophy professor of considerable accomplishment in matters of political theory (Szporluk 1981). The Czechoslovak experience was unusual in Eastern Europe in its democratic accomplishments, however. Military governments were the more likely outcomes of postimperial politics in Eastern Europe. But even in this project, intellectuals remained central.

In Poland, although the military ruled for most of the interwar period, intellectuals were placed in leading positions of formal government. Mathematician Kazimierz Bartel and chemistry professor Ignacy Moscicki were appointed premiere and president in the wake of the 1926 military coup, for example. The military tradition also was highly influenced by the broad intelligentsia from which many of its officers came. Of course, some intellectuals served as organic intellectuals for the popular classes, and most intellectuals in the Polish state practiced less political lives. The unity occasioned by the common struggle of intelligentsia and nation against an occupying power ended with the winning of state power, and the class united by sociopolitical aims fragmented into occupationally structured subgroups (Gella 1989, pp. 159-61). Nevertheless, the responsibility of intellectuals to practice politics became an important legacy in Eastern Europe, inspired by the struggle of the intelligentsia to help construct nations and win for them state power before World War I and by their prominence in the postimperial governments.

Intellectual hegemony in movements or states dominated by nationalist discourse is less problematic than in those movements or states whose legitimacy is tied to the discourse of class. In these latter discourses, intellectuals are always potentially suspect for they cannot claim to be completely of the class for whom they speak. This ambiguity facilitates challenge to intellectual claims of representation. Nationalist intellectuals, by contrast, do not have the same problem given the "vertical integration" constructed through their discourse.[2] Intellectuals can be the "natural" leaders of nations or peoples, even when it is the popular or folk traditions that are revered. They merely "discover" or "articulate" the sentiment of that nationalism.

It is not, therefore, surprising that the postcommunist projects of many East European intellectuals are rooted in a politics of nationalism rather than that of class. This tradition of intellectual politics is particularly strong in Eastern Europe, and it is comparatively effective in assuring intellectuals political authority in the construction of national agendas. It remains appealing in the 1990s because nationalist politics did not have the possibility of shedding, through domestic democratic struggles, its early twentieth-century form. World War II and its aftermath in the rule of communist parties transformed nationalist politics either by pushing it abroad or underground or by forcing it into a new communist framework, which in either case undermined the previous status of intellectuals as national spokespersons.

Not only did the Nazis aim to exterminate peoples like Jews and Gypsies, they also sought to destroy the intellectual leadership of the nations they intended to enslave, such as the Poles. The Soviet invasion of Poland also destroyed an important part of its national intelligentsia, exemplified by the murders in the Katyn Forest of its elite officer corps, most of whom were members of the intelligentsia. By war's end, about 45% of Poland's physicians and dentists, 15% of teachers, 18% of clergy, 40% of professors, 57% of lawyers, and 50% of engineers had died (Lukas 1985; Hoser 1970).

When communists came to power after World War II, it is not, therefore, surprising that dealing with a national intelligentsia would figure significantly in their programs. The communists had to construct a postwar generation of intellectuals suitable to the new order. They also had to deal with those intellectuals who survived the war and those who sought to bring forward old traditions into the new era.

THE INTELLECTUAL ENGAGEMENT WITH COMMUNISM

The considerable social injustices of the interwar period, and the destructiveness of the war itself, led many East European intellectuals to increasingly radical positions. In the first years after the war, before it became obvious that national routes to communism would be forced into Stalinist molds, the new superpower spheres of influence in the world did not seem so disastrous, especially in comparison with the codified inhumanity of the Nazi "master race." Coalition governments in Eastern Europe were the rule. Jan Masaryk, the son of the prewar leader, could even be minister of foreign affairs in the Czechoslovak communist-led government. But between 1948 and 1949, optimism became less tenable.

Czeslaw Milosz, the Polish-Lithuanian Nobel prize winner for literature, bore an awkward, but typical, relationship to the regime. He finally broke with the Polish government in 1951 after serving as cultural attaché in its U.S. and French embassies. *The Captive Mind* ([1953] 1981) was written within the next year as a challenge to French intellectuals sympathetic to Stalin. In it, he portrays several responses by Polish writers to communism, responses based on contemporary authors: Jerzy Andrzejewski was the basis for Alpha the Moralist, Tadeusz Borowski for Beta the Disappointed Lover, Jerzy Putrament for Gamma the Slave of History, and Konstanty Galczynski for Delta the Troubador. This work is especially useful for suggesting the initial East European intellectual engagement with communism, not only for the case studies it offers but also for Milosz himself as among the most influential East European intellectuals of the postwar world.[3]

Communism offers much to the intellectuals,[4] writes Milosz. Intellectuals long to belong to the masses and this New Faith offers them such an association. Membership even can be based on scientific foundations. Thus intellectuals gain new significance, for this scientific faith elevates their function to a new height, simultaneously destroying their old rivals in business and aristocracy. But this philosophy also casts the intellectual into an ambiguous position.

While intellectuals were once distinguished by their ability to think independently, in the new philosophy, intellectuals were to be a part of the stream of history, moved by its own dialectical laws, which were in turn supported by a new state machinery that guaranteed the success, or failure, of an intellectual career. Thus, while the intellectual was guaranteed prominence in the new order, and the prospects of becoming a full-time intellectual improved, the distinction of the intellectual was undermined. Eastern intellectuals may have accepted in 1951-52 that "the basic means of production should belong to the State, that it should be regulated according to a planned economy, and that their proceeds should be used for hygienic, cultural, scientific and artistic ends," but they also wanted to create outside the binds of the official philosophy (Milosz [1953] 1981, p. 40). They could not, however, because of their dependence on the state. Intellectuals, therefore, practiced "Ketman."

Ketman is a political strategy of dualism, where individuals avow in public what the powerful want to hear while in private maintaining a different, more genuine, perhaps creative intellectual life.[5] Although Ketman had become regular practice for intellectuals by 1950, the intellectual engagement with communism did not begin so, Milosz writes. After World War II, the party sought to establish some kind of better link with the society, by, among other means, inviting the cultural elite to join the communist movement.

Intellectuals of different kinds joined the movement for a variety of reasons, but their survival as intellectuals was endangered by their very entry. Formerly Catholic writer Alpha joined the movement reluctantly, making small compromises at first to realize a greater good, but his small compromises eventually avalanched into a complete dereliction of personal morality. By contrast, moralist Beta found in communism the ideal vehicle for his critique of injustice, but Beta also was destroyed by communism's insistence on intellectual and personal compromise, with suicide as his only moral response. Troubador Delta suffered a variety of communist impositions so that he might reach a larger audience, but he could continue to do so only so long as his considerable cleverness enabled him to continue dancing that difficult step between censorship and art. Political careerists like Gamma thrived under these conditions but at the cost of losing their intellectuality.

Milosz escaped these dilemmas through exile. He nevertheless gained worldwide prominence through the Nobel prize and retained a considerable following in Polonia, the emigrè community. Milosz also was read in the underground in Poland itself, but it was not until after Solidarity was formed in 1980 that he could return to Poland and receive the honors national poets normally enjoy. Thus, by emigration, Milosz managed to become Poland's leading writer, influencing not only the country's arts but also its politics. His emigrè intellectual life enabled him to defy the obligatory Ketman and its violation of intellectuality faced by those who remained in Poland. By so doing, Milosz helped to construct the vision of communism that so many adopted by 1980: Communism was something that could not be reformed from within, and it was something that could not be made Polish.

This was not the image all Polish intellectuals had in the beginning of communist rule. Despite the internal turmoil Milosz paints, other intellectuals, formed more by the system than by adapting to it, were comparatively optimistic. If Stalinism were but an aberrant feature of the system's personnel, and not a consequence of the system itself, another leadership free of the old's errors could make socialism as it should be. Then Stalinism, not communism as such, would be the source of intellectuality's destruction, and communism could then be fulfilled by unleashing intellectuality (Kolakowski 1968). Intellectuals would thus reconstruct communist leadership with their own superior sensibilities. Such a revisionist program could become the call of intellectuals, and so it became in Hungary with Lukacs and those in the Petöfi Circle, in Czechoslovakia among philosophers like Karol Kosik and economists like Ota Sik, and in Poland especially among economists, sociologists, and philosophers. Leszek Kolakowski was in fact one of the leading East European revisionists to emerge in the wake of Stalin's death.

Kolakowski's career exemplifies a current of Polish intellectuality separate from Milosz's. When Milosz rejected communism and left Poland in the early 1950s, Kolakowski taught at the Polish United Workers Party Central Committee's Institute for Training of Scientific Workers. Between 1955 and 1957, he edited a weekly paper called *Po Prostu,* one of the leading periodicals associated with the 1956 "Polish October" when a new, more democratic and Polish route to socialism was proclaimed. He became a lecturer in 1954, then professor in 1959, of the history of modern philosophy at Warsaw University, where he remained until 1968. In that time, he became a leading voice of "Marxist humanism" not only in Poland but throughout the world. In 1968, Kolakowski and several other leading Polish intellectuals were forced into exile in the wake of anti-Semitic and anti-intellectual party politics. In exile, with posts at the University of Chicago and Oxford University, Kolakowski has drifted away from the Marxist humanism of his youth toward a fundamental critique of Marxism, claiming that within it are the seeds of totalitarianism. Given that he was a leading revisionist, and that leading Polish intellectuals, including Jacek Kuron and Adam Michnik, consider him their principal teacher, his reflections on revisionism acquire special significance.

Kolakowski (1981, pp. 456-78) writes that revisionism promoted, in the language of Marxism and socialism, (1) the democratization of public life, with broader civil liberties based on independent workers' councils and trade unions, even if the existing autonomous institution, the Church, figured nowhere in their arguments; (2) sovereignty and equality among socialist countries; (3) an end to the extralegal privileges bureaucrats enjoyed; and (4) economic changes, including more markets and profit incentives and less coercion, but without the promotion of private ownership of property. In these revisions, Kolakowski finds the reinvigoration of Marxism and intellectual life generally. Further, he writes that the revisionism maintained that

Marxism should be based more on its intellectual power than on the power of the state. In revisionism, Leninist-Stalinist Marxism was considered intellectually sterile, especially when approached from the vantage point of a Marxism based on human subjectivity. In this alternative viewpoint, cognition did not simply reflect the material but was the consequence of the interaction between the social and biological. Determinism was likewise criticized, for being at best a useful mythology. Morality especially could not be deduced from laws of history. The politics of revisionism faced different chances in Poland, Hungary, and Czechoslovakia, however.

The Hungarian revisionist movement was more orthodox than the Polish, finding in particular that freedom could be realized within the one-party system. As such, revisionism ultimately was left behind in the 1956 revolution that was crushed by the Soviet invasion. Polish revisionism, on the other hand, died from its own power. The revisionist critique led party authorities to abandon ideological commitments and adopt a narrow careerist mentality that made the party impervious to intellectual opposition from within. The intellectual movement itself came to treat Marxism as but one of many currents useful to critical intellectuality. In conditions where Marxism survives by maintaining its isolation from other traditions, as in Poland, exposure to the novel leads to Marxism's extinction from relevant political discourse, Kolakowski argues. After 1968 and the Warsaw Pact extermination of the Prague Spring, Marxism had become virtually irrelevant to the Polish opposition and to intellectual life in Poland. But precisely because revisionism was destroyed by force, and not by its own bankruptcy, Czechoslovak revisionism retained for the future some political possibilities.

Kolakowski's discussion of revisionism stands up relatively well in the light of the revolutions of 1989-90. The Hungarian Socialist Workers party dissolved itself, with its leading politicians moving to embrace a social democratic identity that still left them far behind in the 1990 spring elections. The Hungarian revisionists in the democratic opposition abandoned their old Marxism in favor of liberal democratic politics, but their Alliance of Free Democrats lost the elections to the nationalist Hungarian Democratic Forum. Because of the deal worked out in the spring 1989 roundtable agreements, the Polish United Workers' party was able to retain influence in the postcommunist Solidarity-led government. In less than a year after those agreements, the Polish communists dissolved their party in favor of new social democratic parties, but these parties face even dimmer electoral hopes in future free elections than the former Hungarian communists found in theirs.

In general, the discourse of communism's opposition in all of these countries finds revisionism, if a theme at all, one of the weakest threads in alternative politics. It is perhaps strongest in the German Democratic

Republic. The transformed Communist party, now called the Party of Democratic Socialism, fared the best of all "native" East German groups in the March elections, but the politics of postcommunist transition are now being determined by West German political parties. In Czechoslovakia, the political leader of the Prague Spring, Alexander Dubcek, returned from enforced obscurity to become the president of the Federal Assembly, and other former communists turned Charter 77 activists, notably Jaroslav Sabata, have played important roles in the transition. This does not mean that revisionism will regain hegemonic status, for anticommunist forces have sought to destroy politically even those proven democrats like Sabata, considering their distant past sufficient grounds for exclusion from Czechoslovakia's postcommunist parliament. But Czechoslovakia's relatively successful experience with revisionism might leave a legacy without parallel in Poland, Hungary, or East Germany.

The postcommunist discourse of Havel and Civic Forum is much closer to the themes of revisionism than any other national discourse in postcommunist Eastern Europe. Both discourses emphasize the importance of individual responsibility and the centrality of consciousness over material being. And both have treated nationalist politics and matters of political economy as secondary to the cultivation of critical intellectuality and emancipatory political practice. Indeed, emphasis on individual dignity and disdain for political economy have been common themes of the opposition intellectual politics that laid the intellectual foundations for the revolutions of 1989. But nationalism could be its successor, as these liberal politics of civil society prove difficult to practice in authority.

THE INTELLECTUAL FOUNDATIONS OF POSTCOMMUNIST POLITICS

The distinction of intellectuals resides in their capacity to redefine their distinction.[6] Even while the Soviet-type system elevated the intellectual by eliminating class rivals and promoting a knowledge-based class order (Szelenyi 1982), it also sought to take away from intellectuals their distinction in the name of a supraindividual rationality. Where, in other social orders, intellectuals were privileged not only by rank but also by a qualitatively separate status based on their distinction, in the new order, they were placed on top of a hierarchy that denied their qualitative difference.

Most obviously, state censorship denies intellectuals the capacity to define their product. Imposed styles, such as socialist realism, reduce intellectual distinction. Even in more subtle ways, the Soviet-type system oppresses this distinction. The idea that intellectuals, as others, should serve some common interest means that intellectuals are denied the privilege of defining their master. Collectivism, even based on some order favorable to the material interests of intellectuals, works to deny the individualistic foundation that makes the intellectual as actor distinctive. As Bahro (1978) argued, the Soviet-type system produced "surplus consciousness," where bureaucratic domination supressed the creative capacity of individuals, especially of intellectuals.

Communists need not have made intellectuality an anachronism in their alternative society. While a dominant discourse based on class justice may challenge intellectual privilege more than other discourses, it need not undermine intellectuality. Indeed, the burst of revisionism in Eastern Europe in the 1950s and 1960s suggested that the Soviet-type system could spawn a considerable measure of intellectual creativity within, or compatible with, the Marxist tradition. But to the extent political authorities reified socialism by defining the essence of the system according to substantive rather than procedural features (as in centralized planning or in the leading role of the party rather than on the basis of the expansion of democracy and of human rights or the end to alienation), an explosion of intellectuality could only have undermined the system by attacking its sacred prescriptions.

Formal traits defining the good society can be defended as essential only if they themselves are sacred, something intellectual criticism cannot touch. If the formal features of the system cannot be changed, revisionism as such must die. In other words, the system must be transformable for revisionism to be meaningful. But once the system became available for transformation in the end of the 1980s, revisionism was no longer available to become the soul of change. Intellectuality came to be defined in opposition to Marxism. The evolution of Polish discourse on opposition and transformation illustrates better than any other discourse the logic of revisionism's decline in Eastern Europe.

Adam Michnik's "The New Evolutionism" ([1976] 1985) was one of the first programmatic statements to suggest the course the Solidarity movement followed later. Michnik argued against revisionism and neopositivism, the prevailing political strategies for opposition. Neopositivism, represented by the Catholic group Znak whose ranks had included Tadeusz Mazowiecki, argued that participation in existing institutions, even if one rejects decisively their lasting value, was the best means for assuring progressive change. Both strategies depended, however, on the activities of elites, not on mass public pressure. This dependence on initiation from above thus led them to choose the wrong sides in periods of open conflict. The only political strategy that might consistently lead to the right choice is that which is based on "an unceasing struggle for reform and evolution that seeks an expansion of civil liberties and human rights" (Michnik [1976] 1985, p. 142). Michnik ([1976] 1985, p. 148) concludes,

> In searching for truth, or, to quote Leszek Kolakowski, "by living in dignity," opposition intellectuals are striving not so much for a better tomorrow as for a better today. Every act of defiance helps us to build the framework of democratic socialism, which should not be merely or primarily a legal institutional structure but a real day-to-day community of free people.

Michnik's essay helped to lay an intellectual foundation for the Solidarity movement in Poland. It constructed a program that was unambiguously on the side of society against the authorities and without possibility for compromise with them. It could not easily be attacked from any ideological position, especially because most political groups at least pay lip service to the idea of human rights. And it promised a new universality, one that could eclipse the claims of Marxism. Here, human rights were in everyone's interests, serving equally well workers, peasants, and intellectuals. But perhaps even more significant than the essay, Michnik and other intellectuals formed a group that demonstrated in practice what the essay suggested.

The Committee in Defense of Workers (Komitet Obrony Robotnikow, or KOR) was formed to help those workers, and their families, who were victimized by the authorities after the 1976 strikes and demonstrations. They not only tried to raise money to help them but also tried to facilitate directly the self-organization of society by advocating independent trade unions through the Charter of Workers' Rights (Lipski 1985). The Solidarity movement, although not a product of these intellectuals' efforts alone (Laba forthcoming), was certainly influenced by this new image of opposition: civil society against the state (Arato 1981).

This civil society was tied closely, although not entirely, to the Catholic church. Lay Catholic intellectuals, organized in clubs of Catholic intellectuals, were frequent advisers and contributors to the movement. Church premises could be used as meeting places. Religious clerical networks connecting pulpits, and, therefore, congregations, could provide a means for communicating a coherent message to a significant proportion of Poles. The elevation of Krakow Archbishop Karol Wojtyla to pope also gave Poles a new charismatic figure with whom to identify. His visit to Poland in 1979 was organized by civil society itself, without state assistance, thereby providing an important lesson in self-organization. Perhaps equally important, the pope's language provided to Polish citizens a new vocabulary for expressing their resistance to the regime.

The traditional language of liberation had been appropriated by the authorities. Terms like "socialism," "self-management," and "class struggle" compromised those who uttered them (Staniszkis 1979). The pope provided instead a language that expressed emancipation in terms of "human dignity," "truth," and "solidarity." These terms could be used without compromise to express the common interests of civil society against the authorities. Pope John Paul II's invectives against the language of class struggle in liberation theology reflect this background of struggle against Poland's communist authorities. This opposition to Marxist language also had an important function in Polish politics, as class antagonisms were one of the foundations for the reproduction of the communist order.

In Soviet-type systems as elsewhere, workers typically resent intellectuals' arrogance and privilege, while intellectuals often distrust workers' fundamentalist or populist politics. The communist authorities have exploited this distrust in their effort to quell any kind of unified opposition to them (Kostecki and Mrela 1984). The idea of civil society, and the terminology of dignity and solidarity, allowed an escape from this principal barrier to an organized civil society.

The civil society project was also successful because it contained no substantive politics. It said nothing about the distribution of wealth, ownership of the means of production, or division of labor. Strategically, it offered a means for the construction of cross-class alliances, as intellectuals could offer their support in the defense of the civil liberties and human rights of those with weaker ties to the media and poorer skills at publicizing their oppression. In return, the collective strength of self-organized workers could build public pressure on the authorities to respect the rights and liberties the intellectuals moved to the public sphere. This was the alliance that made Solidarity ultimately so potent.

The civil society project also could incorporate, however, both nationalist and democratic discourses. Civil society was defined in opposition to the communists, not only in terms of human rights but also in terms of national identities. As such, liberals like Adam Michnik and nationalists like Leszek Moczulski in Poland, or liberal Janos Kis and nationalist Jozsef Antall in Hungary, could define one another as allies in the common struggle of civil society against the state. But in the aftermath of revolution, they become the principal contestants for power.

THE IMPLICATIONS OF EASTERN EUROPE FOR CRITICAL INTELLECTUALITY

The relationship between intellectuals in Eastern Europe and critical intellectuals elsewhere has been problematic. Milosz's *The Captive Mind* ([1953] 1981) is one early example of the attempt by East European intellectuals to explain their politics to Western critical intellectuals. Kolakowski's (1974, 1981) contributions to discussions of Marxism and socialism also communicate, on a more philosophical level, the East European intellectual life world. Feher and Heller's (1987) contributions on the relationship between Eastern left and Western left are also noteworthy in this regard. In these explanations and in others, the motivation for explaining East European intellectual politics was not mainly political. Of course, Western intellectuals could influence, in a limited way, the repressive practices of communist regimes by direct protest and participation in human rights groups. But emancipatory politics depended mostly on domestic initiatives. Post-communist Eastern Europe faces different challenges, however, and demands an even more international intellectual politics.

The projects for civil society's reconstruction in the face of communist rule are showing the fault lines around which they were constructed. Nationalists and liberals are vying for power, with the former more likely to foster a climate in which there will be interstate war and repression of national minorities. At the same time, however, the liberals appear less sensitive to the dangers of capitalist transformations and more likely to provoke militant working-class oppositions. It is the nationalists who are more likely to speak of a "third way" and identify with the legacy of interwar Europe, whereas the liberals seek full integration with Western Europe and assert a common "European" identity. Indeed, the extent of East-West European integration might establish the basic alternatives for intellectual politics in the coming decade. To the extent the East Europeans struggle to find a "third way," their politics will likely increasingly resemble those of Latin America, with alterations between military dictatorship and tentative electoral democracies.

If the East Europeans are not included in the European Community in the near future, their civil societies will come to resemble more those of the semiperiphery in Latin America than any core country. Whether underdevelopment results from solely economic integration with the core, or from an attempt to construct a third way without the resources to do it, it is likely that similar problems that have confronted Latin American politics will find expression in Eastern Europe. Militaristic authoritarian regimes are likely responses to problems of developing economies, and they have a legacy in Eastern Europe upon which they can draw. Under these conditions, working-class needs and interests will probably be hidden in a co-opted Mexican-style corporatism, with additional integration provided by nationalist passions. Under these conditions, dialogue between East European and Latin American critical intellectuals may become increasingly helpful to each.

It will be too easy for the core to pit one region against the other in the emerging world order. Already, Latin America and Africa are suffering losses of U.S. financial aid as Poland and Hungary receive increases. Latin American representatives have been critical of the favorable treatment on debt repayment that East European regimes receive at the expense of Latin America. As the weak alternative offered by the Soviet-led economic association disappears, and the world capitalist system grows more dominant, it will become ever more important for the semiperipheries and peripheries of the world system to establish new alliances to defend their interests. There are several barriers that stand in the way, however, the most prominent of which may be Marxism.

In the Third World, Marxism remains a legitimate and important tradition for the construction of an emancipatory alternative. Upon his release from prison on February 12, 1990, Nelson Mandela saluted the South African Communist party "for its steady contribution to the struggle for democracy." The Sandinista experience also suggests that pluralism, egalitarianism, and self-management, the value frame of Solidarity, might be derived from Marxism instead of opposed to it. But East Europeans are unlikely to accept the association of Marxism, and especially of communism, with democracy. Pope John Paul II's hostility to Latin American liberation theology is illustrative of the tension that an East European-Latin American dialogue will generate. When an associate of the pope, the Polish priest and "theologian of Solidarity" Jozef Tischner (1987), was asked about liberation theology, he could only say that it was hopelessly naive about Marxism and communism. As the Soviet-type system reified Marxism, so too have its opponents.

Marxism, socialism, and communism have been constructed in particular historical conjunctures with various cultural legacies. One of the greatest barriers to an internationalization of emancipatory politics has been the divergent, often diametrically opposed, experiences of various regions with this construction. It is remarkable, for instance, to note the compatibility between contemporary Chinese and East European intellectual politics and to note the difficulties faced by dialogue between Chinese and Indian intellectuals or East Europeans and Latin Americans. As the Soviet Union loses its own systemic distinction, a new opportunity for emancipatory politics might emerge within Europe, however. The new period may be characterized by a different attitude toward Marxism, much as the East European revisionists suggested, one by which it is viewed as but one of many potential emancipatory traditions. Once Marxism is thus demoted from either its sacred or its demonic status, the possibilities for East European dialogue with the Third World will increase. But, until that time, divergent understandings of the Marxist legacy may hamper international emancipatory alliances.

The impetus for such a link between critical intellectuals in Eastern Europe and in the Third World will decline, however, to the extent Eastern Europe's position in the world economy is mitigated by its integration into the European Community. But such integration will likely open up East

European politics and encourage democratic possibilities far more than will the isolation of Eastern Europe as new European dependents. As such, the position of the European liberals might offer greater opportunities for a new East European politics, even if at the expense of dialogues between North and South.

Before the revolutions of 1989, networks connecting new social movements in the West with activists in the East helped to establish new politics in the latter. For instance, the contact of European peace activists and West German Greens with Polish activists helped to establish a discourse about peace never before heard in Polish society (Tymowski 1984; Kennedy 1990b). While the end of the cold war may make peace movements with a European focus a theme of the past, the environmentalist project can only become more important given the destruction of the biophysical environment. Already, some of the most vital and innovative East European movements are ecologically informed. Once better ties are established with greens in the West, environmentalism might become a dominant theme of opposition in East European, or even pan-European, politics. The growth of new social movements thus will become more likely in Eastern Europe to the degree these movements have ties to those similarly inclined in Western Europe. And, as that occurs, the possibilities for a new critical intellectuality will grow.

One form of critical intellectuality has been noticeably absent in the dominant discourses of oppositional intellectual politics in Eastern Europe. Although there are feminist circles in Russia (Noonan 1988) and Yugoslavia (Jancar 1988), they have generally faired even more poorly in countries with Soviet-imposed communist regimes. Feminism has suffered in all these countries from prohibitions on self-organization and from the importance of traditional family roles given limited consumer goods and services. One of the most significant barriers to feminist politics, however, has been its association with the authorities and its incompatibility with strategies of social self-organization. To the extent that feminism was identified as "leftist" and in opposition to national traditions, and to the extent that the struggle for self-organization required the maintenance of traditional family roles to ensure domestic tranquility while public conflict raged, feminism stood hardly a chance. But as civil society is reconstructed with an especially patriarchal face, both the tolerance for and the necessity of feminist politics have become much greater.

Warsaw feminist Hanna Jankowska (1989) has noted how women's politics was virtually ignored in the Polish roundtable agreements. Even women's participation in the new politics is extremely limited; only 12% of delegates to the National Assembly are women. Henzler (1989) notes that even fewer, only 8%, of the Solidarity nominees for Senate and Sejm were women. As women were especially active in Solidarity's grass-roots politics, even if not at the regional or national levels in 1981, women might be prepared to initiate a feminist politics, especially as the Catholic church tries to limit reproductive rights in the postcommunist order. But these politics will have to construct a new feminism that is not identified so closely with the communist politics against which most Poles have struggled for decades. This project ought to become easier too as the intellectual political field loses its convenient dichotomies based on civil society and communism.

Finally, the end to the dichotomy between communism and civil society might open a new forum for class politics, especially if these systems are not incorporated into the European Community and are integrated with Western Europe only economically, for instance, through membership in the European Free Trade Association. Under these conditions, it is likely that a new working-class militance will emerge. In Poland, it is possible that an alliance between the old communist trade union associated with Alfred Miodowicz and disgruntled Solidarity militants associated with the Workers' Group (including Andrzej Gwiazda) and Fighting Solidarity (Kornel Morawiecki) could be formed. But it is unlikely that Polish intellectuals in authority will point to, much less facilitate, the development of such militance, given that they now have the responsibility for making Poland attractive to foreign investors.

It is too easy to understand such reluctance on the part of Polish intellectuals as confirmation of the thesis that, once one abandons Marxism and socialism, one also abandons critical intellectuality. On the contrary, I believe that one of the lessons of Eastern Europe is that critical intellectuality cannot depend solely on the critique of capitalism or any other single, even if "basic," form of domination. Instead, the practice of a critical hermeneutics—in which readings of other world experiences help the reconstruction of both analytical and normative foundations for emancipatory praxis—is as fundamental to emancipatory praxis as the analysis of any systemic tendency. And while East Europeans currently are not particularly inclined to understand the politics of dependency in the capitalist world system, neither are critical intellectuals from without their life world well prepared to contribute to the challenges facing East European intellectuals.

The tasks facing these intellectuals are not entirely unlike those facing the Bolsheviks through Lenin's death. The Bolsheviks were not prepared to construct an entirely new system, especially one limited to a single country. They retained and imported many elements from the dominant sectors of the capitalist economy, even if they adopted them believing that they were beginning to construct a new kind of society. East European intellectuals in authority have no such grand dreams, and many of them want to import wholesale that which the West already has. But others retain a critical spirit, even in authority. This is especially evident in their attempts to introduce an ecologically sound element to their economic transitions. The dilemma for these critical intellectuals, however, is that alternative visions are weak and alternative resources are even more limited. Unlike the Bolsheviks, who at least had the vision of socialism to inspire them, contemporary East European intellectuals are limited not only by their economic dependence but also by the tendency of contemporary Western critical intellectuals to theorize only the politics of opposition and not that of authority. East European intellectuals do not have that option.

One of the principal challenges before critical intellectuals today is to make the revolutions of 1989, and the histories that moved them, central to the reconstruction of the emancipatory project. That begins with being able to read intellectual politics in their own context, for, by so doing, one establishes the possibility for real dialogue across radically different life worlds. In the 1990s, such a dialogue emerged between Eastern and Western Europe over the meanings and politics of peace and disarmament. That dialogue is by no means over in the 1990s, but it must be extended to other places and to new themes so that the transformations of Eastern Europe facilitate the generation of emancipatory alternatives instead of helping to bury them.

NOTES

1. "Intellectual" and "intelligentsia" in social scientific discourse have had as many as seven different meanings. Sometimes the former is a subset of the latter and, other times, the latter is of the former. In the first, most general, case, "intellectuals" are distinguished from the larger category by their creative powers and capacity for self-definition. In the second, the "intelligentsia" is distinguished from the larger category by their inclination for teleological reasoning or their distinctive cultural identity. In this framework, the "intelligentsia" is also distinguished from another kind of intellectual, professionals, whose technical know-how and occupational distinction mark their distinctive identification, not their teleological reasoning or their culture (Szeleny 1982). Even within these two general categories, "intelligentsia" is a controversial term in Eastern European discourse.

So understood, the "intelligentsia" can also refer to, third, a statistical category (such as all those with higher educations in Eastern Europe; Szczcpanski 1962); fourth, a social group with a special ethos of morality and responsibility (as the old Polish intelligentsia claimed to be the moral government of the nation; Gella 1971); or, fifth, a class with particular consciousness or interests, possibly en route to domination, as Jan Waclaw Machajski through Ivan Szelenyi have suggested.

"Intellectual," the concept, also can become an object of controversy, for it can become, sixth, a category of relative exclusiveness based on some special responsibility, experience, or achievement, as Baranczak (1986-87) suggests; or it can refer to, seventh, a capacity of all men and women that is exaggerated or repressed under various social circumstances, as Gramsci (1971) would emphasize. Each of these understandings of "intellectual" and "intelligentsia" must be kept in mind when discussing Eastern Europe, even though I will usually use these terms in the general, second sense, unless otherwise indicated.

2. Recent discussions in the Program of Comparative Studies of Social Transformation at the University of Michigan have addressed these relationships between nation and class. Especially important to my own thoughts on the subject is a recent discussion paper by Ronald Grigor Suny (1990) on class and nation during the Bolshevik Revolution and Civil War, wherein he discusses the patterns of horizontal and vertical integration of classes and nations in this period.

3. Milosz's (1968) "autobiography" is also useful for this purpose, although he is less literal in the treatment of his engagement with communism than one would expect. Nevertheless, the same "Ketman" comes through there.

4. Milosz ([1953] 1981) uses the term "intellectual" as I do when explicating *The Captive Mind*, in the first, general sense and in the sixth, particular sense. See note 2.

5. Charles Lemert suggested an interesting parallel between this East European Ketman and the dualities of African American culture discussed in Gates (1988).

6. Here, I use "intellectual" more in the particular, seventh sense. See note 2.

REFERENCES

Arato, Andrew. 1981. "Civil Society Against the State." *Telos* 50:19-47.

Bahro, Rudolph. 1978. *The Alternative in Eastern Europe.* London: New Left Books.

Baranczak, Stanislaw. 1986-87. "The Polish Intellectual." *Salmagundi* 70-71:217-28.

Bauman, Zygmunt. 1987. "Intellectuals in East Central Europe." *Eastern European Politics and Societies* 1(2):162-86.

Feher, Ferenc and Agnes Heller. 1987. "Eastern Left-Western Left: Part I: Reflections on a Problematic Relationship." *Socialist Review* 89:25-48. "Part II: After 1968." *Socialist Review* 90:33-48.

Gates, Henry Louis, Jr. 1988. *The Signifying Monkey.* Oxford: Oxford University Press.

Gella, Aleksander. 1971. "The Life and Death of the Old Polish Intelligentsia." *Slavic Review* 30:1-27.

———. 1989. *Development of Class Structure in Eastern Europe.* Albany: State University of New York Press.

Gramsci, Antonio. 1971. "The Intellectuals." Pp. 5-23 in *Selections from the Prison Notebooks.* London: Lawrence and Wishart.

Havel, Vaclav. 1990. [Address to the Joint Session of the U.S. Congress, February 21.]

Henzler, Marek. 1989. "Wygrali w Prawyborach." *Polityka* 21(May 27):3.

Hertz, Aleksander. [1961] 1988. *The Jews in Polish Culture.* Chicago: Northwestern University Press.

Hoser, Jan. 1970. *Zawod i Praca Inzyniera.* Warsaw: Ossolineum.

Jancar, Barbara. 1988. "Neofeminism in Yugoslavia: A Closer Look." *Women and Politics* 8(1):1-30.

Jankowska, Hanna. 1989. "Mowienie Wlasnym Glosem." *Polityka* 33 (August 22):10.

Kennedy, Michael D. 1990a. *Professionals, Power and Solidarity in Poland: A Critical Sociology of Soviet-type Society.* Cambridge: Cambridge University Press.

———. 1990b. "The Constitution of Critical Intellectuals: Polish Physicians, Peace Activists and Democratic Civil Society." *Studies in Comparative Communism.*

Kennedy, Michael D. and David A. Smith. 1989. "East Central European Urbanization: A Political Economy of the World System Perspective." *International Journal of Urban and Regional Research* 13(4):597-624.

Kolakowski, Leszek. 1968. "Intellectuals and the Communist Movement." In *Toward a Marxist Humanism.* New York: Grove.

———. 1974. "The Myth of Human Self-identity: Unity of Civil and Political Society in Socialist Thought." In *The Socialist Idea: A Reappraisal,* edited by Leszek Kolakowski and Stuart Hampshire. London: Weidenfeld and Nicolson.

———. 1981. *Main Currents of Marxism.* Oxford: Oxford University Press.

Kostecki, Marian and Krzysztof Mrela. 1984. "Collective Solidarity in Poland's Powdered Society." *The Insurgent Sociologist* 12:131-42.

Laba, Roman. Forthcoming. *The Roots of Solidarity.* Princeton, NJ: Princeton University Press.

Lipski, Jan Jozef. 1985. *KOR: Workers Defense Committee in Poland.* Berkeley: University of California Press.

Lukas, Richard. 1985. *Forgotten Holocaust: The Poles Under German Occupation, 1939-44.* Lexington: University of Kentucky Press.

Mandela, Nelson. 1990. "Transcript of Mandela's Speech at Cape Town City Hall: 'Africa It Is Ours.' " *The New York Times,* February 12, p. A10.

Michnik, Adam. [1976] 1985. "The New Evolutionism." Pp. 135-48 in *Letters from Prison and Other Essays.* Berkeley: University of California Press.

Milosz, Czeslaw. [1953] 1981. *The Captive Mind.* New York: Vintage.

———. 1968. *Native Realm: A Search for Self Definition.* Garden City, NY: Doubleday.

Noonan, Norma C. 1988. "Marxism and Feminism in the USSR: Irreconcilable Differences?" *Women and Politics* 8(1):31-49.

Spechler, Martin C. 1989. "The Economic Advantages of Being Peripheral: Subordinate Nations in Multinational Empires." *Eastern European Politics and Societies* 3(3):448-64.

Staniszkis, Jadwiga. 1979. "On Some Contradictions of Socialist Society: The Case of Poland." *Soviet Studies* 31:167-87.

Suny, Ronald Grigor, 1990. "Nationality and Class in the Revolutions of 1917: A Reexamination of Social Categories." Paper discussed in the Program for Comparative Study of Social Transformation, University of Michigan, February 15.

Szczepanski, Jan. 1962. "The Polish Intelligentsia: Past and Present." *World Politics* 14:406-20.

Szelenyi, Ivan. 1982. "The Intelligentsia in the Class Structure of State-Socialist Societies." Pp. 287-326 in *Marxist Inquiries,* edited by M. Burawoy and T. Skocpol. Chicago: University of Chicago Press.

Szporluk, Roman. 1981. *The Political Thought of Thomas G. Masaryk.* New York: Columbia University Press.

———. 1988. *Nationalism and Communism.* Oxford: Oxford University Press.

Tischner, Jozef. 1987. [Group Interview at the University of Michigan, October 5.]

Tymowski, Andrzej. 1984. "Underground Solidarity and the Peace Movement." *Poland Watch* 5:114-31.

Wallerstein, Immanuel. 1976. *The Modern World System.* New York: Academic Press.

Chapter 7

THE IDEOLOGY OF INTELLECTUALS AND THE CHINESE STUDENT PROTEST MOVEMENT OF 1989

CRAIG CALHOUN
University of North Carolina, Chapel Hill

WHEN CHINESE STUDENT PROTESTORS said in the spring of 1989 that they were acting as "the conscience of the nation," and that this was not just a simple choice but a responsibility they had to live up to, they were speaking in line with a long tradition. Earlier intellectuals had remonstrated with emperors at great personal risk. During the declining years of the Qing dynasty, both students and older intellectuals had been in the forefront of the struggle for reform. They helped to lay part of the foundation for communism in China by reevaluating traditional culture, encouraging critical thought, and importing or developing a range of challenging ideas. Many intellectuals played key roles in the revolutionary struggle itself or returned from safe positions abroad to help build a new China. Under communist rule, they did not fare very well. Yet, paradoxically, the vilification of intellectuals at various points under communist rule—especially during the Cultural Revolution—reinforced the salience of the category, even while it added a complexity to normative evaluations of its members.[1] And the events of the last 13 years, since the end of Maoist rule, only enhanced this sense of a crucial role for intellectuals.

Yet it is not obvious or clear just what "intellectual" means. The category is an ideological construction, a claim about the unity among a variety of people, not simply a reflection of it. The Chinese term, *zhishifenzi,* is usually taken simply to mean all educated people, though that is still a fuzzy definition. During the "antirightist" campaigns and the Cultural Revolution, avoiding the label "intellectual" often made political sense. As the idea of expertise took on prestige once again in the 1980s, some provincial cadres began to claim startling numbers of intellectuals in their units because they counted everyone with primary, or perhaps secondary, educations. An

AUTHOR'S NOTE: I am greatly indebted to my students in Beijing for including me in their activities of spring 1989 and trying to explain them. I have also benefited from many discussions since then with Chinese students and intellectuals in the United States; regrettably, to thank people by name may be to put them at risk in China.

official definition includes all those people at the middle level of expertise, equivalent to "assistant engineer" or above. A standard rule of thumb includes all university graduates and "others of comparable levels." Intellectuals include writers, professors, scientists, and others who make their living by the production or dissemination of "knowledge" or "culture." But they also include doctors, lawyers, town planners, sanitation engineers, and other people with higher education. Especially at the more elite end, this notion of "intellectuals" reflects a process of class formation through which intellectuals have come to share a variety of ideas and interests and a common sense of themselves and their role in China.

Chinese students constitute a specific, generationally defined segment of the more general class of intellectuals. The protestors of 1989 had strong identities as budding intellectuals and as students in particular. They were different from other intellectuals not only in their youth and the lesser development of their ideas and skills but in the fact that they didn't have families to support or jobs to risk (at least in the immediate sense). They were, therefore, understood to be freer than their elders to act through public protest as a "conscience of the nation." In this understanding of themselves, the students echoed older Chinese precedents, most notably the student and intellectual movement of May 4, 1919, whose anniversary they celebrated in the second of this year's really large marches. Of course, the student "fraction" of the intellectual class also had its own complaints: crowded, poorly constructed dormitories, inadequate stipends, a shortage of good jobs after graduation, and the like.

More senior intellectuals had exerted an enormous influence on students through their writing, public speaking, and teaching in recent years. During the protest movement, they offered advice, tried to protect young activists, and pushed for change in quieter ways (though a special respect was paid to those elders who did put themselves on the line in public protest). But protesting students did not simply follow the lead or advice of older intellectuals. They learned much during discussions with those individuals during the months and years before the movement took off on April 15. They continued to pay attention to what senior intellectuals said and were much heartened by support from more established figures. But the younger generation had its own orientation. Its members—who, of course, had heterogeneous views of their own—absorbed some aspects of the ideology of their elders more than others and recombined elements in new mixes. In particular, the older generation, what the Chinese call both young and middle-aged intellectuals as well as the very senior, was shaped profoundly by its response to the Cultural Revolution. Though these intellectuals did not, for the most part, reach the same conclusion as China's aging leadership, they did share the fear of widespread turmoil. They often argued that students were going too far and should pull back, not just because the government might crack down, as indeed it did, but because order might disintegrate. Many of these older intellectuals, including, for example, the most prominent among them, Fang Lizhi, were very radical in their critique of communist rule. But their call ultimately was for a kind of reform in which the best-trained, most elite experts would advise the government, not for a mass mobilization of the Chinese people. Only a few of these prominent older intellectuals could find anything good to say about the Great Proletarian Cultural Revolution during which they had suffered. Liu Binyan (1990) is distinctive in being able to praise the democratic, antibureaucratic ideals of the Cultural Revolution at the same time that he shows how these were negated by the party apparatuses and cliques that maintained power during it. The Cultural Revolution was not the same sort of personal experience for most of the younger students in the protest (and most of the main activists were quite young—22 years or younger). The point is not that they supported the Cultural Revolution, or learned very directly from it; the point, rather, is that memories of the Cultural Revolution did not damn for them the idea of participatory democracy. They were often elitist in their own ways, but they were far more willing to risk turmoil and to call for mass participation as a solution to the evils wrought by established authorities.

In this chapter, I want to describe something of the range of intellectual positions and views that formed the backdrop of the student protest movement. It is important to avoid collapsing diversity. More senior intellectuals had heterogeneous views, and various students combined parts of them with ideas of their own in novel mixes. I will describe some key lines of differentiation in the Chinese intellectual field of the late 1980s, relating different positions in that field to different stances on the question of what protest and/or reform ought to achieve. The basic lines of tension and differentiation are quite long-standing, though various specifics and especially bases of institutional support have changed in the last 100 years. The concerns of the intellectuals thus have somewhat less to do with communism—pro or con— than is often thought. The questions of political and economic reform in the 1980s have a great deal in common with those of the 1920s and before. In both eras, moreover, the most basic question may have been how to deal with a pervasive sense of China's cultural crisis. This concern encouraged many protestors in 1989 to move beyond the narrower programs outlined by Fang Lizhi or reformers close to Zhao Ziyang and contributed to the movement's fundamental emotional strength. Space limitations prevent me from treating the earlier period more than allusively and, indeed, will make my account of the recent period more of a sketch based on key personalities than is ideal. Neither will I here be able to relate this to any very detailed account of the student movement itself (see Calhoun 1989a, 1989b, 1989c, 1989d). This chapter will remain focused on part of the background of the movement. I will, however, return briefly in the conclusion to the argument about how the students differed from their elders even as they learned from them.

"SCIENCE AND DEMOCRACY"

In the early twentieth century, intellectuals developed personifications of science and democracy as part of their effort to spread enlightenment among the less educated in China (and thereby strengthen the nation both domestically and internationally). "Mr. Science" and "Mr. Democracy" (often presented not through the full Chinese terms but as "Mr. Sci" and "Mr. De") were widely touted as solutions to China's problems. These problems were many and varied but were perceived centrally in terms of modernization and relations with the West. Thus the protest of May 4, 1919, was sparked by China's abuse at the hands of its nominal allies in the Versailles treaty negotiations, which ceded large tracts of China to Japanese control. Political weakness was seen simultaneously in traditional terms of a corrupt, declining dynasty and in terms of failed modernization and lack of national strength. Similarly, China's poverty had become an increasing concern, and the importance of both "Mr. Science" and of political reform lay substantially in paving the way for economic modernization and improvement in material standards of living. Last but not least, as the enlightenment imagery suggests, May 4th intellectuals worried about the cultural state of the nation. Illiteracy and in general a low level of cultural attainment among the mass of the population formed part of the story. Beyond it, though, there was a critique of traditional Chinese culture, from the binding of women's feet to the emphasis of stultifying rote learning and the archaic formal essays in the imperial examination system. China, it seemed, needed not only more but different culture.

In the late winter and early spring of 1989, many of China's intellectuals had resumed the May 4th struggle. They held "democracy salons" and open lectures on university campuses, wrote essays, debated the merits of reform proposals, and laid plans for a celebration of the 70th anniversary of the May 4th movement. One group tried to expand the public sphere on a very eighteenth-century European model by founding a coffeehouse, the Enlightenment Cafe, though it was short-lived. Taking even more risks, leading intellectuals even organized a series of petitions, notably calling for the release of political prisoners from previous prodemocracy movements. One key open letter of February 13 read:

We are deeply concerned with Mr. Fang Lizhi's January 6, 1989, open letter to Chairman Deng Xiaoping. We believe that on the occasion of the fortieth anniversary of the establishment of the PRC and the seventieth anniversary of the May Fourth Movement, the granting of an amnesty, especially the release of political prisoners like Wei Jingsheng, will create a harmonious atmosphere conducive to reforms and at the same time conform with the world's general trend that human rights are increasingly respected.[2]

Wei Jingsheng was the most prominent leader of the 1978-80 "democracy wall" movement, a worker-intellectual and publisher of that period's most exciting new magazine. He has languished in prison, mostly without communication with the outside, since that movement's suppression.

There had been repeated movements for democracy throughout the post-Mao era, most notably in 1978-80 and 1986-87. The government itself had made some efforts to cultivate the goodwill of intellectuals, especially more "technocratic" ones, seeing them as central to its attempt to modernize and revitalize the economy. Speech and publication had grown more free; the universities had become centers of discourse about public affairs as well as particularistic concerns. The project of intellectual class formation had been resumed, though each movement forward led to at least a minor government crackdown and temporary reassertion of controls.[3]

In early 1989, intellectuals were beginning to organize themselves and to speak more forcefully in challenge to the government than at any time in the history of the PRC. The petitions to free Wei Jingsheng and other political prisoners were the focus. As Perry Link (1989, p. 41) comments:

> Although the petitions failed to free any prisoners, their very considerable significance was to mark the first time in Communist Chinese history that intellectuals have, as a group, publicly opposed the top leader on a sensitive issue.

Two initial petitions drew a stern warning that things must go no further; the intellectuals responded with a third petition. This was pointedly signed by 43 scholars, precisely one more than had signed the second petition. These intellectuals built on the heroic efforts of figures like the physicist Fang Lizhi (perhaps China's closest analogue to an East European-style dissident, a form not generally characteristic of the Chinese scene) and the investigative journalist Liu Binyan. Crucially, though, they defied the government as an organized group, not simply as courageous individuals.

At the same time, many of these more senior intellectuals were speaking to university students in freewheeling "democracy salons" and open discussion sessions on the major campuses. These discussions built on the previous speeches of national figures like Fang, and the conversations small knots of students held among themselves. In this way, they provided a bit of the associational network the protests would need as well as a forum for spreading ideas. It was important, though, that this diffusion of ideas and awakening of consciousness was not limited to such discussions, to the elite university campuses, or even to the most intensely interested of students. Basic concerns about Chinese society and the appropriate stances to take toward it were spread in a variety of ways and translated from a sophisticated intellectual discourse into a more popularly influential idiom of dissent.

Many of the later student leaders were among those most involved in the discussions in the winter and early spring. They transmitted ideas as they in turn gave speeches to their fellows. They built, however, on a base. Crucial to the provision of this base was the relative freedom of publication that China had begun to enjoy. Thus the speeches of Fang Lizhi not only reached thousands in his immediate audiences but were transcribed and circulated widely. This combined with increasing freedom of travel to encourage common attitudes on campuses all over China (though not necessarily off campuses, let alone outside urban areas). The publications that played important roles were of several kinds. There were academic journals that printed analyses of China's crisis and proposals for reform. Even many university-sponsored and putatively purely scholarly journals in China were devoted not to "ivory tower" academic pursuits but to concrete discussion of the contemporary situation. Beyond them were intellectual journals like *Seeking Facts* (the former *Red Flag*) and newspapers such as the *People's Daily* and the *Guangming Daily* (the so-called intellectuals' newspaper). Literary magazines carried commentary on current events as well as essays and fiction taking up themes of public concern. This was true not only of elite periodicals but of their more popular cousins.

Popular music was also a very important medium for transmission of political dissent. Singers did not attempt to develop major social analyses in their lyrics, of course, but they did give expression to feelings that moved many others. When Cui Jian, for example, sang "Nothing I Have," he expressed something of the sense of social and cultural bankruptcy that many Chinese students felt. His songs in particular gave encapsulated, often repeated, expression to grievances and desires; the very style of much of the music combined Westernization with countercultural critique. Another popular singer's simple lyric, "follow your own feelings," summed up one of the powerful urges, even moral mandates, for Chinese students. Film and performing arts also played similar roles. Last but not least, the proliferation of gathering places from private restaurants to a short-lived coffeehouse provided something of the material basis, the "free spaces" for a nascent public sphere.

Among the intellectual elite, various groupings could be identified. To start with, borrowing typical Chinese categories, there were (1) the scientists and technical workers of whom Fang Lizhi is the most prominent protagonist; (2) the social scientists and advisers to government and party reformers of whom Yan Jiaqi, Su Shaozhi, and Li Zehou are the most famous examples; and (3) the literary intellectuals including journalists like Liu Binyan, critics like Liu Zaifu, and creative writers like Bei Dao and Liu Xinwu.[4] Each of these groups had their distinctive social and institutional bases. Fang Lizhi's main audiences were at Beijing University and the Chinese University of Science and Technology. The social scientists were based especially at the Chinese Academy of Social Sciences, though some were also scattered through party and quasi-private think tanks. The literary intellectuals were sometimes on the faculties of universities or housed in institutions like the Academy for Chinese Culture, but they were most distinctively writers for increasingly open newspapers and magazines, including a host of new, substantially independent publications and book series; they were also engaged in an effort to develop a sort of coffeehouse and salon culture outside of the official institutions of Beijing. Each of these three groups also had its distinctive views and lines of argument on China's current situation; though these discourses sometimes overlapped, of course, they also had their own internal heterogeneity.

NATURAL SCIENTISTS

Relatively few natural scientists were among the most visible leaders of protest. They tended to emphasize freedom to pursue their own scientific and technical work and the economic contributions that work could make to China's modernization and prosperity. Their emphasis was on the first term in the old May 4th slogan of science and democracy. In the same sense, though, the ideology of science colored the notion of democracy far beyond the ranks of scientists. When scientists considered democracy, they tended to identify it very strongly with the rational, efficient management of government by people with trained expertise. Their most general concern was with the project of modernizing China. While most pursued this directly in their scientific careers, a few offered broader critiques or programs for remaking China in the imaged of science. Thus Wen Yuankai, a former vice president of the Chinese University of Science and Technology (CUST), wrote a widely read book, *Reform and Remolding of National Character.*

Another former vice president of CUST, Fang Lizhi, became the most influential of these scientists and indeed of all spokespeople for Chinese intellectuals. His arguments are heavily colored by an ideology of science but also have a resonance far beyond the ranks of scientists; he thus transcends the category in which he is placed here. Fang will get more attention here than any other individual, both because of his enormous influence and because his speeches are so frequently concerned with the question of what role intellectuals should play in Chinese society. Fang was also unusually radical in his positions. For example, natural scientists in general tended to be strong supporters of Westernization. Fang (1987, p. 87) went further, embracing the government's very condemnation: "Talking about China's modernization, I personally like the idea of Westernization at full scale." What Fang thematized about the West, however, was quite specific—an idealized notion of science, an empiricist discourse of truth, democracy as embodied in conventional electoral institutions, and, above all, an account of modernity as an evolutionary ideal more or less independent of cultural particularity.[5]

Like other scientific and technical researchers, Fang sought institutional arrangements in which to make practical contributions without the distortion or impediment of corrupt and ideological leadership:

> As an intellectual, one should be a driving force for society. One major aspect of the effort to push the society forward is to do a better job in our professional field so that we can give more to society. . . . Our social responsibility, so to speak, is for each of us here to work for a better social environment that will allow our intellectuals to make good use of their talent and work more efficiently. . . . One important sign of a developed society is that intellectuals have a say in social development and enjoy considerable influence. (Fang 1988a, pp. 68-69)

Fang illustrated the influence he imagined intellectuals to have in the West with the story of attending a scientific conference in Rome at which both the Italian president and the Pope listened to the scientists. The contrast to senior Chinese leaders who never meet with even the most eminent scientists or take an interest in scientific work was telling to Fang and his listeners on several levels. The Italian president, for example, sat in the front row, not on state: "The president himself must sit down there because he was a citizen like all of his compatriots" (1987, p. 127). Even more impressive was the interaction with the pope:

> The following day, we had a scientific popularization meeting with the Pope in a church. We scientific researchers took pains to explain scientific knowledge to him because we wanted him to believe in our research. Since he represents the power of God . . . we sat before him. . . . But we and the Pope sat face to face. Thus, we explained our latest discoveries to him. These two meetings impressed me deeply, very deeply! I learned what position knowl-

edge has attained in the modern age. After we finished with our explanations, the Pope made a speech to thank us. . . . what he said concerned chiefly with scientific knowledge. He said he understood our explanations about the Halley's Comet, cosmic dust, black hole, and the universe. His speech contained almost nothing irrelevant to science. . . . After these two meetings, I came to the conclusion that in those developed, democratic countries, knowledge has an independent position. It has its own value and independent position. Moreover, everyone must understand the importance of knowledge. Everyone, from those who occupy high positions such as the president of a nation and the Pope to ordinary people, must understand this. . . . If one wants to be a noble man or a man in a high position, one must not be ignorant. Therefore, I feel that there is truly a great difference between those nations and ours. (Fang 1987, pp. 127-28)

Having leaders who couldn't understand their work, and didn't care to, was obviously bad for intellectuals. But Fang emphasized that it was also bad for society as a whole. Repeatedly, Fang argued, in a fashion indebted to Daniel Bell and his popularizers Alvin Toffler and John Naisbitt (both of whose books are widely read in Chinese translation), that modern technology has made knowledge, rather than labor or other material means of production, basic: "Intellectuals, who own and create information and knowledge, are the most dynamic component of the productive forces; this is what determines their social status" (Fang 1986, p. 17).

Like other reform-oriented Chinese intellectuals, Fang spoke frequently of democracy. His emphasis, however, was not egalitarian. Rather than mass participatory institutions, he advocated a government by experts. At the extreme, it seemed as though he would like to see government by physicists. Thus he argued:

It's up to the intellectuals as a class, with their sense of social responsibility, their consciousness about democracy, and their initiative to strive for their rights, to decide whether the democratic system can survive and develop in a given society. (Fang 1988b, p. 85)

Fang did not argue that the decision on whether democracy would survive might more properly—more democratically—belong to the society as a whole. He clearly thought the society was not ready:

You can go travel in the villages and look around; I feel those uneducated peasants, living under traditional influence, have a psychological consciousness that is very deficient. It is very difficult to instill a democratic consciousness in them; they still demand an honest and upright official; without an official they are uncomfortable. (quoted and translated by R. Kraus 1989, p. 298, from same speech as Fang 1988c)

Fang's conception of democracy was not essentially participatory. It turned on (1) human rights, (2) the importance of honest, expert officials, and (3) the responsibility and right of intellectuals to criticize the government.

The rhetoric of human rights has been very important and potentially radical in China.[6] Like many intellectuals, Fang Lizhi hesitated before the radical implications of human rights, for example, the notion of granting the "uneducated" equal standing in public discourse with the intellectuals. Like most of the students I talked to during the protest movement, he did not consider democracy to be inherently a process of education through participation in political activity. Education was something intellectuals would offer to peasants, workers, and soldiers; democratic discourse was by and large a right of the educated.

This said, Fang did make good points in stressing that democracy should not mean simply a relaxation of controls (as the CCP seemed sometimes to imply) and that it ought to flow from bottom to top (even if he was a bit inconsistent in deciding just where the social "bottom" lay).

> What is the meaning of democracy? Democracy means that every human being has his own rights and that human beings, each exercising his own rights, form our society. Therefore, rights are in the hands of every citizen. They are not given by top leaders of the nation. All people are born with them. (Fang 1987, p. 137)

Thus Fang argued persuasively that students ought not to believe the party's claim that it had "given" them an education. Their education, he suggested, was a right. If it was based on anyone's "gift," the donors were their parents, who had labored hard to provide for them (1987, p. 139; 1988b, p. 84). On the one hand, this scored an excellent point against the party's (in this case highly traditional) claims as authoritarian benefactor. On the other hand, it ignored the extent to which educational opportunities remained class stratified in the China of the 1980s; the university students to whom Fang spoke were virtually never the children of peasants and seldom the offspring of ordinary workers.

Similarly, Fang did recognize the importance of critical discourse to the development of a democratic public sphere:

> I hope we may all benefit from this interchanging discussion method. I don't want you to listen to me only. . . . I think, if I have said something wrong, you may refute me. Thus, we shall advance toward democracy. I must stress this. I insist on expressing my own opinion. When I see something wrong, I say it. If my criticisms are incorrect, you may always refute me. This [expression of one's own opinion] may be gradually realized when "both sides are not afraid of each other." I think, democracy is still far away, but at least, outspoken criticisms may create a democratic impression. I mean, we intellectuals are able

to play a certain role in democratization. (1987, p. 135; alternative translation, 1988b, p. 80)

But, ultimately, Fang (1988c, p. 92) linked democracy very closely to science; "science and democracy are running parallel." In the tradition of May 4, 1919, science meant, first and foremost, rationalism as against tradition. Fang railed against China's feudal heritage as much as against communism; indeed, he saw the two as closely linked. His individualism entailed rejection of both Confucianism and communism, which shared a definition of personhood in terms of social relations and obligations to others (see Kraus 1989, p. 297).

"Learn truth from facts" is an old Maoist epigram that Deng Xiaoping made emblematic of the pragmatism of the reform era. For many intellectuals, however, including Fang, it had a more profound if ultimately ambivalent meaning. On the one hand, "learn truth from facts" could refer to the ideology of empiricist science, and, in Fang Lizhi's case, this is a powerful part of his rhetorical claim to attention. On the other hand, the same saying could refer not to "external" verification of factual evidence but to an extreme subjectivism by which the "facts" are understood to be those of irrefutable personal experience. This is a more important rhetorical trope for many of the literary intellectuals of the 1980s, especially for creative writers, but it is not insignificant for Fang as well. "I cannot control myself," he said in one speech, "I feel that if I don't speak out, I shall neglect my duty as a citizen of this nation" (1987, p. 125). Frequently, Fang insisted in his speeches on the importance of talking about his own experience. He adopted what Adorno called "the jargon of authenticity." But this was not just a part of Fang Lizhi's rhetoric, it was also a powerful component of the intellectual complaint against communist rule. The slogan of Czechoslovakian rebels in 1989 states it clearly: "to live honestly," that is, to end the thousand daily ways in which protecting oneself from the regime meant compromising one's values and indeed one's very identity (see the discussion of creative writers below).

Fang saw the need for honest self-expression as especially important for scientists:

> Scientists must express their feelings about anything in society, especially if unreasonable, wrong and evil things emerge. . . . Since physicists pursue the unity, harmony and perfection of nature, how can they logically tolerate unreason, discordance and evil? Physicists' methods of pursuing truth make them extremely sensitive while their courage in seeking it enables them to accomplish something.

> Let's take a look at the events of the postwar years. Almost invariably it was the natural scientists who were the first to become conscious of the emergence of each social crisis. (Fang 1986, pp. 16-17)

Here Fang is mobilizing two of his favorite rhetorical tropes at once: his claim to speak from the privileged standpoint of science and his claim to special insight because of his knowledge of the West. The rhetoric of science is not just window dressing. It is closely linked to Fang's basic self-understanding and his conception of democracy and modernization. It is important to see how Fang sets his priorities and how he conceptualizes democracy, for his account of the Chinese situation and the role of intellectuals was among the most directly influential on the student protesters of 1989. And in the conclusion to one of his most famous and widely circulated speeches, here is how he orders and sums up his points:

> We should have our own judgment about what is right, good, and beautiful in our academic field, free from the control of political power, before we can achieve modernization and true democracy, and not the so-called democracy. (Fang 1988c, p. 93)

This is the call, first and foremost, of an academic scientist, one who sees democracy primarily in terms of rationality, not participation, and as crucially dependent on the leadership of specialized elite intellectuals. This is not entirely objectionable. Surely few of us would disagree with statements like this: "What I pursue is a more reasonable society that is pluralistic, nonexclusive, a society that incorporates the best in the human race" (1988a, p. 73). Yet one has to consider also that Fang almost never mentions peasants or workers as significant or desirable forces in society, that his conception of freedom is couched almost entirely in terms of intellectuals' rights to carry on their work and criticism of the government, and that his notion of democracy is overwhelmingly a call for rational, scientific leadership, for modernization in the May 4th sense, not for anything like "government of the people, by the people and for the people."

SOCIAL SCIENTISTS

Social scientists by and large would agree with Fang's criticisms. Many went further, however, in developing specific views about market reforms and other economic policies, even advocating increasing private ownership and stock trading (see Schell 1988, pp. 44-55). Social scientists were also much more likely to add a specifically political argument about reform of the Communist party, loosening of central controls, or even free, multiparty elections. Some of the social scientists, like Su Shaozhi (Director of the Institute of Marxism-Leninism-Mao Zedong Thought at the Chinese Academy of Social Sciences) and Zhang Xianyang (of the same institute), tried to develop a more intellectually serious Marxist theory suitable to China's reform and modernization.[7] Attempting to revitalize Marxism did not necessarily make these intellectuals less radical (or safer in the eyes of authorities). Su publicly endorsed the students' protest and is now in exile.

Closely related, but somewhat more prominent in 1989, was a second group that tried to work within the party framework, this time with much less reference to Marxism. Yan Jiaqi, former director of the Institute of Political Science of the Chinese Academy of Social Sciences, was among the most visible of this group. One of Zhao Ziyang's closest advisers, he helped to coordinate the activities of the various intellectual "think tanks" that developed policy analysis and proposals for the party reformers.[8] Econometricians, demographers, and others often saw their roles as essentially applied scientists furthering the cause of China's modernization. Many had views very similar to Fang's not just on the failings of the Chinese government but on the nature of democracy and on modernization as a process best directed by experts. They placed less emphasis on institutional autonomy than the physical and biomedical scientists, though, and often worked closely as advisers to different parts of the party and government. Social scientists were apt to be both more closely involved with concrete reform activities (e.g., rewriting laws on private companies) and more often vocally critical of the conservative forces in the government.[9]

Social scientists with technocratic visions were not necessarily moderate in their views on reform. They might want vast changes, but changes in which professionally trained elites played a crucial managerial role and in which popular democratic decision making was a negligible factor. The one-child family policy of the early to middle 1980s, for example, was a radical reform. It reversed Mao Zedong's Marxist anti-Malthusianism with an image of inevitable competition for limited goods, and it flew in the face of traditional Chinese values. Its proponents made extensive use of projections based on Western demographic techniques and argued for the need to gather better statistics and train more demographers to analyze them. The policy could simply be decided upon when expert analysis convinced top government and party officials; it did not require mass democratic consideration and indeed was considered to be too important to trust to such procedures even if they had been considered. Similarly, many of the major economic reforms involved attempts to transform the economy from the top down. Explicitly, the Dengist vision argued that it was possible to pick various economic reforms from the capitalist world, without needing to add democratic political institutions. Even in the political realm, many reformers were more interested in improving administrative efficiency than popular participation. They focused, for example, on increasing the education and training of middle-level cadres. Indeed, many of these intellectuals were themselves the recent recipients of foreign educations who had been promoted over more senior colleagues to positions of considerable influence. Of course, there was enormous room for variation here. Arguments for decentralization of economic decision making could be taken as implying the need for private ownership of firms, or not; as implying the need for democratic institutions within those firms, or not; as implying the need for similar decentralization and/or democratization of political decisions, or not. Some reformers argued (not unlike the USSR's Gorbachev) that the strong authority of the party center was necessary to carry out the radical transformation of the economy, even though a policy goal of that transformation was to lessen the reliance on central planning. Gorbachev, however, emphasized the need for political openness and restructuring to coincide with, or even pave the way for, economic change. The Chinese leadership resolutely maintained a strict priority on economic matters. Perhaps as a result, even in its recent crisis, China's economy never was in quite the shambles of its Soviet counterpart. But perhaps the crucial reason for the difference was that Gorbachev saw political reform as the only way for him to bring adequate pressure to bear on factory managers and economic planners entrenched in the Soviet bureaucracy, while China's enterprise managers and planning bureaucrats did not have any substantial basis for resistance or challenge to the central government's directives. Moreover, Deng does not seem to have faced such deep challenges on this aspect of his reforms as Gorbachev has.

By Chinese definitions, many journalists were also social scientists, including notably Wang Ruoshui, former editor of the *People's Daily*. These journalists not only wrote social commentary themselves, they managed the major organs of widespread public dissemination of ideas. Qin Benli (editor of the *World Economic Herald*) achieved fame in the West when demonstrations followed the decision of Jiang Zemin and the Shanghai government to close his paper down a few months before the 1989 student protest movement began. Influential economic analysis was as likely to appear in his paper as in professional journals. Qin also figured among a substantial group of social scientists who had major impacts as purveyors and translators of Western thought for Chinese consumption. A number of book series had been founded in the late 1980s, for example, including, notably, the Towards the Future series in Sichuan (edited by Jin Guantao, Bao Zhunxin, and Xie Xuanjin). Bao was also a member of the Institute of History at the Academy of Social Sciences. Jin had become widely known for his saying, "The experiment and failure of socialism in one of the main inheritances of humankind in the 20th Century." Xie was coauthor, with Beijing Normal Institute lecturer Wang Luxiang and journalist Su Xiaokang, of *He Shang* ("Yellow River Elegy"), the remarkable television film series that galvanized viewers across China with its portrayal of Chinese culture as trapped in cycles of self-destruction and unable to meet the challenge of international competition.[10]

Counterpoised to these radical Westernizers was a group more dedicated to revitalizing traditional Chinese culture and finding the basis for dissent and reform in a distinctively Chinese heritage. Li Zehou was officially a philosopher at the Chinese Academy of Social Sciences but best known as an intellectual historian who had written influentially on "the six generations" of modern Chinese intellectuals (see Li and Schwarcz, 1983-84) and on traditional Chinese aesthetics (Li 1988). Liang Congje, editor of a magazine called *Intellectuals,* the historian Pang Pu, and the philosopher Tang Yijie of Beijing University were also prominent. Their reconstruction of traditional Chinese culture explicitly focused on the important role allocated to intellectuals. The newly founded International Academy of Chinese Culture provided them with a base and brought young scholars from all over the country to its headquarters near People's University. This last group held perhaps the greatest prestige in the intellectual community, but it was the Westernizers who commanded the most widespread popularity.

LITERARY INTELLECTUALS

Finally there were the literary intellectuals. This categorization can cover a variety of kinds of writing in China. First and foremost, perhaps, there were creative writers—poets, novelists, and some essayists (genric distinctions are not always clear or always demarcated exactly as we would find them in the West). Second, there were literary critics. Third, but very prominently, came investigative reporters.

Chinese radicals and reformers had long seen literary efforts as central to the basic changes they wanted to produce. As Liang Qichao wrote in 1902:

> To renovate the people of a nation, the fictional literature of that nation must first be renovated . . . to renovate morality, we must renovate fiction, to renovate manners we must first renovate fiction . . . to renew the people's hearts and minds and remold their character, we must first renovate fiction. (quoted by Schwarcz 1986, p. 33, following Sato Shin'ichi)

In the Chinese case, reform of the very language itself was crucial, so much was the very classical language tied up with Confucianism and imperial rule. Yu Pingbo, a veteran of the May 4th protest, wrote in a commemorative poem on the 60th anniversary in 1979, "We did not worry if our words were sweet or bitter / We just wrote in the newly born vernacular" (quoted in Schwarcz 1986, p. 20).

Poetry and fiction had become controversial again in reform-era China. Authors had experimented with new styles, from a sort of vague, evocative poetry that came to be known as "misty" to stream-of-consciousness novels. The most important common thread was a new preoccupation with individual experience and especially its distinctiveness—a theme previously forbidden in communist China. When poets like Bei Dao, Shu Ting, and Jiang He began to write the new sort of poetry, particularly in the journal *Today,* founded during the 1978-80 democracy movement, it was widely understood to carry simultaneous political, cultural, and personal messages. In Shu Ting's famous 1982 poem, "The Wall," for example, her opening and closing verses read:

I have no means to resist the wall,
Only the will.

Finally I know
What I have to resist first:
My compromise with walls, my
Insecurity with this world. (translation from Barmé and Minford 1988, p. 18)

[Excerpt from "The Wall" from *Seeds of Fire* by Geremie Barmé and John Minford. Copyright © 1988 by Geremie Barmé and Joh Minford. Reprinted by permission of Hill and Wang, a division of Farar, Straus and Giroux, Inc.]

A factory worker as well as a poet, Shu was initially celebrated in part for the particular female strength she brought to her writing. More recently, she has been criticized for making accommodations with the literary and party establishment. This complaint itself suggests the extent to which followers of the new poetry want a radical authenticity from their writers.

Older poets like Ai Qing attacked the new poetry, likening it to an intellectual version of the Red Guards, even calling it the "Beat and Smash Poetic School." Indeed, it did have roots in the Cultural Revolution, both in the intensity of the commitment and later disillusionment of young participants and in the wounds with which so many Chinese people were left. It was this poetry, more than any directly political texts, that established the crucial link between the protesting Chinese students of 1989 and their forebears of 1978-80. The Beijing University critic Xie Mian became a minor hero for standing up against the old poets and defending the "misty" poems as an authentic and important part of modern Chinese literature. Protesting students in 1989 frequently quoted Jiang He's "Motherland, O My Motherland" and Bei Dao's "The Answer," particularly the stanzas reading:

Baseness is the password of the base,
Honour is the epitaph of the honourable.
Look how the gilded sky is covered
With the drifting, crooked shadows of the dead.

I come into this world
Bringing only paper, rope, a shadow,
To proclaim before the judgment
The voices of the judged:

Let me tell you, world,
I—do—not—believe!
If a thousand challengers lie beneath your feet,
Count me as number one thousand and one.

I don't believe the sky is blue;
I don't believe in the sound of thunder;
I don't believe that dreams are false;
I don't believe that death has no revenge. (Barmé and Minford 1988, p. 236)

[Excerpt from "The Answer" from *Seeds of Fire* by Geremie Barmé and John Minford. Copyright © 1988 by Geremie Barmé and John Minford. Reprinted by permission of Hill and Wang, a division of Farrar, Straus and Giroux, Inc.]

One marcher I saw on May 4th carried aloft a sign with no words, simply a piece of paper, a bit of rope, and a cutout shadow.

Novelists and short story writers of the same era were perhaps less radical and struck less often to the very heart of their Chinese readers, but they were also influential. "Exploring" writers such as Jiang Zilong, Chen Rong, and Liu Xinwu (editor of *People's Literature*) also took up the implicit critique of the Cultural Revolution and remaining "leftist" tendencies and tried to rehabilitate a certain individualism. In his famous "Black Walls," Liu has his protagonist paint the apartment entirely black, only to confront the puzzlement and ultimately hostility of his neighbors. The point is made apparent even by an orthodox literary critic who claims he cannot find it:

A certain fellow by the name of Zhou—a man recognized as being a little "odd"—paints the walls and ceiling of his apartment black without providing the slightest explanation. An egotistical "indulgence" of this nature can hardly be seen as normal or acceptable . . . the problem, however, is that the author . . . regards the "abnormal" as "normal," and is critical of the attempted suppression of Zhou's desire to express his quirky individuality.[11]

The stifling of individuality was linked to the stifling of artistic and literary creativity. As Wang Ruowang put it, turning a government condemnation on its head, "we should say that those people who opposed the freedom of creativity are themselves the greatest source of contamination in spiritual pollution" (interview in Guan 1988, p. 44).

Literary critics such as Liu Zaifu and Liu Xiaobo (as well as Xie Mian) played important roles in China. Not only did they help to elucidate themes in literature, and act as arbiters of taste and reputation, they engaged in the ongoing project of linking contemporary literature to Chinese culture. Critics were also in the center of debate over that culture. Liu Zaifu sought both to reform Marxist criticism from within, emphasizing subjectivity, and to show the continuing importance of the Old Chinese literary tradition, Liu Xiaobo was more of an enthusiastic Westernizer and a radical. In this context, "traditional" means seeking a good balance of emotion and rationality and a stress on the collectivity and the social responsibility of the artist. "Radical," by contrast, means a focus on the expression of personal feeling, individuality, auratic art (to borrow Benjamin's term), the autonomy of artistic production, and its potential independence of national particularity in the modern metropolitan culture.

Something of this tension was played out in differences between the "creative writers" and the "investigative reporters." The latter were positioned between social scientists and literary intellectuals (though in China even literary critics were often housed in the Academy of Social Sciences). The Communist party, long holding that social reportage (and sometimes only social reportage emphasizing the morale-building good side of socialist society) was the main responsibility of writers, saw reporters as central to literature. Younger writers were more likely to disagree, wishing to claim that turf for art. In 1989, the younger writers Su Xiaokang and Dai Qing were attracting more and more of a readership (Su was one of the coauthors of "Yellow River Elegy" and had close ties in academic circles; he was also a lecturer in the Beijing Broadcast Institute). Much more famous, Wang Ruowang and Liu Binyan were the senior statesmen of this group, long-standing communists who wielded considerable influence as writers in official periodicals. Both Wang and Liu had been attacked repeatedly as rightists and periodically accepted discipline (including, in Liu's case, temporary expulsion) by the party throughout their careers. Even in their most critical writings, they are remarkable for retaining a commitment to some of the ideals that had made them communists in the first place. In one of his articles, for example, Liu spoke of "another kind of loyalty" to the party, one that put ideals and the interests of the people ahead of the dictates of the bureaucracy and discipline of the hierarchy (see Schell 1988; Liu 1990). He tied his efforts very much to the reform branch of the Communist party exemplified by Hu Yaobang. After the fall of the Gang of Four, the project of rediscovering the forward momentum of Chinese liberation seemed urgent and seemed also to depend on uncovering the various ways in which old "leftists" clung to power despite rectification campaigns.

From 1979 on, Wang became increasingly bold and unrepentant when his views were, as he admitted, "heterodox" (Guan 1988). He was one of the few writers willing to look seriously at the implications of Deng's policies following the slogan "to get rich is glorious." Class polarization, he argued, was an inevitable consequence of the policies being pursued. Wang did not argue for reversal of the reforms but for taking seriously the consequences:

If we go on emphasizing that we don't want inequalities to develop, we may as well attack the economic reforms and turn everything back to the egalitarians. Let them carry on their highly authoritarian management. Let them decisively and fearlessly cut down to size those who were so bold as to get rich sooner than others. (quoted in Schell 1988, p. 173)

Ultimately Wang was dismissed from the party for his refusal to recant such views; Deng was determined to maintain an egalitarian myth even as he opened up a market economy with hints of capitalism. Yet this was a serious problem. One of the main ideological problems China faced in the spring of 1989 was that the government had neither developed—nor allowed others the possibility of a public discourse to develop—a rationale for economic inequality. Nearly all serious and novel inequalities of wealth looked to many ordinary people like corruption.

Even more famous than Wang was (and is) Liu Binyan. The two played an enormously popular role as gadflies of authority and a sort of conscience of the nation. Liu specialized in documenting the corruption of local Communist party officials and the failure of the party hierarchy to do anything about it. As he was himself a party member, and writing in an officially controlled press, his exposés sometimes carried more weight than those in Western papers; people sought him out to try to get their problems resolved. He maintained voluminous files on investigations all over China, often working with teams of assistants. When he felt he had documented a wrong that needed to be righted, he might send a file directly to a senior party official, like Hu Yaobang, as well as (or instead of) publishing an article about it. Of course, Liu was not always successful, and often his articles backfired, bringing retaliation rather than redress to those whose grievances he documented (see Liu 1988, 1990). Liu had been writing much the same sort of report for more than 30 years when he was finally expelled from the party in 1987.

Liu Binyan had joined the Communist party as a teenager, five years before the 1949 revolution. He was active in underground struggle first for liberation of China from Japanese occupation and then for communist victory over the Guomindang. After the war, he returned to his plans for writing. "I wanted to use my pen to slash the pall hanging over China, to dispel the gloom and open up the mental horizons of the people" (Liu 1990, p. 52). Unfortunately for Liu, he thought that dispelling the gloom depended on honest reporting of the causes of China's problems. In one of his first major articles, Liu had told of two engineers. One had built bridges entirely according to party directives, failing to take emergency measures when floods came early in 1954. The floods washed away the bridge support his team had built. The other refused to wait for orders from above, changed the plans, and saved his construction team's work. The party promoted the first and demoted the second. And so it has been for Liu, though he continues to exhibit the second sort of loyalty, along with his incorrigible optimism. Liu lost some 22 years of his life to labor reform among the peasants and other punishments. He had only been rehabilitated a few months from his condemnation as a rightist when in 1966 the Cultural Revolution broke out and he was again attacked. Yet, the Cultural Revolution began with a promise to democratize China. Even in the midst of his sufferings, Liu could see positive potential in its attack on bureaucratism, corruption, and special privileges for party leaders. Though one of the most resolute and effective opponents of those who came to power during the Cultural Revolution, Liu is set apart from other intellectuals in his ability to see something important in its ideals. In this, as in having genuinely been a revolutionary, Liu is quite different than Fang Lizhi, for example. He still believes in the ideals that motivated him to become a communist in the first place. He is not just a spokesman for intellectuals but a man who cares about all sorts of people; he wants their freedom and their democracy as well as his own.

Liu maintained his investigative reporting not only in the face of party pressure but in the face of a changing fashion among writers.

> In recent years, with the exception of a very small number, writers with a similar set of experiences as mine have turned their attention to subjects that are less politically or socially sensitive, devoting themselves to the pursuit of art. Consequently, even more than ever I have stood as the odd man out. (Liu 1988, p. 33)

> Fewer and fewer Chinese writers think they should use their writing to help the Chinese people to reorganize society. One common view is that it would destroy the artistic purity of their work and cause it to lose the value of timelessness. (Liu, Ruan, and Xu 1989, p. 25)

Liu regarded those writers and artists who turned away from "reality" as people whose sense of mission had never been strong and who turned to commercialism, the ideology of art for art's sake, or the pursuit of a Nobel prize partly out of timidity in the face of hostile authority (Liu 1990, p. 171). As far as he was concerned, the purpose of writing, for a person of conscience, was social improvement. At a conference in California in April 1989, Liu (already living in the United States) clashed with the modernist Bei Dao over just this issue. As Perry Link sums up, quoting each man:

> "Our job is to tell the truth," said Bei Dao, "and if we don't, we indeed *are* inferior to bean curd vendors, who do their jobs quite well." But there was no consensus on how much an intellectual's independence should be devoted to

social action as opposed to pure scholarship or art. "I see a terrible incongruity," said Liu Binyan. "On one side, 500,000 people massed in Tiananmen Square; on the other, in our literary magazines, essentially a blank—*avant garde* experiments, read only by a few, understandable sometimes by none."

Bei Dao bluntly disagreed. "True art does not ask about its own 'social effects.' We will understand this problem more adequately only when we understand why foreign writers, unlike Chinese writers, sometimes commit suicide. . . . It's because they're concerned with life itself, not social engineering." (Link 1989, p. 40)

Liu has no doubt about his grasp of reality. His style is simple and straightforward, a flat statement of telling facts punctuated by condemnations in the strongest terms. Readers were unlikely to miss the point of his articles, even when references were oblique out of political necessity. And his pieces were simultaneously reports for the party and publications for the people. He was, thus, the sort of socially responsible writer that communist activists said they wanted, and praised until they were in power and apt to bear the brunt of the criticism. To label Liu a bourgeois individualist was merely to say that he insisted on civil rights and liberties, including his own right to publish the truth as he saw it as well as the rights of the victims of party excesses about whom he wrote. The new poets and younger fiction writers, however, have often expressed something much more akin to the "bourgeois individualism" of the West, an emphasis on self-expression as an end in itself and an understanding of art as the product solely of inner consciousness.

It is, nonetheless, important to realize that the sense of Chinese cultural crisis, and a concern for the fate of the nation, did drive these younger, less political writers as well. Liu Binyan, for example, reports on the young scholar Liu Xiaobo:

Liu Xiaobo was not very interested in politics; in fact, he despised and hated politics. After Hu Yaobang died, Liu published an article in the *China News Daily,* a Chinese-language New York newspaper, in which he said he did not think much of the student movement. His opinions were unusual: For instance, he thought Hu Yaobang was only the leader of the Party, and that we should not honor him so. Instead, we should honor Wei Jingsheng, who had been imprisoned by the Communist Party ten years earlier for fighting in the Democracy movement. (Liu, Ruan, and Xu 1989)

Nonetheless, Liu Xiaobo (unlike Liu Binyan) did return to Beijing and, moreover, was one of the intellectuals who caused a stir by announcing a hunger strike of their own at the monument to the people's heroes only days before the massacre. He was arrested and reportedly tortured.

In terms of the broad mass of the Chinese people, the work of Liu Binyan and similar investigative reporters no doubt loomed much larger than the experimental, often obscure poetry and fiction of the 1980s. Yet, in the student movement, the two influences merged. Students responded both to a straightforward account of the corruption of the communist regime and to a more nebulous sense of cultural crisis—and potential. They responded both to simple logical arguments for civil liberties and human rights and to more mystical literary expressions based on a claim to those rights. They responded also to the physical presence of older intellectuals. As Liu Binyan and Xu Gang remark:

> Literary critics could be seen shouting in streets and alleys, calling people to block army vehicles; famous writers ran around in a sweat, buying urinals for students. Scholars of the Chinese Academy of Social Sciences were also very active. Groups of people from many research institutes came to join the movement. University professors plunged in, also abandoning their usual discreet and retiring behavior. (Liu, Ruan, and Xu 1989, pp. 25-26)

The student protest movement took older intellectuals partly by surprise. A few retired to their apartments but many came forward to support the students. Though these intellectuals gave advice, they did not run the movement behind the scenes, as some have charged (and a few intellectuals have claimed). Their greatest influence was through the ideas that shaped the students' consciousness.

CONCLUSION

Student demands initially reflected their particularistic concerns rather closely: for recognition of an autonomous students' association, improvement of a variety of conditions in universities, and more choice and meritocracy in the assignment of graduates to jobs. Yet, once the protest took root, a variety of deeper, longer-range ideas also came to the fore. Grievances specific to students and intellectuals flowed together with a discourse about democracy, modernization, and China's cultural crisis.

At first, students sounded much like Fang Lizhi. His views both shaped and reflected a very broadly shared orientation. Thus students saw the project of democracy through lenses colored by class. For example, when they spoke of the relationship of education to democracy, they always spoke of the need for them, and others like them, to "educate the masses of people." They did not speak of democracy as itself a process of public education as well as of self-government. On the other hand, the basic self-identification of the students in Tiananmen Square—and not just their intellectual self-categorization but their lived identity—was transformed and was for a time radicalized. Their consciousness expanded beyond class concerns to include national ones and, in important ways, universal ideals. The movement itself helped to liberate their thoughts from concerns like where they would work after graduation, and turn them toward the question of China's future. This still reflected practical concerns of the kind stressed by Fang and various social scientists. But it also called for a more radical, emotionally inspiring vision. For this, students drew more on literary intellectuals.

It was this only half-explicit vision that made sense of the risks students took, the sacrifices they made. In the same way, when the ordinary people of Beijing rallied to protect the student hunger strikers starting May 19, this was not only because they saw students speaking for ideals they shared but because the act of refusing sustenance and courting government reprisals impressed people that the students were not just seeking personal gains but sacrificing themselves for the people as a whole. In the midst of the struggle, it became possible to identify emotionally with a general category—the Chinese people—that, under more ordinary circumstances, would be rent by numerous divisions. Despite their own elitism, students were in many ways much more committed to democracy than most older intellectuals. Repeating the old May 4th slogan, "science and democracy," the older generation always seemed to put the emphasis on science, while the younger generation put it entirely on democracy. To them, moreover, democracy meant not just administrative reform or proper respect for expert advice but, at least in many cases, genuine participation.

This is the source of the radicalness—and indeed the arrogance—of students' demand for high-level dialogue. From early in the protests, students had called for a "dialogue among equals" with top policy-making officials. They were disappointed that they were able to have this dialogue only with Yuan Mu, the spokesman of the State Council, and that he did not treat them as equals. Later, when Li Peng did speak with students, they challenged him directly for making a (rather haughty) speech and not truly engaging in a dialogue. Yet, from the standpoint of Chinese history, the fact that the students were able to get even this approach to dialogue was quite remarkable. The call for such a dialogue was only seemingly a mild demand; in fact, it asked for a very radical act of political symbolism. On the one hand, it reflected the students' very high opinion of their own importance as young intellectuals (and directly echoed Fang Lizhi's emphasis on how Western leaders listen to scientists, quoted above). On the other hand, this call for dialogue reflected an egalitarian ideology and offered echoes of young Red Guards interrogating senior officials in the 1960s. Of course, the student protesters had no intention of acting like Red Guards, but the similarities were quickly noted by others. Undergraduates thought nothing of summoning the president of my university out to a rather forced dialogue one morning in May, but even some Ph.D. candidates were enough older to be reminded of the Cultural Revolution and slightly chilled by the action. One argued with the students at the edge of the crowd, but his views were dismissed.

Underlying some of these tensions are varying conceptions of the intellectual's role in Chinese society. I met no students in 1989 who were prepared to defend a strong ideal of "redness" and party discipline. The opposition of professional-technical expertise to personal-literary expression carried a good deal of weight, however. Linked to this is the difference between analyses of China's current predicament that focus on purely economic issues, that complement this with emphasis on political reform, and that go beyond either of these notions of reform to emphasize the need to confront a basic crisis in Chinese culture.

This sense of crisis was a crucial ingredient in the concerns of students involved in the spring protests. It is also the ingredient most overlooked by Western observers. And it linked the China of 1989 with that of 1919 as surely as the slogan "science and democracy," the rhetoric of modernization, or the concern with how to gain wealth and power in the world. Indeed, the sense of cultural crisis was linked with all these things. It was born in large part of China's relations with the Western world, the uncertainty about whether China's weakness should be blamed on something intrinsic to Chinese culture or character.

To understand what intellectual orientation, and what strength of feeling, lay behind the willingness of so many of China's brightest young people to become martyrs, one has to go beyond the conventional Western focus on capitalism and democracy. Some party leaders, to be sure, wanted economic reform without political change or threats to their power. They pursued the virtually impossible line of trying to import Western technology, economic thought, and bits of business practice without accepting any political or cultural baggage. Many reformers were primarily interested in the same economic goods, but, even in pushing for purely technocratic economic solutions, saw some need to streamline administration and reform the structure of power. Like nearly everyone, student, professional, intellectual, worker, or peasant, many of these reformers saw the need to do at least something about corruption. More radical reformers—and most of the students in Tiananmen Square—added political democracy to their demands. They meant, first and foremost, civil rights and liberties: free speech, freedom to publish, acknowledgment of free associations. Beyond this, elections and other forms of participation were possibilities desired by some with varying degrees of urgency. Having a government truly interested in the will of the people, and willing to listen to the views and needs of the people (especially as interpreted by intellectuals), was a more basic desire.

All of these goals motivated student protesters. But they are not adequate to explain the depth of emotions in the square or the capacity of students to identify with the Chinese nation. Behind or beyond these various practical goals was a concern for just what it could mean to be Chinese as the twenty-first century approached. This was a compelling question of personal identity that was not solved adequately by pursuit of Westernization any more than by appeal to traditional Chinese culture. This question linked the individual with the social in ways few could articulate explicitly. But it is important that all the expressive individualism of youth in the 1980s was not *just* selfishness (though goodness knows it was often that as well). It was also an attempt to rethink identity and options for human action. Students could turn from apparent selfishness to self-sacrifice partly because external conditions changed but also because their own discourse even at its most individualistic was not just about themselves but about China.

The students who protested in Tiananmen Square were young or budding intellectuals. They saw China's problems through lenses that focused attention on their own role. But they were concerned with China's fate and saw the existing government policies as denying them not only privileges and income but a proper chance to contribute to meeting the country's challenges. Technological improvements and economic reforms certainly required intellectual expertise, and students felt that the government did not invest enough in preparing them or paying them for this role. More basically, democracy required a public discourse, and students saw intellectuals as playing the most central role in this arena, as watchdogs for government accountability, proposers of policies, interpreters of the demands and desires of more inarticulate masses. Finally, the sense that China was wracked not just by material underdevelopment but by cultural crisis seemed more than anything else to call for contributions that intellectuals alone could make.

NOTES

1. On the shifting fortunes of intellectuals, see Goldman (1981), Shapiro and Heng (1986), Spence (1981), Thurston (1987), White and Cheng (1988).

2. Translated and published in *Issues and Studies* (Vol. 25, No. 3, 1989, p. 1).

3. Though analytic orientations differ substantially, Cheek (1988), Goldman (1987), Goldman, Cheek, and Hamrin (1987), Link (1986), Schell (1989), and Suttmeier (1987) all fill in parts of the general picture of Chinese intellectuals in this period. Useful selections are translated in Barmé and Minford (1988).

4. And at the same time that, for convenience, we may see the intellectual field organized into the traditional categories of natural scientists, social scientists, and lierary intellectuals, we must realize that this draws on folk constructs that may misrepresent much of the actual organization. See, for comparison, Pierre Bourdieu's (1987) arguments about the need to break with such folk categorizations of the French academic field and with the self-interestedness of most of the analysts who deploy them about their own academic field.

5. This was distinctive in a discourse in which nationalism played a major role. Fang spoke out against nationalism as a guiding force in Chinese reform, arguing that "patriotism should not be our top priority" and that feelings of national pride were apt to block the way to progress. Liu Binyan and others objected, arguing that patriotism was still one of China's most precious resources (Link 1989, p. 40). On this point, Liu seems to come closer to sensing where the strength of feeling motivating radical protest came from in 1989.

6. One wall poster I saw during the 1989 student protest saw this as the essential contribution of Western thought to the discourse. After a listing of more authoritarian views from Chinese tradition and the Communist party, it concluded simply: Believe in human rights—foreigner

7. Among other contributions, Su encouraged a return to serious study of Marx's original texts as distinct from the Soviet-style summaries reflecting the party positions of any particular moment (see Su 1988).

8. Now in exile, Yan has emerged as a key leader of the democratic movement among the Chinese diaspora, working closely with Wu'erkaixi. Wan Runnan, general manager of the Stone Computer Corporation (China's largest private company), and Cao Shiyuan, president of the Stone Corporation's Institute of Social Development (a remarkable private think tank), also fit into this group as did a great many of China's economists. The last was arrested after the June massacre and remains in prison.

9. Very few social scientists of any note actually spoke out against radical reform. Certain conservatives in the government did try to promote the work of He Xin, a youngish but prolific researcher at the Chinese Academy of Social Sciences, precisely because he was critical of radical reform; after June 4, he became even more visible but not more popular or typical.

10. Two other particularly influential members of this grouping were Ge Yang, editor of *New Observations,* and Liu Xiaobo, a popular Beijing Normal University lecturer who was among the intellectuals who began a hunger strike near the end of the occupation of Tiananmen Square in May.

11. The story is translated in Barmé and Minford (1988) and the criticism reprinted on page 29.

REFERENCES

Barmé, Geremie and John Minford, eds. 1988. *Seeds of Fire: Chinese Voices of Conscience.* New York: Hill and Wang.

Bourdieu, Pierre. 1987. *Homo Academicus.* Stanford, CA: Stanford University Press.

Calhoun, Craig. 1989a. "Revolution and Repression in Tiananmen Square." *Society* 26(6):21-38.
———. 1989b. "The Beijing Spring, 1989: Notes on the Making of a Protest." *Dissent* 36(4):435-47.
———. 1989c. "Protest in Beijing: The Conditions and Importance of the Chinese Student Movement of 1989." *Partisan Review* 56(4):563-80.
———. 1989d. "Tiananmen. Television and the Public Sphere: Internationalization of Culture and the Beijing Spring of 1989." *Public Culture* 2(1):54-70.

Chang, Chen-pang. 1989. "The Awakening of Intellectuals in Mainland China." *Issues and Studies* 25(3):1-3.

Cheek, Timothy. 1988. "Habits of the Heart: Intellectual Assumptions Reflected by Mainland Chinese Reformers from Teng T'o to Fang Li-chih." *Issues and Studies* 24(3):31-52.

Fang, Lizhi. 1986. "Intellectual and Intellectual Ideology" [interview with Dai Qing]. *Beijing Review,* December 15, pp. 16-17.

———. 1987. "Intellectuals and the Chinese Society." *Issues and Studies* 23(4):124-42.

———. 1988a. "The Social Responsibilities of Young Intellectuals Today" [originally December 1986]. *Chinese Law and Government* 21(2):68-74.

———. 1988b. "Intellectuals and Chinese Society" [speech of November 15, 1986; alternative translation of 1987]. *Chinese Law and Government* 21(2):75-86.

———. 1988c. "China Needs Modernization in All Fields—Democracy, Reform, and Modernization" [speech of November 18, 1987]. *Chinese Law and Government* 21(2):87-95.

———. 1988d. "Intellectuals Should Unite" [originally February 1987]. *Chinese Law and Government* 21(2):96-102.

Goldman, Merle. 1981. *China's Intellectuals: Advise and Dissent.* Cambridge, MA: Harvard University Press.

———. 1987. "Dissident Intellectuals in the People's Republic of China." Pp. 159-88 in *Citizens and Groups in Contemporary China,* edited by V. Falkenheim. Ann Arbor: University of Michigan Press.

Goldman, Merle, Timothy Cheek, and Carol Hamrin, eds. 1987. *China's Intellectuals and the State: In Search of a New Relationship.* Contemporary China Series, no. 3. Cambridge, MA: Harvard University Press.

Guan, Yuqian. 1988. "Wang Ruowang Discusses Literary Policy and the Reform." *Chinese Law and Government* 21(2):35-58.

Krauss, Richard. 1989. "The Lament of Astrophysicist Fang Lizhi: China's Intellectuals in a Global Context." Pp. 294-315 in *Marxism and the Chinese Experience,* edited by Arif Dirlik and Maurice Meisner. White Plains, NY: Sharpe.

Li, Zehou. 1988. *The Path of Beauty: A Study of Chinese Aesthetics.* Beijing: Morning Glory.

Li, Zehou and Vera Schwarcz. 1983-84. "Six Generations of Modern Chinese Intellectuals." *Chinese Studies in History.* 17(2):42-57.

Link, Perry. 1986. "Intellectuals and Cultural Policy After Mao." Pp. 81-102 in *Modernizing China: Post-Mao Reform and Development,* edited by A. D. Barnett and R. N. Clough. Boulder, CO: Westview.

———. 1989. "The Chinese Intellectuals and the Revolt." *The New York Review of Books* 36(11):38-41.

Liu, Binyan. 1988. "Self-Examination" [originally October 1986]. *Chinese Law and Government* 21(2):14-34.

———. 1990. *A Higher Kind of Loyalty: A Memoir by China's Foremost Journalist.* New York: Pantheon.

Liu, Binyan, Ruan Ming, and Xu Gang. 1989. *"Tell the World" : What Happened in China and Why?* New York: Pantheon.

Schell, Orville. 1988. *Discos and Democracy: China in the Throes of Reform.* New York: Anchor.

Schwarcz, Vera. 1986. *The Chinese Enlightenment: Intellectuals and the Legacy of the May Fourth Movement of 1919.* Berkeley: University of California Press.

Shapiro, Judith and Liang Heng. 1986. *Cold Winds, Warm Winds: Intellectual Life in China Today.* Middletown, CT: Wesleyan University Press.

Spence, Jonathan. 1981. *The Gate of Heavenly Peace: The Chinese and Their Revolution, 1895-1980.* Baltimore: Penguin.

Su, Shaozhi. 1988. *Democratization and Reform.* Nottingham: Spokesman.

Suttmeier, Richard P. 1987. "Riding the Tiger: The Political Life of China's Scientists." Pp. 123-58 in *Citizens and Groups in Comtemporary China*, edited by V. Falkenheim. Ann Arbor: University of Michigan Press.

Thurston, Anne. 1987. *Enemies of the People: The Ordeal of the Intellectuals in China's Great Cultural Revolution*. Cambridge, MA: Harvard University Press.

Tu, Wei-ming. 1987. "Iconoclasm, Holistic Vision, and Patient Watchfulness: A Personal Reflection on the Modern Chinese Intellectual Quest." *Daedalus*, Spring, pp. 75-94.

Wakeman, Frederick. 1988. "All the Rage in China." March 2, 1989:19-21. *The New York Review of Books*.

White, Lynn and Li Cheng. 1988. "Diversification Among Mainland Intellectuals." *Issues and Studies* 24(9):50-77.

PART III

Social Theory of Politics and the Politics of Theory

Chapter 8

IDEOLOGY AND OCULARCENTRISM
Is There Anything Behind the Mirror's Tain?

Martin Jay
University of California, Berkeley

IN WHAT IS SURELY ONE of the most widely remarked metaphors in all of his work, Marx compared ideology to a *"camera obscura,"* that "dark room" in which a pinhole in one wall projects an inverted image of an external scene onto its opposite. The famous passage from *The German Ideology* reads as follows (Marx and Engels 1970, p. 47): "If in all ideology men and their circumstances appear upside-down as in a *camera obscura,* this phenomenon arises just as much from their historical life-process as the inversion of objects on the retina does from their physical life-process."[1]

Marx's selection of a visual metaphor to distinguish upright from distorted knowledge is by no means surprising or unusual, for Western thought has long privileged sight as the sense most capable of apprising us of the truth of external reality. Whether in the guise of Platonic ideas in the "mind's eye," Cartesian "clear and distinct" ideas available to a "steadfast mental gaze,' or Baconian observations empirically grounded in "the faith of the eye,"[2] our most influential epistemologies have been resolutely ocularcentric. Accordingly, as Hans Blumenberg (1957, pp. 432-47) has demonstrated, light has been the privileged metaphor for truth, and enlightenment the metaphor for its acquisition.

But if vision has enjoyed a special status as the noblest of the senses, its capacity to deceive has also been a source of frequent concern. Trusting in the mind's eye, what Carlyle once called "spiritual optics,"[3] has sometimes led to a distrust of the actual perception of the two physical eyes. Both the Platonic and the Cartesian traditions have been deeply suspicious of the imperfections of what might be called "material vision" and have sought to distance themselves from the eye as concretely embedded in the human body.[4] Religious thinkers, believing more in the Word of God and the hermeneutic project of interpreting it than in divine manifestation, have often echoed this suspicion. In its more extreme forms, hostility to pagan idolatry has produced a full-fledged iconoclasm. One of its stimulants has been the fear that the eye is responsible for exciting restless yearnings—what Augustine called "ocular desire"[5]—whereas the ear is credited with the ability to listen patiently for an authoritative voice from above.

For all these reasons and many more that we do not have time to adduce, vision has served both as the model for truth and as a source for falsehood, an ambiguity cleverly exploited in Marx's metaphor of ideology as a *camera obscura*. Here the contrast is between a false vision that is reversed and inverted and a true one that is straightforwardly adequate to the object it sees. The darkness and obscurity of the closed box is also implicitly set against the transparent clarity of a *"camera lucida,"* in which ideology is banished in the glare of enlightenment. Although the analogy between retinal vision and ideological misprision is not really precise—the mind, after all, has no problem setting its images straight,[6] whereas ideology's inversions are not so easily dispelled—Marx's choice of a visual metaphor was a rhetorically powerful ploy at a time when ocularcentrism still reigned supreme.

In our own century, however, the premises of that assumption have come increasingly under attack. Indeed, a great deal of recent intellectual energy has been directed, as I have tried to demonstrate elsewhere (Jay, 1986) at dismantling the traditional hierarchy of the senses, which placed vision at the summit. As a result, it has been dethroned in many quarters as the allegedly most noble of the senses. With its departure has gone the assumption that the alternative to a distorted, ideological sight, inverted and reversed, obscure and opaque, is a clear and distinct vision of the truth as it actually is.

In fact, if anything, confidence in the truth-telling capacity of vision in any of its various guises has become itself a widely reproached mark of ideological mystification. This reversal is evident, for example, in the recent proliferation of attacks on the idea of the totalizing gaze from above, the God's eye view of the world, and the practices of surveillance and discipline to which it contributes. Foucault is, of course, an obvious example here, but another would be someone who comes from a very different tradition, the phenomenology that Foucault always criticized: Claude Lefort. Drawing on Merleau-Ponty's attack on "high-altitude thinking," Lefort (1986, pp. 196-202) has specifically linked the belief in a God's eye view with a mistaken concept of ideology:

> We cannot . . . undertake to delimit ideology with reference to a reality whose features would be derived from positive knowledge, without thereby losing a sense of the operation of the constitution of reality and without placing ourselves in the illusory position of claiming to have an overview of Being. . . . If we were to regard as ideology the discourse which confronts the impossibility of its self-genesis, this would mean that we would be converting this impossibility into a positive fact, we would believe in the possibility of mastering it; we would once again be placing ourselves in the illusory position of looking

down at every discourse in order to "see" the division from which it emerges, whereas discourse can only reveal this in itself.

Another manifestation of the distrust of the visual can be discerned in the frequent appearance of attacks on specularity and speculation, mirroring and the metaphysics of reflection. In the Marxist tradition, this critique was most vigorously elaborated by Louis Althusser. Borrowing Lacan's categories of the mirror stage and the imaginary, Althusser (1971, p. 153) insisted that ideology is "a representation of the imaginary relationship of individuals to their real conditions of existence." Such imaginary relationships are not equivalent to false consciousness, however, because they are permanent and inevitable elements of all social systems, no matter how emancipated. The most fundamental mechanism through which ideology constitutes these imaginary relationships is what he calls the interpellation of individuals as subjects, a process which, despite the verbal hailing also implied, is essentially specular. The individual subject is but a reduced mirror image of the meta-subject that is an abstraction generated by the contradictions of the system to occlude their operations. Whether it be called God, the Absolute Spirit, the State, or even Humanity, this meta-subject is fundamentally the same phenomenon. The little "I" of the ideological subject is thus based on the meta-subject's specular "eye" that duplicates only itself in a process of reflective narcissism.

Althusser's critique of the ocularcentric basis of ideology was, to be sure, based on a contrasting notion of Marxist science, which somehow escaped mystification. Although not identified with "true consciousness" in the traditional sense of clear and distinct ideas or representations of an external reality, it nonetheless presupposed the possibility of access to a more fundamental level of structural relations that ideology worked to veil. Insofar as Althusser remained beholden to the structuralism that he always protested he had surpassed, his version of science was itself hostage to an ocular notion of penetrating vision, which could see the outlines of the deep structures transparent through the seemingly opaque surface of ideology. Althusser's confusing and ambiguous concept of scientificity has been the target of a number of devastating critiques and there can be few, if any, adherents left who hold to it with any confidence. But his critique of specularity, shared as we have seen by Lacan, remains very powerful in non-Marxist as well as Marxist circles.

In feminist thought, for example, it has been most extensively articulated in the work of Luce Irigaray (1985). The flat reflecting mirror of Western metaphysics, she has contended, has been complicitous with the phallocentric privileging of male subjectivity. Here the visibility of the male genitalia is invidiously contrasted with the apparent *rien à voir* of the female. The classical psychoanalytic account of castration anxiety with all its sexist implications is also indebted to the privileging of visibility over the invisible. For feminists like Irigaray—and one could adduce evidence from others like Cixous or Kristeva—it is ideological, at least from a woman's vantage point, to assume sight is nobler than other senses like touch and smell.

Even more radical critiques of ocularcentrism have come from deconstructionists like Sarah Kofman, who are less willing than Irigaray to affirm another sensual hierarchy. In Kofman's (1973) study *Camera Obscura—de l'idéologie,* she explicitly confronts the implications of Marx and Engels's visual metaphor in *The German Ideology* (1970). Noting its continued importance in Freud as well, she argues that it mistakenly reproduces the traditional binary, metaphysical oppositions of clarity/obscurity, transparency/opacity, rationality/irrationality, and truth/falsehood. By merely hoping to reverse the illusory image of ideology, Marx and Freud betray their nostalgia for a hierarchical and binary order of their own. Although Marx does not simply posit scientific consciousness as the antidote to false consciousness—a mistaken characterization of his position that ignores his stress on the need for a practical resolution of the contradictions in the world that necessitate ideological mystification—his ideal, Kofman (1973, p. 33) claims, "remains that of a perfect eye, a pure retina."

Only Nietzsche, Kofman concludes, transcends the inadequate use of the *camera obscura* metaphor. He does so by recognizing its metaphoricity, embracing an artistic rather than a scientific notion of truth and multiplying the perspectival implications of the device itself. Everyone, Nietzsche realizes, has his or her own *camera obscura,* so that no collective or intersubjective vision of reality is possible. "The *camera obscura,*" Kofman (1983, pp. 59-60) writes approvingly, "is never a *camera lucida* and in the usage Nietzsche makes of such metaphors, there is no nostalgia for clarity. Nietzsche strategically repeats this classical metaphor precisely to denounce the illusion of transparency."

In his recent defense of the philosophical legitimacy of deconstruction, *The Tain of the Mirror,* Rodolphe Gasché extends this argument even further. Claiming that the mainstream of Western philosophy has been a metaphysics of specularity, he argues that it came to a head in the absolute reflection of German Idealism, most notably Hegel. In his thought, all otherness, difference, and heterogeneity are recuperated in a grand gesture of perfect mirroring, in which the meta-subject sees only itself. What is lost in the process is the unseeable silver backing of the mirror, the material "tain" in the title of Gasché's book. It is on this reverse side of the mirror, according to deconstruction, that dissemination writes itself. But the result is not total blindness, Gasché (1986, p. 238) insists:

At first the mirror that Derrida's philosophy holds up seems to show us only its tain; yet this opaque tain is also transparent. Through it one can observe the play of reflection and speculation as it takes place in the mirror's mirroring itself. Seen from the inside this play gives an illusion of perfection, but observed through the tain, it appears limited by the infrastructural agencies written on its invisible side, without which it could not even begin to occur.

There is, therefore, a certain place for sight in deconstruction, but all it can show is the limits of specularity and the interference of the mirror's tain in its functioning.

Lacking a positive notion of clear truth, unmediated objectivity, and transparent vision, all of these antiocular arguments might well appear to have abandoned any critical notion of ideology as well. Althusser's denial that ideology can be overcome, which is even more troubling once the poverty of his scientific alternative is exposed, may serve as the telos of virtually all of these writers. For if we live only in a world of individual perspectives, as Kofman contends, if we are forever trapped in a network of imaginary relationships based on the specular interpellation of the subject, as Althusser argues, if we cannot fully break through the looking glass of phallogocentrism because of our sexual divisions, as Irigaray implies, and if the gaze through the mirror's tain shows us only the limits of pure specularity, as Gasché argues, it is difficult to discern what the antidote to ideology can be. To put it in slightly different terms, once the "other" of ideology is jettisoned as a contrasting concept, the term loses its critical edge and becomes purely descriptive, as in certain mainstream sociological uses of it.[7]

How, we must ask, is it then possible to defend the practice of ideology critique in a nonocularcentric age? If we cannot see the fully visible truth, naked, pure, and upright—a phallocularcentric image, if there ever was one—can we establish another standard by which we can measure ideological distortion? If, to play on Lacan's famous distinction between "le petit objet a" and "le grand objet A," we must give up a visual "other" of ideology with a capital "O," can we at least still find nonvisual ones with a small "o" instead?

For those who have distrusted the illusions of our senses and sight in particular, a frequent alternative has been sought in the realm of language. The religious tradition that, in the broadest sense, we can call Hebraic (as opposed to the more visually oriented Hellenic) has always trusted more in the divine word than in imagistic idols. It is not surprising that many more secular critics of ocularcentrism have also turned to language as a way to preserve a critical notion of ideology. But here, of course, there is no simple community of opinion about what language is or how it operates to mystify or tell the truth.

Of all the possible tendencies that one might choose to discuss, let me for the sake of brevity stress an opposition between two, which we can roughly call deconstructionist and critical hermeneutic. Both are suspicious of a monologic, scientific vision, which claims to see the truth beneath the surface of a mystified level of appearances. Both abandon the assumption of what Richard Rorty (1979, p. 37) calls the mind as a "glassy essence"[8] mirroring objects external to it. Both reject the ocularcentric implications of Marx's *camera obscura* metaphor. But in offering an alternative, each foregrounds a different dimension of language.

At first, deconstruction—if indeed we can homogenize it into such a coherent entity—may appear hostile to any concept of any ideology. This would certainly be the implication one can draw from Sarah Kofman's radically Nietzschean perspectivalism. And it is also symptomatic that the index to Gasché's book carries no reference to "ideology" at all. But, if we turn to the work of another major champion of deconstruction, the late Paul De Man, we can see that at least one of its spokespersons did still argue for its importance. In the opening essay of his collection *The Resistance to Theory*, De Man (1986, p. 11) writes:[9]

> What we call ideology is precisely the confusion of linguistic with natural reality, of reference with phenomenalism. It follows that, more than any other mode of inquiry, including economics, the linguistics of literariness is a powerful and indispensable tool in the unmasking of ideological aberrations, as well as a determining factor in accounting for their occurrence. Those who reproach literary theory for being oblivious to social and historical (that is to say ideological) reality are merely stating their fear at having their own ideological mystifications exposed by the tool they are trying to discredit. They are, in short, very poor readers of Marx's *German Ideology.*

How then does literary theory in the deconstructive mode better read *The German Ideology* without regressing to the ocularcentric notion of setting right reversed and inverted images? De Man (1986, p. 11) answers:[10]

> It upsets rooted ideologies by revealing the mechanics of their workings; it goes against a powerful philosophical tradition of which aesthetics is a prominent part; it upsets the established canon of literary works and blurs the boundaries between literary and non-literary discourse. By implication, it may also reveal the links between ideology and philosophy.

The implications of De Man's own position are not difficult to discern. For deconstruction, the major mystifying ideologies of Western culture are the occlusion of the rhetorical moment in philosophy and science, the mistaken conflation of linguistic reference with the reality of an external object, the hypostatization of such categories as the Aesthetic or the Literary, the smoothing over of the mechanics of literariness in every text, the confinement of textuality itself to what appears between the covers of a book, and so on. All of these questionable practices are indeed worth challenging as possible sources of obfuscation, and we are certainly in debt to deconstruction for exploring their implications.

And yet, we may well feel uneasy with the contradictions lurking behind De Man's attempt to salvage a critical concept of ideology. Looking closely at his own rhetoric gives cause for alarm. Who, for example, is the "we" in his first sentence? If the Nietzchean perspectivalism of Kofman is taken to its individualist conclusions, where is there room for a collective subject in deconstruction, a subject able to get outside of its own *camera obscura* long enough to share a common view of the nature of ideology? Furthermore, De Man tells us that ideology is the confusion of linguistic with natural reality, reference with phenomenalism. The "other" of ideology in this sense—other with a small "o"—would be presumably the overcoming of that confusion. But this achievement would not mean that we could tell when we are talking about linguistic "reality" and when we are not. For one of the main lessons of deconstruction is surely that we can never make a sharp distinction between two such putative approaches to the world.

Our knowledge of nature, or anything else for that matter, is always already "linguistic" in the strong sense of the term. All that we can overcome, therefore, is the false belief that we can bracket our rhetorical mediations and see the world straight. As a result, we must remain agnostic about our external reality against which we can measure our understanding and find it appropriate or not. To know that we have hitherto been confused in our attempt to disentangle reference from phenomenalism may be an advance over blithely thinking we are not, but it is not much of a step beyond ideology as an inevitable and irremediable dimension of the human condition. For along with the deconstruction of the boundary between rhetoric and the perception of nature goes the sober realization of its inevitable restoration in our everyday practice. There is no radical cure, no revolutionary therapeutic benefit, to be derived from the acknowledgment of our false belief, for it is impotent to prevent our lapsing back into error. Deconstruction, like poetry in Auden's celebrated line, makes nothing happen.

De Man, however, does contend that "the linguistics of literariness is an indispensable tool in the unmasking of ideological aberrations." But if there are aberrations, there must be a norm by which they are measured, a state presumable free of ideology itself or else closely approximating it. But it is precisely such a state of full presence, immediacy, and transparence that deconstruction has been at such pains to refute. If there is a normative *point d'appui* beyond the deceptions of ideology, it is only the Nietzschean rejection of the whole problematic of true and false consciousness based on a discredited subject/object metaphysics of adequation between idea and its referent. But here we are faced with the time-honored problem of how to judge such an assertion as itself true or false, when the whole basis for distinguishing between the two is denied. To say we are somehow beyond that dilemma because we have learned that language cannot be reduced to its constative, predicative function and, therefore, measured against a putative object outside it may be satisfying to some, but it provides very little basis for a workable concept of ideology.

Finally, De Man tells us that deconstruction will upset "rooted ideologies by revealing the mechanics of their working." This contention is, of course, the old formalist program of baring the device, which in the hands of Brecht and his followers found its way into Marxist aesthetics as well. Although it is certainly an indispensable tool in exposing the illusion of authorial genius or the organic integrity of the work of art, it too is unfortunately very problematic as a basis for ideology critique. First of all, the goal of revealing hidden mechanisms is itself tacitly grounded in an essence/appearance model, which deconstruction is normally at pains to discredit. Although he himself questions the surface/depth distinction, De Man's rhetoric of revelation suggests otherwise. For it entails that very ocularcentric premise of being able to see through an apparently opaque surface to reveal the hidden depths beneath, which the antiocular turn of much twentieth-century thought has called into question. The Derridean metaphor of a bottomless chessboard suggests in fact that, once we reach a putative hidden mechanism, it too will be subject to further deconstruction *ad infinitum,* so that no ultimate, essential level of explanation can ever be reached.

Second, there is precious little evidence to show that baring literary devices really changes anything outside of the practice of literary criticism. It was, moreover, already anticipated by modernist art, among whose central strategies were the foregrounding of its own artifice, the revelation of the materiality of its media, and the problematizing of its authorial voice. This deaestheticization of art, as Adorno would have called it, was useful in debunking certain earlier notions of the aesthetic, but it was the founding moment of a new aesthetics of a different kind, which we call modernism.[11] Whether or not it in its turn may be ideological in some respects can also be debated and, of course, has been by critics from Lukács to Jameson. De Man himself contributes to the suspicion that it may be by his tendency to call it the essential quality of all literature, self-consciously modernist or not. For, in so doing, the historical specificity of different literary practices is lost.

Finally, as Brecht knew, but his less politically committed followers have sometimes forgotten, ideology is really weakened not by the exposure of its workings alone but only when the larger constellation of forces making it necessary are themselves changed. De Man, to be sure, acknowledges the importance of this insight in passing, when he says that the linguistics of literariness is "*a* determining factor" in accounting for the occurrence of ideology, but he never offers any real analysis of the linkages between it and the other unnamed determining factors. Instead, we have to take on faith the contention that subverting the mystifications deconstruction is most concerned with challenging—those I listed above—will work in common cause with subverting the others, whatever they may be. But in fact the links between them are not very easy to establish, especially as deconstruction can be turned itself against many of the values that oppressed groups have, perhaps in their benighted way, thought they were fighting for, values like solidarity, community, universality, popular sovereignty, self-determination, agency, and the like. In the absence of a more developed notion of what is not an ideological aberration, the suspicion will remain that deconstruction can be corrosive not only of mystifications but also of any possible positive alternative to them.

For all its determined undermining of many of the most fundamental assumptions of Western thought, for all its soliciting—in Derrida's sense of shaking but leaving still standing—the traditional hierarchies of that thought, for all its self-proclaimed subversiveness, it is hard to avoid the conclusion that the deconstructive alternative to a discredited ocularcentric version of ideology critique is by itself insufficient. For it provides little guidance in suggesting the other of ideology, with either a small or a large "O," outside of suggesting that its own Sisyphean labors are it.

What then of the alternative I have, for shorthand purposes, designated "critical hermeneutics"? Here the major spokesman is Jürgen Habermas, although the contributions of other thinkers like Paul Ricoeur and Karl-Otto Apel should also be acknowledged. This is not the place to spell out Habermas's introduction of a linguistic turn into the Frankfurt School's Critical Theory or to examine the mountain of commentary devoted to it. Let me make only a few remarks that bear on the question of ideology. Although Habermas's work does contain discussions of various substantive ideologies that he considers particularly important today—the fetish of science and technology, for example (Habermas, 1970)—the main contribution he has made to ideology critique concerns its formal underpinnings.

Based on a pragmatic rather than structural linguistics, composed of insights from a variety of traditions, his argument has emphasized the process of communicative interaction through intersubjective discourse. He posits as a counterfactual telos of language the assumption of an undistorted speech situation in which the power of the better argument rather than prejudice, manipulation, or coercion creates a consensus of opinion about both cognitive and normative matters. What defines "better" is not congruence with an

external reality but its ability to persuade after a process of rational deliber-
ation is carried out, a process always open to later revision. Such a state of
affairs is, of course, a regulative ideal, which can be approached only
asymptotically. The main advantage of this argument over hermeneutic
theories that assume meaningful communication always already exists or can
be realized through interpretive effort alone—what makes it a critical rather
than pure hermeneutics—is its linkage of language to power. For it argues
that the undistorted speech situation can only be approximated when social
conditions are themselves free of hierarchical domination. A conflict of
interpretations can be rationally adjudicated only when a formal structure of
rules and procedures is in place, which permits the unconstrained interchange
of views leading to the ultimate triumph of the better argument. This condition does not mean the naive suspension of power, as some of Habermas's
critics have charged, but the challenging of systematically asymmetrical
relations of power. The power that remains is not in the service of domination,
which is the *raison d'être* of ideology, but in that of acting in concert to
overcome illegitimate authority. Such an overcoming can only be achieved
by an intersubjective effort that goes beyond the radical individualism of
Sarah Kofman's Nietzschean perspectivalism and the anti-individualism of
such theories as Althusser's with its claim that the subject is only an effect
of specular ideology.

By squarely facing the thorny problem of how to distinguish between a
consensus based on manipulation, prejudice, and mystification and one
grounded, at least in principle, in rational discourse supported by symmetrical power relations, Habermas helps us to establish a vantage point from
which ideology can be called an aberration. As John Thompson (1984,
p. 194) puts it in his recent *Studies in the Theory of Ideology,* "to study
ideology . . . is *to study the ways in which meaning (or signification) serves
to sustain relations of domination.*" That is, ideology is not a function of
occluded vision; it is a distortion in the process of communicative rationality
in the service of blocking the achievement of symmetrical power relations.
Ideology critique, in other words, is meaningful only when it goes beyond
baring the device and subverting received wisdom to challenge the conditions
that necessitate ideology in the first place. For ideology is not merely a
mistaken understanding of reality; it is an element in the exploitation and
domination of human beings.

Habermas's project, therefore, is in the service of emancipation through
social change, not merely textual reinterpretation. Because he is willing to
defend in a nuanced way the values of the enlightenment tradition, it is not
surprising to discover that he is somewhat less virulently hostile to vision
than some of the other figures discussed above. In fact, the process of
ideology critique as he understands it contains a certain role for the objectivist

epistemology that is so closely tied to the privileging of vision. Not only is it an indispensable tool in our intercourse with nature, it also helps us make sense of those aspects of a reified social order that act as if they were a "second nature," to use the familiar Hegelian Marxist concept. That is, insofar as hierarchical, asymmetrical relations of domination permeate our society, it is necessary to investigate them from without, even as we try to undermine them from within. Although the point of view of total outsiderness is, of course, a fiction, embedded as we are in the flesh of the world and possessed of only a limited horizon from which to look about, it is nonetheless a useful "as if" concept in our attempt to grasp the larger structural constraints that limit our communicative interaction. Deconstructionists like De Man tacitly acknowledge this necessity in their assumption that we can reveal the mechanism of ideology's workings. We cannot entirely relinquish the cold eye of dispassionate analysis, losing the advantage given by gaining some perspective on a problem, in order to listen to each other for the purpose of coming to a rational consensus about our potentially common interests. As Ricoeur has also often stressed, we need a moment of distantiation, a more synoptic overview, as one positive condition of all historical understanding.

There is obviously a great deal that can be said about the implications of all this, much of which may well seem problematic without further development, but let me close by taking a different tack, which will lead us toward a certain cautious rapprochement between the two linguistically informed alternatives to an ocularcentric concept of ideology. Neither of them alone provides a sufficiently powerful basis for an ideology critique that will survive the charge of arbitrariness hurled by those who deny the escapability of ideology. The deconstructive position tends to an ahistorical preoccupation with language and textuality per se. As a result, its exponents often lean toward a certain homogenization of the metaphysical tradition of Western thought as a whole, which is characterized as logocentric, specular, and so on. Symptomatically, when Derrida was asked at a recent conference to explain the rise of deconstruction itself during the last generation, he brushed the question aside by asserting that language always calls itself into question.[12] This type of hostility to historical change is, needless to say, fatal for any critical theory of ideology that wants to go beyond the crippling assumption that mystification is a universal constant of the human condition.

Still, by challenging a whole host of received truths, deconstruction has opened up an enormously stimulating series of issues for ideology critique to consider. The point, however, is to foster the conditions under which such a debate might be carried out with the hope of working through their implications. Here only a theory that takes seriously the linkages between linguistic manipulations and social domination in particular historical circumstances can help us. There is no guarantee, to be sure, that a perfectly symmetrical speech situation, if it is indeed more than a counterfactual, regulative ideal, can provide anything like the certainty of the old ocularcentric notion of true consciousness as congruence between idea and its object. But it does at least give us some procedural standard by which our fragile capacity to reason may lead us beyond ideological illusions and the domination they abet. Without such a criterion, we may well fall back into a resigned acceptance of the coercive power of institutionalized authority, which cannot be challenged by anything outside it (e.g., Stanley Fish). For such a position, the "other" of ideology is an utterly meaningless concept.

One final word on the relationship between ideology and the visual is in order. In the ocularphobic context of much twentieth-century thought, it often seems as if the old religious hostility to idolatry has been resurrected to thwart any positive appreciation of the visual. One of the sources of the religious distrust of sight, as we have noted, was the anxiety unleashed by ocular desire. In our more secular context, this emotion sometimes appears to have been transformed into a deep distrust of what Guy Debord (1970) made famous as "the spectacle" of modern consumer capitalism. Alongside of surveillance, the spectacle is attacked as one of the visual mainstays of the current order, one that operates by stimulating yearnings that are never really satisfied in a positive and fulfilling way.

It would be foolish to reject this insight into the way wants are generated in our society, at least in part by the seductions of sight. But it has also been noted by writers like Castoriadis (1975) and Ricoeur (1976, pp. 17-28) that what can be called the "social imaginary" contains elements that cannot be reduced to mere ideological mystifications. For, in addition to illusory phantasms, it also projects utopian images of another possible social order. From an Augustinian point of departure, ocular desire is to be condemned because it distracts us from listening to the divine word in scripture, but for those of us no longer so certain of the power of that word, it may have a more laudable function. As a stimulant to dissatisfaction, however open to manipulation it may be, it is also a source of yearning for something better. The critique of ideology can exist only when such yearnings are still accounted viable. The old metaphor of a *camera obscura* showing ideology as a reversed and inverted image of a truly existing world may, as we have remarked, be difficult to sustain in our antiocular age, but another link between ideology and the visual may not. That is, what we are looking *for* when we criticize the distortions of ideology may be present in what we are looking *at* in certain manifestations of ideology itself.[13] The images of specular reciprocity, transparent meaning, standing in the light of the truth, and so on may all be easy to deconstruct as chimeras, but they are perhaps also ciphers of that unattainable "Other" of ideology—this time with a capital "O"—on which all critique must ultimately rest.

NOTES

1. For a recent consideration of the metaphor, see W. J. T. Mitchell (1986).

2. For useful discussions of these and other visual metaphors in Western epistemologies, see Hans Jonas (1982) and Evelyn Fox Keller and Christine R. Grontowski (1983).

3. This was the title of an essay by Carlyle printed in Froude (1982, pp. 7-12). For a discussion of the Romantic attitude toward vision, see M. H. Abrams (1973, p. 373).

4. For a critique of the disembodied eye, see Maurice Merleau-Ponty (964). It might be noted that Descartes, for all his hostility to the imperfections of the actual human eye, did advocate the usage of the newly discovered telescope in his *Dioptrique* of 1637.

5. Augustine discusses ocular desire in Chapter 35 of his *Confessions*, where he links it to the temptations of idle curiosity.

6. G. M. Stratton (see 1897) performed an experiment wearing an inverted lens for eight days and discovered that he was able to reacquire normal straightforward vision.

7. A classic example is the use of the term in Daniel Bell (1960). Other proponents of this view included Edward Shils, Raymond Aron, and Seymour Martin Lipset.

8. The phrase is taken from Shakespeare's *Measure for Measure.*

9. See also his remarks on the need for "critique of ideology" and the relevance of Adorno and Heidegger to such a project (de Man 1986, p. 121).

10. See also the discussion of ideology in Michael Ryan (1982, p. 39). Ryan contents that a belief in an ideal meaning prior to its textual expression is the equivalent of the idealism Marx was attacking in *The German Ideology.*

11. For an account of the crisis of the traditional aesthetic assumptions before the actual emergence of modernism, see Catherine Gallagher (1985). She demonstrates how the nineteenth-century realist novel also experienced a breakdown of formal consistency as it tried to incorporate new material from nonliterary discourses.

12. This occurred at the conference "The States of Theory," at the University of California, Irvine, California, May 1987.

13. If we recognize the ambivalent quality of ideology as containing both a yearning for something better and a consolation for its unattainability under current circumstances, we may see it as derived from the deconstructionist critique of either/or formulations. It may, however, also be understood as evidence of a dialectical concept of ideology, which can be traced back to Marx's usage itself.

REFERENCES

Abrams, M. H. 1973. *Natural Supernaturalism: Tradition and Revolution in Romantic Literature.* New York: Norton.

Althusser, Louis. 1971. *Lenin and Philosophy and Other Essays.* New York: Monthly Review Press.

Bell, Daniel. 1960. *The End of Ideology.* Glencoe, IL: Free Press.

Blumenberg, Hans. 1957. "Licht als Metapher der Wahrheit." *Studium Generale* 10: 432-47.

Castoriadis, Cornelius. 1975. *L'Institution imaginaire de la société.* Paris: Seuil.

Debord, Guy. 1970. *The Society of the Spectacle.* Detroit: Black and Red.

De Man, Paul. 1986. *The Resistance to Theory.* Minneapolis: University of Minnesota Press.

Froude, James Anthony. 1882. *Thomas Carlyle 1795-1835.* Vol. 2. New York: Scribner.

Gallagher, Catherine. 1985. *The Industrial Reformation of English Fiction 1832-1867*. Chicago: University of Chicago Press.

Gasché, Rodolph. 1986. *The Tain of the Mirror: Derrida and the Philosophy of Reflection*. Cambridge, MA: Harvard University Press.

Habermas, Jürgen. 1970. "Technology and Science as 'Ideology.'" In *Toward a Rational Society: Student Protest, Science and Politics*. Boston: Beacon.

Irigaray, Luce. 1985. *Speculum of the Other Woman*. Ithaca: Cornell University Press.

Jay, Martin. 1986. "In the Empire of the Gaze: Foucault and the Denigration of Vision in Twentieth-Century French Thought." In *Foucault: A Critical Reader*, edited by David Couzens Hoy. London: Blackwell.

Jonas, Hans. 1982. "The Nobility of Sight." In *The Phenomenon of Life: Toward a Philosophical Biology*. Chicago: University of Chicago Press.

Keller, Evelyn Fox and Christine R. Grontowski. 1983. "The Mind's Eye." In *Discovering Reality: Feminist Perspectives on Epistemology, Metaphysics, Methodology, and Philosophy of Sciences*, edited by Sandra Harding and Merrill B. Hintikka. Dordrecht: D. Riedel.

Kofman, Sarah. 1973. *Camera Obscura—de l'idéologie*. Paris: Seuil.

Lefort, Claude. 1986. *The Political Forms of Modern Society: Bureaucracy, Democracy, Totalitarianism*. London: Polity.

Marx, Karl and Friedrich Engels. 1970. *The German Ideology*. London: International Publishers.

Merleau-Ponty, Maurice. 1964. "Eye and Mind." In *The Primacy of Perception*. Evanston, IL: Northwestern University Press.

Mitchell, W. J. T. 1986. *Iconology: Image, Text, Ideology*. Chicago: University of Chicago Press.

Ricoeur, Paul. 1976. "Ideology and Utopia as Cultural Imagination." *Philosophic Exchange* 2(Summer):17-28.

Rorty, Richard. 1979. *Philosophy and the Mirror of Nature*. Princeton, NJ: Princeton University Press.

Ryan, Michael. 1982. *Marxism and Deconstruction*. Baltimore: Johns Hopkins University Press.

Stratton, G. M. 1897. "Vision Without Inversion of the Retinal Image." *Psychological Review* 4(5):341-60.

Thompson, John B. 1984. *Studies in the Theory of Ideology*. Cambridge: Polity.

Chapter 9

BRINGING DEMOCRACY BACK IN
Universalistic Solidarity and the
Civil Sphere

JEFFREY C. ALEXANDER
University of California, Los Angeles

IN THE LAST 18 MONTHS, as one nation after another has embarked on the long and difficult road to a liberal and responsive social order, "democracy" has once again become a fashionable term. In sociology, this revival could lead to a disciplinary crisis, for about democracy contemporary sociology has precious little to say. When democracy was sociology's concern, moreover, it was never successfully theorized.

In the days of the cold war, ironically perhaps, social scientists considered democracy to be something rather easily achieved, a heritage that the world deserved and would eventually receive. It was conceptualized as a necessary implication of the classical dichtomies that structured the field, of *Gesellschaft* as compared with *Gemeinschaft,* of modernity in contrast with traditionalism. We would become democratic by default, by virtue simply of our modernity. Systematic distinctions were rarely made within the concept of modernity itself. Nondemocratic societies were understood simply as not yet modern enough.

Two languages informed this postwar discourse. One stressed efficiency. Democracy was adaptive because it was flexible. Because it was flexible, it would survive. It was an evolutionary universal (Parsons 1963). The other vocabulary was taken from the voluntary rationality of the Enlightenment. In the postwar world, democracy was formally introduced into other nations by the Allies; constitutions were put into place, legal guidelines established. These normative expectations, it was believed, would be cherished and followed in due course (Parsons 1971).

We see now that these earlier efforts failed to understand the requisites of democracy. They were either technocratic and determinist (e.g., Lerner 1958, p. 40; Rostow 1960, p. 133) or hopelessly rationalist and optimistic (Lipset 1960, pp. 27-63). To continue such theorizing in the present day is not only anachronistic, it is also irresponsible.[1]

THE TURN TOWARD "REALISM"

In the last two decades, we have learned that this is not, after all, the best of all possible worlds and that democracy does not come easily. This education has been a salutary one, but the shift in social scientific understanding that has accompanied it has not been equally so. Cynicism has replaced optimism, materialism and "realism" have replaced the concern with morality (Collins 1975). Instead of exploring politics, social scientists now explore society. They investigate the social origins of political arrangements (Moore 1966) and downplay the effects of constitutions and political norms (e.g., Rex 1961). Conflict theories (Dahrendorf 1959) have replaced theories about the possibility of social integration. Even when the specificity of politics is acknowledged, the independent state is conceived of in a purely instrumental way (Skocpol 1979). It is a power bloc of its own, one more environment within which egoistic interest can be pursued (Evans et al. 1985).

This does not mean that political ideals have disappeared from the sociological discourse about politics. It means that they are now pursued in a "tough-minded" way. Democracy is considered merely a formal arrangement. What is important is the distribution of power and force, the balance of material resources. Equality has become the central focus, class conflict and power structure the topics of elaborate analysis.[2] If there is unequal economic or political power, it is assumed, dominant groups will pursue their interests by any available means. It is means that count, not ends. It is concrete goals that matter, not the moral frameworks that can possibly frame them.[3] Citizenship results from class struggle. Rights cannot be conceptualized in an independent way. Democracy can be explained only as the product of a truce between conflict groups that have achieved relative but temporary parity (Rex 1961), a political manifestation of capitalism that provides "the material bases of consent" (Przeworski 1985, pp. 133-70).[4]

Those who write about the political condition of contemporary societies express little confidence in the possibilities for democracy. When Marcuse (1963) attacked capitalist democracies as one-dimensional and totalitarian, he was considered a radical iconoclast. Thirty years later, Foucault has gained increasingly wide acceptance for a theory that, while more sophisticated and precise, emphasizes the same repressive qualities in Western societies while virtually ignoring the meaning of a democratic state (e.g., Foucault 1979, 1980).[5] Citizens of Western societies are seen as monitored, as subject to surveillance (Giddens 1981). They are selfish and do not engage in public life (Sennett 1977; Habermas 1989). When democratic discourse does become the focus of analysis, it is conceived of as ideology, not as values, as simply another means to pursue strategic ends (Edelman 1964; Thompson

1984). Debunking rhetoric, of course, cuts pretentious authority down to size. It has always been a mainstay of democratic politics. Without more of a theoretical perspective on democratic and antiauthoritarian struggles, however, social scientific understanding cannot be gained. Social science thinking about democratic societies has become part of the practice of democratic politics. Under these conditions, the development of a realistic theory of democratic societies has become impossible.

THE TRADITION OF THRASYMACHUS

We are left with the tradition of Thrasymachus, for whom one of the first conflict theorists wrote an essay in praise (Dahrendorf 1968). Thrasymachus provided the foil for Plato. Against Socrates' vision of an ideal and transcendent justice, he insisted on base motives and the necessary cruelty of political life: "In all states alike, 'right' has the same meaning, namely what is for the interest of the party established in power, and that is the strongest" (Plato 1965, chap. 3, p. 18). This hardheaded caution about idealism is clearly important. It is reflected in the long tradition of normative political theory that has insisted that democracy depends on the separation of powers. The ever practical Aristotle (1963, *The Politics,* Book 4, sec. E, chap. 14) argued against Platonic idealism that well-ordered constitutions would have to be divided against themselves. Montesquieu (1977, *The Spirit of Laws,* Book 11, chap. 6, p. 202) believed that, if independent institutions were not pitted against each other, tyranny, arbitrary control, and "all the violence of the oppressor" would be the result. In the *Federalist Papers,* Hamilton and Madison said much the same.

Classical social science writing about democracy has largely followed a similar path. Marx ([1848] 1962) economized Thrasymachus when he argued that democracy was a sham because classes had grossly unequal economic power, concluding that class power had to be separated from political governance. Weber ([1917] 1968) sociologized him when he argued that democracy depended on the creation of powerful counterweights to state bureaucracies, on the emergence of political demogogues and ruthless party organizations. Following upon Marx and Weber, Michels ([1911] 1962) argued that socialist parties and unions became oligarchical because their leaders could monopolize the organization's material resources. When Lipset, Coleman, and Trow wrote *Union Democracy* (1956)—the most important single sociological study of democracy in the postwar era—they followed in Michels's footsteps. Arguing that organizational democracy can be defined as the opportunity for effective competition between groups, they demonstrated that such competition is possible only if the means of struggle are pluralized.

This line of thinking is certainly essential to any realistic thinking about democracy. The return to it is an important antidote to the ideological innocence and theoretical simplification of earlier postwar thought. The self-interested dimension of human action must be firmly respected, as must the significantly self-aggrandizing character of every social group. It is for this reason that sustained participatory democracy in any large organization (Mansbridge 1980, pp. 278-89) is impossible. Oligarchies form in every organization. If these elites are not given what they consider their due, they will seek to dominate society in turn. Every serious theory of democracy must cope with this fact. Democracies depend on social structures that allow egoism to be pursued but that make the aggregation of egoism impossible. No society can prevent the formation of elites; a society will be democratic, however, to the extent that the interests of these elites can be differentiated in a manner that makes them competitive rather than convergent (Etzioni-Halevy 1989; Alexander and Colomy 1989). If society cannot prevent elite formation, it can prevent the monopolization of power and resources by any single elite (Walzer 1983).

POLITICS AS A SYMBOLIC CODE

Elite conflict and structural differentiation cannot, however, form the exclusive point of our interest. The tradition of Thrasymachus is not adequate to understand politics, much less the phenomenon of political democracy. Within its narrow confine, we cannot understand the interior domain—the realm of feeling, moral sense, and perception—that makes living together possible. We cannot illuminate the mysterious process by which citizens agree to uphold rules whose utility they scarcely understand. The tradition of Thrasymachus explores only the "base" of politics. But power is a medium of communication, not simply a goal of interested action or a means of coercion. It has a symbolic code, not only a material base (Parsons 1969).

To understand this code, we must introduce a normative and cultural dimension into our theory of democratic society. This will mean returning to some earlier thinking about normative and cultural integration and trying to understand it in new ways. It will also mean connecting our discussion of politics to other important and contemporary intellectual themes (Alexander 1988a; Alexander and Seidman 1990).

Because politics has reference to a symbolic code, it can never be simply situational; it has a generalized dimension as well. This generalized reference makes politics not only contingent and rational but stylized and prescribed. To understand it, we need anthropological concepts about rhetoric and ritual and structural theories about language and codes. The symbolic medium of politics is a language that political actors themselves do not fully understand. It is not only situationally motivated speech but a deep symbolic structure. What Lévi-Strauss (1963, p. 50) has said about the code of kinship, we can say about the language of politics: "It exists only in human consciousness; it is an arbitrary system of representations, not the spontaneous development of a real situation."[6]

There is a tradition of contemporary political theory—often called "normative" in contrast with "empirical" or "behaviorist"—that similarly rejects the consideration of politics in utilitarian terms alone. Drawing inspiration from the ancient Greek Polis, thinkers like Arendt (1958), Wolin (1960), Unger (1975), and MacIntyre (1981) describe democracy as a participatory political community whose citizens have a commitment to the public interest that transcends private and egoistic concerns. They call for a "politics of vision" and criticize contemporary politics as instrumental from the perspective of this ideal, democratic norm. Their communitarian approach argues that democracy can be sustained only if a sense of altruistic civic virtue permeates political life.

The problem here is not with the emphasis on morality and internal commitments or with the injection into political theory of explicit normative criteria. The problem is with the manner in which these commitments and criteria are understood. The normative aspirations of this tradition are conflated with behavioral possibilities, the moral *ought* is confused with the empirical *is*. If political life is not fully participatory, this tradition judges it to be egotistical and instrumental, ruled by interests rather than values. If it is not virtuous in a liberal or progressive sense, it is judged to be without any reference to any conception of virtue at all. Similar problems detract from sociological reactions to political utilitarianism. When Bellah (Bellah et al., 1985) demands new "habits of the heart," and Bell (1976) a new "public household," they too draw upon this romantic conception of the possibility for a powerful and controlling civic virtue. While morally admirable and politically provocative, such thinking seems not only utopian but a bit sociologically naive.[7]

If there is to be a more value-oriented conception of democratic politics, it must start from a more realistic conception of the difficulties and challenges of complex societies. Self-interest and conflict will never give way to some all-embracing communal ideal. Indeed, the more democratic a society, the more it allows groups to define their own specific ways of life and legitimates the inevitable conflicts of interest that arise between them. Political consensus can never be brought to bear in a manner that neutralizes particular group obligations and commitments. To think that it can be is to repeat the fallacy of Rousseau's belief in the General Will as distinct from the actual will of particular individuals and groups. A more differentiated conception of political culture is needed, one that will be more tolerant of individual differences and more compatible with the pluralization of interests.[8]

To arrive at such a conception, one must differentiate among various levels of political life (Parsons and Smelser 1957, chap. 7; Smelser 1959, 1963). The existence of broadly shared moral ties does not mean that individuals and groups pursue similar or even complementary goals and interests. At the same time, divergent and conflictual goals do not mean that shared understandings are not highly significant. Generalized commitments inform and influence goals even if they do not create them. While the concrete situation has its own exigencies, it does not create goals and interests out of a whole cloth. The articulation of this more specific level is always informed by the logic of more generalized patterns, by norms and by values, by deep symbolic structures that provide a common medium of communication for conflict groups despite their strategic and divisive aims. Without returning to an earlier innocence or idealistic naïveté, this cultural dimension must be studied if any plausible sociological theory of democracy is to emerge. If we do so, we will find that the tradition of Thrasymacus that has dominated social science in recent years is a cultural discourse rather than an empirical description of contemporary political life; and the language of community and integration, while no more empirical and no less culturally constructed, is a code that sustains democracy wherever it even fleetingly appears.

Hegel ([1807] 1977, para. 440) saw this when he criticized the theoretical illusion, so common to mechanistic theories, that individuals and institutions are entirely separated from some broader *Geist*. The reasons such actors offer for their actions, he insisted to the contrary, are in fact deeply embedded in moral conceptions of which they are often unaware. Simmel (1955) argued in the same way when he suggested that social conflicts are embedded in "concepts," in implicit, idealized, and highly generalized notions that define the rewards that conflict groups are fighting for and even their conceptions of others and themselves.[9] More recently, Walzer (1970, pp. 3-23) has argued that the structure of political obligations is much the same. Justifications for political actions and opinions may be forcefully expressed in the language of free will and individual desire; yet the very fact that actors feel obligated to speak or act in these ways reveals that they do so as members of communities. The groups to which they belong impose these obligations in the name of their particular, higher ideals. Individuals must act at the level of situationally specific demands; in doing so, however, they typically invoke the more general understandings of their groups (Walzer 1970, pp. 3-5).

DEMOCRACY AND SYMBOLIC UNIVERSALS

The cultural reference of politics is a constant. In particular situations, there is always some reference to generalized codes. In thinking about political democracy, however, the differential capacity to make these references becomes particularly salient, for the specific content of the reference can be defined in variable ways. Democracy depends on the regulation of diverse particular actions by rules that are broadly accepted and hence inclusive. If the cultural reference of action does not have a far-reaching scope, it cannot be inclusive in effect; because it is narrowly defined, it will be exclusive. The more general the symbolic reference to which specific actions are subject, moreover, the more they can be subject to demands for justification. These demands are made in relationship to the general referents that are acknowledged by participants as guiding their specific actions. The more general the scope and inclusiveness of the cultural reference, therefore, the more action can be subject to criticism and reformulation.

Breadth of scope and inclusiveness of effect can be understood in terms of the contrast between universalism and particularism. I will spend some time discussing this contrast, both because I believe it to be so central to any conception of democratic politics and also because the contrast seems largely to have disappeared from the discussion that still remains of political culture itself.[10]

Aristotle (1963, p. 47) first defined this contrast in terms of the qualities of actual things.

> Now of actual things some are universal, others particular. I call universal that which is by its nature predicated of a number of things and particular that which is not; "man," for instance, is a universal, Callias is a particular.

If one relates to Callias as a "man," one judges him according to criteria that are broad, general, and all embracing. This cultural reference creates a psychological or intellectual separation from the particular situation within which Callias is encountered, allowing one to compare Callias's actions with others' and to develop a critical perspective. If one relates to Callias simply under the rubric "Callias," by contrast, one employs categories of understanding that are peculiar to this particular situation alone. The culture reference reflects Callias's uniqueness. This particularism may encourage intimacy, but it does not allow the separation from situational immediacy that encourages critical judgment.

This contrast between universalism and particularism has been intrinsic to every significant effort to understand the culture of critical social action and democratic and inclusive societies. In his *The Phenomenology of Spirit,* Hegel ([1807] 1977) described human development as involving the perception of ever more universalistic categories, each of which would include under a higher and more general rubric the particular antitheses of the preceding stage. Because Hegel believed the spirit of God to be even more general and inclusive than the reason of man, he described the end point of human development as the regulation of every particular interaction and social institution by a mutual reference to this powerful universal force. If such regulation, or interpenetration, were achieved, there would be the integration of the particular and universal, which Hegel called the "concrete universal."

When Parsons formulated his pattern-variable scheme (e.g., Parsons 1951), the same distinction was stated in a less metaphysical way. He argued that interactions are regulated by norms that specify the dimensions of universalism and particularism with great precision. Norms may allow more or less affect and more or less diffuseness in role obligations. They may define an interaction as oriented more to self or other concerns. To the degree that normative orientations are more neutral, less diffuse, and more other oriented, they are more universalistic. Parsons and others demonstrated that the tension between universalistic and particular patterns is central to a wide range of social situations, from parent-child and doctor-patient interactions (Parsons 1951; Barber 1980) to race relations (Williams 1960) and the structure of national communities (Lipset 1963, pp. 237-312).

The most important psychological studies of human development have focused on the transition from particularistic to universalistic capacities. While its direct implications for social life have never been precisely formulated or experimentally proved, Freud's theory that decathexis from objects of intense desire is essential for the development of ego rationality has had a pervasive effect on modern thought (see, e.g., Rieff 1959). Piaget's developmental psychology has had a more delimited effect, but it has been subject to much stricter experimental controls and its social implications are direct.

In his cognitive and moral theory, Piaget (1972) focuses on "generalization," which he defines as the ability to separate ideas from things. Children learn to separate their thoughts from their actions and the things encountered in their environments as the result of the "interiorization" of objects that were once "out there." The result is cognitive and moral objectification, the emergence of concepts and orientations that allow children to decenter themselves from the outside world and to manipulate it. With further development, the capacity for abstraction from particular details increases. From the ability to perform simple concrete operations, children learn universal, generalizable principles that allow formal operations. In this more adult stage, "knowledge transcends reality." Because of such generalization, universalistic moral standards become possible. Moral development depends on similar capacities for universalism and generalization. Younger children cannot participate in games because their understanding is so particularistic that they cannot even understand the concept of "rule." Children can play together spontaneously in organized games only if they can understand their own and others' actions as instances of more generalized frames. Only when they do is spontaneous and cooperative group interaction possible. Only with this kind of generalization, moreover, can critical orientations to actions, and even to rules themselves, be sustained.

More explicitly sociological treatments of socialization have argued in the same way. In Parsons's sociological translation of Freud and Piaget, he (1955) demonstrated that socialization involves the increasing capacity for generalizing beyond primary familial relations. To move beyond the Oedipal fixation on his particular father, Parsons argued, the male child needs to encounter other adult men outside the home. This transition from family in the worlds of school and play accentuates the tension between universalism and particularism, as the male child asks, "Is father a man, or are all men fathers?" The capacity to treat future authority figures in a critical and rational way depends on developing the capacity for invoking the more general category. Dreeben (1968) and others have demonstrated that this capacity is precisely what is learned in the increasingly impersonal and critical environment of primary and secondary schools.

Mead's (1964) theory of the "generalized other" points to the same phenomenon. In the play of early childhood, he suggests, children learn to take the role of the particular others with whom they interact. As they do so, a more universalized understanding emerges of what membership in this broader society requires. By referring to this more generalized element, older children can take the same attitude toward their own behavior as they do to others', which is precisely what following rules means. Such universalism allows there to be spontaneous play in organized games. The capacity for generalized reference also allows individual flexibility and critical, innovative behavior.

By referring to these studies in psychological development, I do not mean to suggest a causal relationship between socialization and democratic culture. It is evident that most individuals in most societies develop the capacities for universalistic action and judgment, whereas only a few societies have democratic political systems. I do want to suggest, however, that there is a significant homology between these seminal studies and the more general thinking that must be done about political culture and democratic society. Because these psychological theorists were concerned with cooperation and rationality, they had to focus on the tension between universalism and particularism. This contrast between general and inclusive orientations, and situationally specific and exclusive ones, illuminates a central distinction in human behavior. When actors are engaged in practical politics at the expense of general principles, when they exercise personalistic judgments without reference to office obligations, when they are guided by prejudice rather than mutual respect, when they act for self-interest alone without reference to higher laws, when they accept capricious authority without demanding justification or when authorities refuse to recognize the legitimacy of demands for justification when they are made—in all these situations actors are behaving in particularistic rather than universalistic ways. While these actors no doubt possess the psychological capacity for generalization, it has not informed their practice as members of the political community.

UNIVERSALISM AND CIVIL SOCIETY

The concept of universalism is applied to such political communities in the discourse about civility, civil society, and citizenship. It is unfortunate that, in the recent and very promising theoretical discussion about civil society that has emerged from within post-Marxist political theory (e.g., Keane 1988a, 1988b), the close connection between civil society and cultural universalism has not been made. For universalistic attitudes and codes are concretized in political communities by the construction of an independent civil sphere, with the civility and citizenship that this implies. Civility implies respect for others and control of oneself and also the adherence to a social code of behavior. Freud ([1930] 1961) argued that civilization depends on the substitution of ego-ideals and sublimated modes of participation for the direct emotional gratification of interaction; only in this way could supra-familial ties be established and the sphere of cooperation enlarged. Elias ([1939] 1978) traced the emergence of such control and refinement in a more historical way, showing how important it was to the construction of the first early nation-states and how it allowed broad social classes to be established and political bureaucracies to emerge.

In his earlier response to the rationalism and individualism of contract theory, Adam Ferguson ([1767] 1966) argued that an increase in self-control and "subtlety," and a decrease in brute impulse, were crucial to the "history of civil society." He described the latter as the social bond that defined a nation, the fellow feeling among members of a community that guaranteed respect for law, protection of property, and democratic regulation of authority. Hirschman (1977) has shown that, in the seventeenth and eighteenth centuries, there emerged a powerful backlash against the passionate glory seeking and hero worship of the late middle ages. Only by softening and polishing the manners of men, by creating psychological and hence social calm, would the arbitrariness of rulers be curbed by social rules and stable political order be achieved. Hirschman has shown that, for thinkers like Montesquieu, democratic constitutions and the separation of powers would be one result.

It is not often recognized that similar themes—civility, civil society, universalism, and citizenship—have also been central to certain traditions of social science. Weber ([1917] 1968, pp. 1212-372) argued that modern legal-rational societies depended upon the increasing "fraternization" that occurred for the first time in the city-states of the late middle ages. Christianity defined all men as brothers in the abstract community of Christ, rejecting ethnic or even national ties as valid criteria for community membership. Only because of the universalism of this cultural reference, Weber believed, were Western cities able to define urban dwellers as citizens, in principle extending that status to every male inhabitant of the city. In Eastern or ancient cities, by contrast, membership was defined irrevocably by family, ethnic, or class ties.

Marshall (1965) took the increasing density and power of these enlarged group ties as the dynamic factor in the expansion of citizenship. In the eighteenth century, citizenship was a crucial innovation in social organization, yet it entitled members of a national society simply to the protection of their legal rights. In the nineteenth century, with the emergence of nationalism and demands for recognition by lower classes, cross-group solidarity was strengthened, and citizenship was extended to the political right to vote of all community members. In the twentieth century, with its great solidarizing experiences like World Wars I and II, citizenship came to guarantee social and not just legal and political rights. Members of the newly developed "welfare states" had the ability to make legitimate demands for a wide range of educational and social services (see Bendix 1964).

What Parsons (1967, 1971, pp. 86-121) did was to reformulate Marshall's theory in a manner that tied it directly to the expansion of social solidarity. Increased market relationships, political participation, and religious activism are not only significant in themselves but contribute to the construction of an independent solidary sphere of society, which Parsons defined as the societal community. More specifically integrative processes are also involved, such as geographical and social mobility, intermarriage, migration, education, and the emergence of new forms of mass communication. For all of these reasons, the intensity and frequency of interaction increases; members of national societies see themselves as more like one another; cross-group ties become closer; and the societal community expands. Modernizing social change must be defined, therefore, not only as shifting the economic, political, or value spheres but as increasing inclusion via the societal community.[11]

In earlier and more simple societies, membership in the community was defined by the particularism of kinship and blood. For most members of feudal societies, it did not extend past the limits of immediate consanguinity (Banfield 1958). With the construction of a civil society, these particularistic definitions of membership are broken through; they are replaced by abstract criteria that emphasize simple humanity and participation in the nation-state. Citizenship, then, can be understood as a form of social organization that is anchored in universalistic bonds of community that define every member as equally worthy of respect. These are highly generalized ties and abstract and differentiated rules that regulate the political game. Members of a civil society can refer to these universalistic values to gain distance from their immediate relationships, in order to change them or criticize them.

I am not suggesting here that a national community should be understood simply as a civil society, any more than it should be understood as a capitalist society, a nation-state, or a cultural community. Civil society must be understood analytically, not concretely. It is not a sphere that one can touch or see, any more than is the sphere of political power, economic production, or cultural life. It is a dimension that is organized by the fact that it subjects those who are its members to distinctive kinds of obligations and acts, which can be distinguished from, and are often in conflict with, those of economic, political, and cultural ideology. The analytic nature of this sphere means that civil society can be understood as interpenetrating with, or permeating, these other spheres, just as the pressures of the latter are often interjected into public life.

Citizens appear to be acting in terms of situational interest; in fact, they are part of a densely structured cultural world. They are acting within a public realm that is the product of a centuries-long civilizing process. They are disciplined by this world even when they feel themselves free; indeed, it is the discipline of their universalistic community that makes them free. Tocqueville emphasized the voluntariness of American political society, the constant formation and reformation of local political groups, the rich and thick existence of a society beneath and outside the state. He understood, however, that these democratic Americans were not, in fact, individualistic. They were held together by the invisible threads of what Tocqueville (1945, pp. 310-13) called America's "voluntary religion."[12] It was universalistic evangelical religion, not the influence of law in and of itself, that for Tocqueville ensured democracy in America.[13]

Civil society does not mean "civilized" in the sense of well-mannered behavior. It should not be equated with trust in an actual government, although it is a necessary condition for that. To trust faithfully in the good of any actual government, indeed, would be to abandon universalism for the particularism of a party or state. Civil society implies something quite different. It means trust in the universalistic values that abstract from any particular society and that provide critical leverage against particular historical actors. It guarantees the existence of a public, not public consensus or consent. Because of their trust in a higher universal order, citizens continually make demands for authorities to justify their actions. The higher order embodies ideal justice; because earthly authorities must inevitably violate this ideal norm, moral outrage is a continual result. In strong civil societies, then, distrust of authoritative action and political conflict are omnipresent. Yet it is this very separation from the endorsement of particular arrangements that makes democracy possible.[14] Because the ultimate loyalty of citizens is to overarching rules rather than to the outcome of any particular game, policies and officeholders can be changed, though the process may be difficult and subject to continual contestation (see Alexander 1988c; Barber 1983).

Constitutions are phenomena that have been almost completely neglected in political sociology, not only in its most recent but in its earlier phase.[15] Yet it is constitutions that codify these universalistic rules, in a legal form that authorizes democratic succession and political dissent. With the exception of legal proceedings, however, when citizens evoke their constitution, it is not to its detailed codifications that they refer; it is to the broad and general cultural standards in relation to which constitutions are signs. In a democratic society, these standards are the codes of the political language. If citizens evoke the constitution, it is because their political speech has become difficult. The constitution is a primer; by referring to it, they are trying to teach recalcitrant citizens how to speak.

THE PROMISE OF A
MULTIDIMENSIONAL THEORY

In their reaction against the naïveté of early postwar theorizing about democracy and social integration, contemporary social scientific students of politics have placed conflict at the center of their analysis and have developed instrumental and materialist understandings of political behavior. Society is depicted as dominated by overwhelming power blocs, and democracy is typically portrayed as merely a formal rationalization for different types of domination. The positive side of this intellectual development is that it has brought back into focus the factors of realpolitik with which every serious theory of democracy must content. No matter how multidimensional the theory, no matter how central a role in it that cultural codes play, it is important to recognize that oligarchies always will form and that elites inevitably will seek to spread their dominion. Democracy will survive only if elite domains can be separated into different spheres. Insofar as this occurs, then, the very efforts that elites and masses make to maintain control over a given sphere of life will involve an effort to maintain the differentiation of each institutional domain. Because elite differentiation prevents monopoly, moreover, the struggles for justice in the distribution of different kinds of institutional resources will have a better chance to succeed.[16]

Political realism, however, can be maintained outside the narrow confines of materialism and conflict theory. It is possible to understand the requisites of democracy in more multidimensional terms. Power is more than its material base; it is also a medium of communication. Every political action has a generalized reference, a relation to meaning that goes beyond the exigencies of its specific situation. For there to be a democracy, this cultural framework for power must be articulated in distinctively universalistic terms. Individuals cannot be seen narrowly, in terms of their particular economic, ethnic, religious, or regional groups alone. Political actors must also be seen in much broader terms, as members of a universal community in which every participant has the same legal, political, and moral status. This universalistic community is a civil society, and the egalitarian status is citizenship. Civil society and citizenship allow public life.

Once the concept of a universalistic civil society has been introduced, it is possible to see how the realistic and idealistic approaches to democracy can be brought together. Civil society can be understood not just as a realm of solidarity and cultural universalism but also as an institutionalized and differentiated social sphere. Most critically, of course, it is differentiated from the state. In a democracy, leaders of the state cannot legally control the activities of civil society, although they often seek informally to do so. Leaders are forced, rather, to participate in public life as citizens. Although they typically bring to this participation unusual resources, like personal authority and prestige, they must contend in this civil arena with elites who possess strategic resources of other kinds. For civil society is also differentiated from other, nonpolitical domains, such as the economic and the religious. These elites too will bring special resources to bear in their efforts to persuade fellow citizens, efforts that take the form of organizing political groups, lobbying power holders, mounting mass educational efforts, and waging election campaigns. Finally, civil society is not without its own elites or without its particular institutional resources. Insofar as they are relatively differentiated, the media of mass communication speak for the societal community, revealing its "public opinion."[17] The legal apparatus articulates the specific demands of civil society, demands that are backed up by force and that, so long as the democratic constitution is maintained, cannot be denied.

These are the social requisites of democracy, in an ideal-typical sense. Any sober look at real societies reveals, of course, that these are never fully achieved. The point of this discussion has been to suggest where to look for the reasons they are not achieved. The more complex and the more differentiated societies become, the more they depend upon centralized and bureaucratic power to provide information and coordination. Bureaucratic power, moreover, is always nonbureaucratic at the top. At the head of every government bureaucracy there stands a personal leader who will develop personal authority in a particularistic way. In times of social crisis, these tendencies for personal domination exacerbate the movements to anticivil social polarization. When rapid social change wrenches the social fabric, the societal community becomes polarized into different camps, left and right, modern and traditional, secular and sacred. As particularistic ideologies become stronger and power blocs threaten the autonomy of different institutional domains, crises emerge that threaten to tear society apart. The struggle to maintain democracy is the struggle to sustain the cohesion and autonomy of civil society. Democracy is preserved only if common ground is sustained, if it proves possible to ensure the generalized, universalistic bonds that allow critical reflection to be sustained without sacrificing social solidarity.

NOTES

1. Despite its elegance and systematic power, Luhmann's approach to democracy exhibits just this kind of anachronistic complacency. In his "Politics as a Social System" (1982, p. 149), he writes, for example: "A political system's ability to absorb social conflicts has to increase when society becomes more complex and conflict-ridden. The political system then changes these conflicts from being cases of outright opposition to being cases of regulated, articulate struggles to influence the decision-making centers."

2. In the outpouring of studies devoted to "power structure research"—which involves arguments about such topics as class versus elite formations in cities and nations and manager versus property control in corporations—there is scarcely any indication that in many capitalist societies these structural issues, and the conflicts they produce, are nested within a democratic political order.

Although the kind of criticism I am making here has typically been the staple of conservative critiques of Marxist work, more recently it has become a perspective for a growing number of post-Marxist critics of "critical theory." Jean Cohen (1982) forcefully argues that the exclusive Marxist focus on class relations is fundamentally mistaken because it misconstrues civil society as a realm without independent normative mediation either in a legal-constitutional or in a more broadly cultural sense. Claude Lefort (1988, pp. 9-11) has put the argument in even more polemical terms, wondering why "there is as yet little enthusiasm" for the analysis of political freedom and democracy among social and political scientists.

3. Collins (1981) argues that the very concept of norms should be expunged from sociological theory.

4. Certainly social democratic theorists like Rex and Przeworski analyze democracy, and theorize about it, in a decidedly more appreciative manner than do orthodox critics of its merely formal character. They conceive of it, however, primarily as an economic adaptation to the growing power of the proletariat, a power whose possibility, they acknowledge, Marx himself did not sufficiently recognize. Thus, for Przeworski (e.g., 1985, p. 140), democracy has succeeded because it allows class conflict to proceed without the destabilizing intervention of physical force. The problem with this approach is that it recapitulates the necessitarian logic of earlier modernization theory. The particularity of democracy is never recognized, its independent history ignored, and its specific structural and historical requisites assumed. "What is most fateful in the continuity between Marx and neo-Marxists," Cohen (1982, p. 5) writes, "is their dislike of the institutions of modern civil society and their reduction of these institutions to mere bourgeois culture and capitalist relations."

5. It is quite extraordinary that Foucault's radically relativistic work on the omnipresence of debilitating discipline throughout modern society seems to have become so widely accepted precisely among those contemporary intellectuals who are themselves committed to the expansion of individual autonomy and social progress. In this regard, it is worth quoting from Charles Taylor's radically humanistic response to Foucault: "Free participatory institutions require some commonly accepted self-disciplines. The free citizen has the vertu to give willingly the contribution which otherwise the despot would coerce from him, perhaps in some other form. Without this, free institutions cannot exist. There is a tremendous difference between societies which find their cohesion through such common disciplines grounded on a public identity, and which thus permit of and call for the participatory action of equals, on the one hand, and the multiplicity of kinds of society which require chains of command based on unquestionable authority on the other" (Taylor 1986, p. 82; see Walzer 1988, pp. 191-209).

6. Invoking the arbitrary character of signs, Saussure ([1976] 1964; see Sahlins 1976) argued that the meaning of a linguistic symbol cand be understood only relativistically—in terms of its difference from, or relation to, a paired sign—rather than by its versimilitude. For a discussion of the impact of this position on contemporary conceptions of culture, see Alexander (1990).

7. Whereas these theorists presuppose the capacity for a quasi-organic political community based on mutual self-regard, Rawls (1971, pp. 105 ff.) believes that fraternity emerges from his "difference principle," a postulate he can defend only by positing either a "natural interest" in association or an innate rationality that perceives the principle's functional benefits. Both defenses ignore the functional tendency toward oligarchy and the arbitrary element of symbolic codes.

8. In light of the distinctive incapacities of the orthodox Marxist tradition I have noted above, it is ironic but highly significant that just this kind of more complex thinking about democracy is beginning to emerge in the recent "post-Marxist" discussions of civil society. These discussions have been stimulated by Marxist reflections that have been based on an explosion of new, nonclass social movements in Western European and North American societies. On civil society, in addition to Cohen (1982), see particularly the essays collected in Keane (1988b) and Keane's own contributions in Keane (1988a). Held's (1987) recent discussion of democracy can be seen as an effort to weld Marxian class analysis with the liberal commitment to pluralism and rights.

9. The convergence in this critical respect between Parsonian and Simmelian thinking about the critical interrelation between conflict and integration has been thoroughly obscured by the association in the 1960s of Simmel with "conflict sociology" and Parsons with "order sociology." For an insightful discussion of the modes of complementarity between Simmel and Parsons, see Levine (1989).

10. This disappearance is one of the principal drawbacks of the semiotic emphasis on the arbitrary that I praised above. Because semiotics largely ignores the key issue of the relation between symbolic code and social structure, the question of the possible tension between these two levels—whether culture is conservative and particularistic, critical and universalist—never arises.

11. Behind this emphasis of Parsons, of course, there also lies Durkheim's insistence on solidarity as the key variable in modernizing society. Shils's work on primordiality, civility, and social integration provides a crucial link between the original Durkheimian tradition and more contemporary sociological concerns (see, e.g., Shils 1975a, 1975b). Geertz (1973) related the perspectives of Parsons and Shils to the contemporary modernization of Third World nations, and Eisenstadt (1987) has reformulated their perspectives into a framework for the comparative analysis of historical civilizations.

In contrast to the explicitly socialist framework of Marshall, the evolutionary and generally optimistic cast of the Parsonian theory of inclusion has made its own critical implications for a theory of expanded civil society more difficult to discern. Still, the social democratic implications of this dimension of Parsons's work are too explicit to ignore (in this regard, see Turner 1986). I have developed a revised, "neofunctionalist" model of inclusion and exclusion, one that places these processes in a more realistic framework of cultural power and social contention, in Alexander (1988b).

12. For a discussion of how a similar kind of "spontaneous conformity" is essential to English democracy, see Lowe (1937).

13. For a compelling analysis of Puritanism as the source for some of the earliest thinking about individual activitivism with a public community, see Mayhew (1984).

14. It is in this sense that Lefort speaks about rights as a "generative principle" of democracy. He argues that rights "cannot be disassociated from the awareness of rights" and that "the symbolic dimension of right is manifested . . . in the irreducibility of the awareness of right to all legal objectification" (pp. 259-60). In other words, the symbolic character of right—its cultural differentiation and universalist form—means that it is always in tension with the so-called objective structures of society.

15. For important exceptions, see Friedrich (1964) and Prager (1986).

16. Walzer (1983) has dealt with these processes in a powerful and eloquent manner in *Spheres of Justice.* While a work of political theory, this book is vital to any sociological considerations of democracy, social differentiation, and civil society.

17. This perspective on the media of mass communication is elaborated in Alexander (1988b). Public opinion polls can be seen as another, related institutional manifestation of civil society. The fact that they sharply and independently articulate public beliefs about a contested issue that forcefully impinges on the actions of political actors is demonstrated in Lang and Lang (1983).

REFERENCES

Alexander, Jeffrey C. 1988a. "The New Theoretical Movement." Pp. 77-101 in *Handbook of Sociology,* edited by Neil J. Smelser. Newbury Park, CA: Sage.

————. 1988b. "Core Solidarity, Ethnic Outgroup, and Social Differentiation." Pp. 78-196 in *Action and Its Environments: Towards a New Synthesis.* New York: Columbia University Press.

————. 1988c. "Culture and Political Crisis: Watergate and Durkheimian sociology." Pp. 187-224 in *Durkheimian Sociology: Cultural Studies,* edited by Jeffrey Alexander. New York: Cambridge University Press.

———. 1990. "On the Autonomy of Culture." In *Culture and Society: Contemporary Debates,* edited by Jeffrey Alexander and Steven Seidman. New York: Cambridge University Press.

Alexander, Jeffrey C. and Paul Colomy. 1989. *Differentiation Theory and Social Change.* New York: Columbia University Press.

Alexander, Jeffrey C. and Steven Seidman, eds. 1990. *Culture and Society: Contemporary Debates.* New York: Cambridge University Press.

Arendt, Hannah. 1958. *The Human Condition.* Chicago: University of Chicago Press.

Aristotle. 1963. *De Interpretatione.* Oxford: Clarendon.

Banfield, Edward C. 1958. *The Moral Basis of a Backward Society.* New York: Free Press.

Barber, Bernard. 1980. *Informed Consent in Medical Therapy and Research.* New Brunswick, NJ: Rutgers University Press.

———. 1983. *The Logic and Limits of Trust.* New Brunswick, NJ: Rutgers University Press.

Bell, Daniel. 1976. *The Cultural Contradictions of Capitalism.* New York: Basic Books.

Bellah, Robert et al. 1985. *Habits of the Heart.* Berkeley: University of California Press.

Bendix, Reinhard. 1964. *Nation-Building and Citizenship.* New York: John Wiley.

Cohen, Jean. 1982. *Class and Civil Society: The Limits of Marxian Critical Theory.* Amherst: University of Massachusetts Press.

Collins, Randall. 1975. *Conflict Sociology.* New York: Academic Press.

———. 1981. "On the Micro-Foundations of Macro-Sociology." *American Journal of Sociology* 86:984-1014.

Dahrendorf, Ralf. 1959. *Class and Class Conflict in Industrial Society.* Stanford, CA: Stanford University Press.

———. 1968. "In Praise of Thrasymachus." Pp. 129-50 in Dahrendorf, *Essays in the Theory of Society,* edited by Rolf Dahrendorf. Stanford, CA: Stanford University Press.

Dreeben, Robert. 1968. *On What Is Learned in School.* Reading, MA: Addison-Wesley.

Edelman, Murray. 1964. *The Symbolic Uses of Politics.* Urbana: University of Illinois Press.

Eisenstadt, S. N. 1987. *European Civilization in a Comparative Perspective.* Oslo: Norwegian University Press.

Elias, Norbert. [1939] 1978. *The Civilizing Process.* New York: Urizen.

Etzioni-Halevy, Eva. 1989. *Fragile Democracy.* New Brunswick, NJ: Transaction.

Evans, Peter, Dietrich Rueschemeyer, and Theda Skocpol, eds. 1985. *Bringing the State Back In.* New York: Cambridge University Press.

Ferguson, Adam. [1767] 1966. *An Essay on the History of Civil Society.* Edinburgh: University of Edinburgh Press.

Foucault, Michel. 1979. *Discipline and Punish.* New York: Vintage.

———. 1980. *The History of Sexuality.* New York: Vintage.

Freud, Sigmund. [1930] 1961. *Civilization and Its Discontents.* New York: Norton.

Friedrich, Carl J. 1964. *Transcendent Justice: The Religious Dimension of Constitutionalism.* Durham, NC: Duke University Press.

Geertz, Clifford. 1973. "The Integrative Revolution: Primordial Sentiments and Civil Politics in the New States." Pp. 255-310 in *The Interpretation of Cultures.* New York: Basic Books.

Giddens, Anthony. 1981. *A Contemporary Critique of Historical Materialism. Vol. 1, Power, Property and the State.* London: Macmillan.

Habermas, Jürgen. 1989. "The Public Sphere." Pp. 231-36 in *Jürgen Habermas on Society and Politics: A Reader,* edited by Steven Seidman. Boston: Beacon.

Hegel, G. W. F. [1807] 1977. *The Phenomenology of Spirit.* Translated by A. V. Miller. Analysis of text and foreword by J. N. Findley. Oxford: Claredon Press.

Held, David. 1987. *Models of Democracy.* Stanford, CA: Stanford University Press.

Hirschman, Albert O. 1977. *The Passions and the Interests.* Princeton, NJ: Princeton University Press.

Keane, John. 1988a. *Democracy and Civil Society*. London: Verso.
————, ed. 1988b. *Civil Society and the State*. London: Verso.
Lang, Gladys and Kurt Lang. 1983. *The Battle for Public Opinion: The President, the Press, and the Polls During Watergate*. New York: Columbia University Press.
Lefort, Claude. 1986. *The Political Forms of Modern Society*. Cambridge: MIT Press.
————. 1988. "The Question of Democracy." Pp. 9-20 in *Democracy and Political Theory.* Minneapolis: University of Minnesota Press.
Lerner, Daniel. 1958. *The Passing of Traditional Society*. Glencoe, IL: Free Press.
Levine, Donald. 1989. "Simmel and Parsons Reconsideration." Prepared for the conference "George simmel e le origini della sociologia moderna," Trento, Italy, October 19-21.
Lévi-Strauss, Claude. 1963. " Structural Analysis in Linguistics and in Anthropology." *Structural Anthropology* 1.
Lipset, Seymour Martin. 1960. *Political Man*. New York: Doubleday.
————. 1963. *The First New Nation*. New York: Basic Books.
Lipset, Seymour Martin, Martin Trow, and James Coleman. 1956. *Union Democracy*. Glencoe: Free Press.
Lowe, Theodore. 1937. *The Price of Liberty: A German on Contemporary Britain*. New York: Hogarth Press.
Luhmann, Niklas. 1982. "Politics as a Political System." Pp. 138-65 in *The Differentiation of Society*. New York: Columbia University Press.
MacIntyre, Alasdair. 1981. *After Virtue*. Notre Dame, IN: Notre Dame University Press.
Mansbridge, Jane J. 1980. *Beyond Adversary Democracy*. Chicago: University of Chicago Press.
Marcuse, Herbert. 1963. *One-Dimensional Man*. Boston: Beacon.
Marshall, T. H. 1965. *Class, Citizenship, and Social Development*. New York: Free Press.
Marx, Karl. [1848] 1962. *Manifesto of the Communist Party*. Pp. 34-65 in *Marx and Engels: Selected Works I*. Moscow: International Press.
Mayhew, Leon. 1984. *The Public Spirit: On the Origins of Liberal Thought*. Davis: University of California, Library Associates.
Mead, George Herbert. 1964. "Selections from Mind, Self, and Society." Pp. 165-282 in *George Herbert Mead on Social Psychology,* edited by Anselm Strauss. Chicago: University of Chicago Press.
Michels, Robert. [1911] 1962. *Political Parties*. New York: Free Press.
Montesquieu. 1977. *The Spirit of Laws*. Berkeley: University of California Press.
Moore, Barrington. 1966. *The Social Origins of Dictatorship and Democracy*. Boston: Beacon.
Parsons, Talcott. 1951. *The Social System*. New York: Free Press.
————. 1955. "Family Structure and the Socialization of the Child." Pp. 35-132 in *Family, Socialization, and Interaction Process,* edited by Talcott Parsons and Robert F. Bales. New York: Free Press.
————. 1963. "Evolutionary Universals in Society." Pp. 490-520 in *Sociological Theory and Modern Society*. New York: Free Press.
————. 1967. "Full Citizenship for the Negro American?" Pp. 422-65 in *Sociological Theory and Modern Society*. New York: Free Press.
————. 1969. "On the Concept of Political Power." Pp. 352-404 in *Politics and Social Structure*. New York: Free Press.
————. 1971. *The System of Modern Societies*. Englewood Cliffs, NJ: Prentice-Hall.
Parsons, Talcott and Neil J. Smelser. 1957. *Economy and Society*. New York: Free Press.
Piaget, Jean. 1972. *The Principles of Genetic Epistemology*. London: Routledge & Kegan Paul.
Plato. 1965. *The Republic,* translated by Francis MacDonald Cornford. New York: Oxford University Press.

Prager, Jeffrey. 1986. *Building Democracy in Ireland: Political Order and Cultural Integration in a Newly Independent Nation.* New York: Cambridge University Press.

Przeworski, Adam. 1985. *Capitalism and Social Democracy.* Cambridge: Cambridge University Press.

Rawls, John. 1971. *A Theory of Justice.* Cambridge, MA: Harvard University Press.

Rex, John. 1961. *Key Problems of Sociological Theory.* London: Routledge & Kegan Paul.

Rieff, Philip. 1959. *Freud: The Mind of the Moralist.* New York: Viking

Rostow, W. W. 1960. *The Stages of Economic Growth.* Cambridge, MA: Harvard University Press.

Sahlins, Marshall. 1976. *Culture and Practical Reason.* Chicago: University of Chicago Press.

Saussure, Ferdinand. [1916] 1964. *Course in General Linguistics.* New York: McGraw-Hill.

Sennett, Richard. 1977. *The Fall of Public Man.* New York: Knopf.

Shils, Edward. 1975a. "The Integration of Societies." Pp. 48-90 in *Center and Periphery: Essays in Macro-Sociology,* Chicago: University of Chicago Press.

―――. 1975b. "Primordial, Personal, Sacred, and Civil Ties." Pp. 111-26 in *Center and Periphery.* Chicago: University of Chicago Press.

Simmel, Georg. 1955. *Conflict and the Web of Group Affiliations.* New York: Free Press.

Skocpol, Theda. 1979. *States and Social Revolutions.* New York: Cambridge University Press.

Smelser, Neil J. 1959. *Social Change in the Industrial Revolution.* Chicago: University of Chicago Press.

―――. 1963. *Theory of Collective Behavior.* New York: Free Press.

Taylor, Charles. 1986. "Foucault on Freedom and Truth." Pp. 69-102 in *Foucault: A Critical Reader,* edited by David Hoy. London: Basil Blackwell.

Thompson, John B. 1984. "Theories of Ideology and Methods of Discourse Analysis: Towards a Framework for the Analysis of Ideology." Pp. 73-147 in *Studies in the Theory of Ideology.* Berkeley: University of California Press.

Tocqueville, Alex. 1945. *Democracy in America.* Vol. 1. New York: Knopf.

Turner, Bryan S. 1986. *Citizenship and Capitalism.* London: Allen and Unwin.

Unger, Roberto Mangabeira. 1975. *Knowledge and Politics.* New York: Free Press.

Walzer, Michael. 1970. *Obligations: Essays on Disobedience, War, and Citizenship.* Cambridge, MA: Harvard University Press.

―――. 1983. *Spheres of Justice.* New York: Basic Books.

―――. 1988. *The Company of Critics: Social Criticism and Political Commitment in the Twentieth Century.* New York: Basic Books.

Weber, Max. [1917] 1968. "Parliament and Government in a Reconstructed Germany." Pp. 1381-1462 in *Economy and Society.* Berkeley: University of California Press.

Williams, Robin. 1960. *American Society.* New York: Knopf.

Wolin, Sheldon. 1960. *Politics and Vision: Continuity and Innovation in Western Political Thought.* Boston: Little, Brown

Chapter 10

THE POLITICS OF THEORY AND THE LIMITS OF ACADEMY

CHARLES C. LEMERT
Wesleyan University

IN THE UNITED STATES, we suffer a more restricted definition of the social role of intellectuals. It is true, of course, that the United States has been home to the many varieties of intellectuals discussed by others in the preceding chapters—grand intellectuals in the French sense, the technical intelligentsia and managers to which New Class theory refers, and organic intellectuals of the dominant and popular classes.

Nonetheless, in the post-World War II period, the most conspicuous intellectuals in the United States have been university professors. As Dick Flacks reminds us, university-based intellectuals in the 1950s were among the most important of the public intellectuals who were to have perfected the American dream by reforming away social evil. Certainly, the university was, outside the business sector, the most radically transformed and expanded institution in the United States after the world war. It was central to this period of American history in at least four important respects: as institutional home for the sciences (including social sciences), which were to produce the knowledge of America's golden age; as avenue to a promised land of economic opportunity for the added millions pursuing a higher education; as reputed haven of eggheads and other objects of civil hatred during the McCarthy and Eisenhower eras; and, at the decade's end, as spawning ground for the New Left, hence, thereafter, a battleground in the 1960s. Among the many ironies of recent history is that one institutional sector, the university, could have been so many things to so many people: equally a source of hope and despair; no less equally to those who would use it to make America "Number One" as to those—beginning with the authors of SDS's Port Huron Statement, in 1962—who protested all that was noxious in such an imperial impulse.

Thus, in the United States, the intellectual of whom one must take note is the academic intellectual. The academy is where intellectuals are usually bred and frequently housed. This, in turn, is one of the reasons, in the last years of the century, we are enmeshed in a public furor over the character, intent, and politics of the American academic intellectual. As a result, the politics of theory is a politics with real stakes. The line variously drawn between the academy and politics divides an important societal battleground.

THE POLITICAL LIMITS OF THE UNIVERSITY

There are today two prominent understandings of the limiting relation between the university and politics. One adheres to the belief that the academy is the bearer of a civilization's truth; hence politics, if they are to be righteous, must be kept out of the academy. A second understanding grants the academy significantly less moral ground; hence political life requires its own truths, truths subject to moral decay if exposed too much to university life. Their starkly different politics notwithstanding, both views draw a line of some sort between politics and the university.

The first understanding can be illustrated by the concluding paragraph from one of the most popular books of the day:

> This is the American moment in human history, the one for which we shall forever be judged. Just as in politics the responsibility for the fate of freedom has devolved upon our regime, so the fate of philosophy in the world has devolved upon our universities, and they are related as they have never been before. The gravity of our given task is great, and it is very much in doubt how the future will judge our stewardship. (Bloom 1987, p. 382)

The passage, you can see, is heavy with purpose. Its talk of fate, gravity, and judgment—each tightly embroidered with "nevers" and "forevers"—concludes a book bearing the portentious subtitle *How Higher Education Has Failed Democracy and Impoverished the Souls of Today's Students*. These terrifying circumstances have arisen precisely because, in this author's view, a false politics has invaded the academy, thereby impoverishing the soul of truth itself upon which rests the true politics for which the American regime is righteous steward.

The second understanding tends more often, though not always, to be frankly suspicious of grand myths of fated freedoms, historical judgments, and responsible regimes. Accordingly, though it recognizes the power of such doctrines, its view of politics is more simply that of the politics of those who struggle against dominant regimes. Hence this view is more honest in identifying its politics, as it is in admitting ambivalence toward the academy. The following passage illustrates sufficiently well an outlook of so many versions that no one can do it full justice:

A specter haunts American universities or, at least, its faculties: boredom. A generation of professors entered the universities in the middle and wake of the sixties, when campuses crackled with energy; today these teachers are visibly bored, if not demoralized. One report found college and university faculties "deeply troubled" with almost 40 percent ready and willing to leave the academy. This subterranean discontent might surface, reconnecting with public life. Conservatives suspect and fear this; hence they continuously rail against what they imagine as the threat from the universities. I think they are wrong. I hope they are right. (Jacoby 1987, p. xiii)

The opening figure reveals the politics of this view. The specter haunts now not all of Europe but the American university, its victims are not so much an alienated working class but bored intellectuals and a public deprived of their radical services. They would be better off to succumb to their discontent in the academy and return to the public engagements of their youth, there to pursue an intellectual life in the service of political emancipation.

Were there only these two choices, I would surely take the latter (illustrated, of course, by a passage from Russell Jacoby's *The Last Intellectuals*) over the former (represented by Allan Bloom's *The Closing of the American Mind*). I believe, however, there are other options. Bloom and Jacoby, it is frequently observed (e.g., Escoffier 1988), are similarly preoccupied with left intellectuals of the 1960s generation. Bloom thinks they are wrecking the university. Jacoby thinks the university is wrecking them. If I can infer, however tentatively, from these two, it is possible that both right and left in the United States desire to establish a limiting boundary between the academy and politics. I also think that many more than these two are odd fellows with respect to the room left social theory ought to keep in the university. Jacoby and Bloom want to move it out—the one so it will thrive, the other so it will go away.

THE POLITICS OF THEORY: THE CASE OF NEW CLASS THEORY

The politics of theory are, therefore, political struggles over who has reason and right to be in the university. At foremost issue is whether or not the generation of the 1960s now in the academy was right to pursue and thereby interject a radical political agenda into curriculum and scholarship. Noting Jacoby's exception (that Bloom has nothing to worry about, we are not only boring but irrelevant), the conservative view is that the cultural left's theory is too political (that is, wrongly political), hence a threat to the essence of the university, the American regime, and all of Western civilization. Never mind that few who might identify themselves with the cultural left trust their ideas to be capable of such revolutionary ends. The attribution is fair enough. This so-called cultural left (usually identified by its opponents, and occasionally its friends, as "Marxists, feminists, deconstructionists, blacks, and other minorities," [1] as though these named assimilable identities) would in fact love to overturn the American regime and the eurocentric West, if not the university.

Whatever the differences that divide it, the cultural left has been a force in challenging the world as seen by Bloom and his sympathizers. The politics of theory, however, entail more than a struggle of right against left. The phrase should also designate the contestations in and among the constituent differences of the cultural left. At stake in this latter case is what constitutes good enough social theory, where "good enough" implies a standard of political adequacy in addition to, or instead of, an epistemological standard. The former dispute between the right and left takes place at so deep a level of difference as to be, for all intents and purposes, beyond any other than political resolution. The controversy within the left, however, still yields debate and product if only because its common ground, so difficult to define, is politically arable.

I propose, therefore, to examine briefly an instance of the latter politics of theory, one that is as fundamental to this book's topic as it is to the development of left social theory in the last generation. In this way, I would hope at the end to return to the wider debate between right and left with some perspective refreshing to the Jacoby position, if not to Bloom's.

Ivan Szelenyi and Bill Martin (1988, p. 645) correctly identify Alvin Gouldner's *The Future of Intellectuals and the Rise of the New Class* as a "milestone both in the Gouldner oeuvre and American social theories of the 1960s and 1970s."[2] It is important to emphasize what they somewhat understate. Gouldner's multivolume study of social theory, beginning with *The Coming Crisis in Western Sociology* (1970) through the New Class book to his final, posthumous *Against Fragmentation: The Origins of Marxism and the Sociology of Intellectuals* (1985), was at its deepest purposes self-consciously political.[3] Gouldner pursued a third force strategy in which he sought to mediate differences between academic sociology and Marxism, then (in the early 1970s) scarcely a presence in the American university. The latent function of his social theory of intellectuals, therefore, was to provide both intellectual justification and, through the prestige and connections he possessed, safe passage for radicals leaving the political struggles of the 1960s for academic careers. Though Gouldner was not the only academic intellectual of his generation to assume such a vocation, he was one of the more successful. His intellectual labor, in these years, was directly related to his politics of theory *and* his belief that political intellectuals in the United States had to be encouraged and protected in their pursuit of academic careers.

Gouldner's theory of New Class intellectuals is, however, rife with uncertainties. The flawed nature of his new universal class, "the best card history has given us to play," is the most familiar of several important qualifications and near contradictions. Gouldner's theory of the New Class was unavoidably flawed due, in large part, to his theoretical politics. He chose to situate himself between Marxism (till then in the United States a mostly public intellectual tradition) and academic sociology. He wanted to normalize Marxism in the academy, while subjecting it to sociological criticism. New Class theory, along with this idea of reflexive sociology, was the answer to his famous question of Marx's theory of ideology ("Where does the camera man fit in?")—an answer composed precisely for the critical intellectuals then entering the academy fresh from public struggles.

The New Class, Gouldner's version, was a political theory in a politics of theory. It was, therefore, conceptually bound by its political purposes. Gouldner knew, in the mid- to late 1970s when the theory was being worked out, that the American university would not stomach a Marxism too pure. True, he was also by nature a critical theorizer with little taste for overly ideological sauces of any kind. But he knew the university as well as he knew Marxism. The flawed New Class was, he thought, a language fluent to both. More accurately, Gouldner's New Class theory was, among other things, a conscious attempt to revise and introduce theoretical elements of Marxian class analysis to American sociology.

Gouldner's theory was received with skepticism as Szelenyi and Martin point out. It is important to say that the skeptics were as much within, as outside, the academic left. but their skepticism can be said, in retrospect, to have been much more than leftish contrariness. The analytic categories themselves were unstable (to borrow an apt phrase from Sandra Harding). We see this more clearly now, in a time when postmodern philosophy challenges the very idea of an analytic category, much less one so totalizing, if not essentializing, as class analysis. Richard Rorty's *Philosophy and the Mirror of Nature* was published in 1979, the same year as Gouldner's (1979) *Future of Intellectuals*. Rorty, like Lyotard and others, who have since become the original sources of postmodern philosophy, rejected not only the metaphysics of essential Truth but, by consequence, the very idea of grand analytic categories—even those so politically correct as class. If Kant and Hegel, then Marx too had to go.

Gouldner was not, by any means, a proto-postmodern. He still believed in a dialectic theory that could tolerate and overcome contradiction. As a result, the foundational culture of the New Class, the Culture of Critical

Discourse, was a "grammar of discourse" rooted in a "speech community," which it transcended insofar as it was "relatively situation free" (Gouldner 1979, pp. 28-29). Gouldner was, therefore, much closer to the neomodernist Habermas than to the early postmodern philosophers. At the same time, he was too much the sociologist ever to have been drawn completely into anything like Habermas's quasi-transcendental universal pragmatics. His theoretical position, like his theoretical politics, was between sides.

The late 1970s, just more than a decade ago, was a crucial moment in the politics of theory. Then, about the time of Gouldner's and Rorty's books, the traditions of the academic left began to strain and tear. Gouldner, in trying to revise class analysis for a new generation, was forced by his politics to choose perhaps the most courageous course but certainly the one least likely to succeed. Habermas, analytic Marxists, and early feminist standpoint theorists like Dorothy Smith (see Bologh's chapter, this volume) determined to keep within modernist philosophical methods while using them to turn the world on its head. On the other hand, Rorty, Lyotard, and the American deconstructionists (e.g., Ryan 1982) were among those who considered this a futile exercise. The whole, somehow, had to be decomposed. Gouldner was among those willing to risk having it both ways. Hence, the oxymoronic intellectual, flawed and universal.

Meanwhile, in the university at the time Gouldner's New Class theory was published, those then younger intellectuals to whom it was in part addressed were coming into positions of tenured security, and many were themselves beginning to train a still subsequent generation of social theorists. Theda Skocpol's *States and Social Revolutions,* for example, was also published in 1979. Though no one in left sociology, then or since, could quite be called typical, Skocpol describes the temper of the times as well, or better, than most. In her words:

> We sixties-generation people do not yearn for one grand sociological theory such as Parsonian structure-functionalism; nor do we imagine that sociology can be pure, cumulative, technically grounded science. Some of us are Marxists and leftists, and all of us know that such folks are valuable to the discipline. All of us have been socialized at a time when the proper research methodologies of sociology broadened from interviews and statistics to include various historical and interpretive methods. And most of us enjoy close intellectual ties to age-peers in one or another different discipline, thus causing us to be less defensive about sociology's boundaries than sociologists were in the late 1950s. (Skocpol 1988, p. 632)

True enough: Left social theorists in the academy were, and still are, more open, more conversant across methodological differences, more interdisciplinary. Yet, it is also true that, compared with social theorists in other disciplines, those in sociology remained, and remain, theoretically cautious.

Here, again, the politics of theory is decisive. The 1960s generation social theorists in sociology, whether deeply influenced by Gouldner or not, ended up in much the same theoretical bind. Skocpol, for example, surely an innovator in the practice of social theory, held tight to traditional attitudes with respect to theory itself. She hates empirically ungrounded theory as much did her teacher, George Homans, and has been known to denounce such theorizing as viciously as Homans, in his day, had denounced Parsons (Skocpol 1986). Within sociology, this seemed a reasonable position, one widely if not universally shared across the 1960s generation. Sociology was, after all, an empirical social science. Its theory must, therefore, not be pure theory. This is science.

But, elsewhere in the academic left, quite a different attitude was emerging. The effect of theoretical work close to that other 1979 book (Rorty's *Philosophy and the Mirror of Nature*) would soon be felt throughout the human sciences just as, in literary studies, deconstructionism was already becoming the position of preference. In this other tradition, that of Rorty and the poststructuralisms, theory was no longer understood to be tied to empirical observations of a real world. *Philosophy and the Mirror of Nature* dismantled the "notion that our chief task is to mirror accurately, in our Glassy Essence, the universe around us" (Rorty 1979, p. 357). Rorty, thereby, took pragmatic philosophy to its conclusion. He attacked the deep tradition (what he later called the Plato-Kant canon) that privileged knowledge over politics and made epistemology the first order of philosophical business. He, thereby, provided the arguments for an attack on philosophy, just as Derrida and Foucault were supplying a growing militia in rebellion against tradition in literary and historical studies in the American university.

Sometime in the next decade, as we know, these otherwise different but related theories came to be known as postmodernism. The tag "postmodern" has become, among other things, emblem for a definite, if complex, position in the politics of theory. It names, thereby, those who doubt reason to be the foundation of knowledge and, especially, science to be "the exemplar of the right use of reason . . . [and] the paradigm for all true knowledge" (Flax 1990, pp. 41-42). An outrageous proposition to some, a silly fad to others, postmodernism nonetheless began to take hold in the United States in 1979. It soon became central to the politics of theory, now more broadly defined to include the cultural left throughout the university in the humanities and social sciences. Postmodernism, thus understood, is a radical theory of theory in which, in the absence of a theory of evidence (that is, epistemology), theory is all there is.

Left social theory in sociology was, however, left at the station by this very fast moving train of thought. Among all the academic disciplines one would expect to be tolerant, if not hospitable, to a deviant new theory, sociology was, and is, surprisingly defensive and resistant to postmodernism. This too is an important story in the recent politics of theory. In a manuscript that circulated widely years before its eventual publication in 1985, Judith Stacey and Barrie Thorne described the extent to which sociology was, even then, unreceptive to feminism, a theoretical tradition that would soon (by the early 1990s) be the most important site of debate over postmodernism. They said: "Feminist sociology . . . seems to have been both co-opted and ghetto-ized, while the discipline [of sociology] as a whole and its dominant para-digms have proceeded relatively unchanged" (Stacey and Thorne 1985, p. 302). This story cannot be told here. But the result, as things now stand, is important. Feminist theory has taken on, though with great skepticism and much disagreement, the postmodern theory of theory, while sociology has ignored it with the consequence of becoming alien to many of those whom it originally welcomed and trained. Anna Yeatman (1990, p. 294), for exam-ple, offers this telling reflection: "I have not abandoned sociology; sociology has abandoned feminism."

CONCLUSION

The story of left social theory in sociology is one instance of the funda-mental theoretical differences that exist within the academic left, but one that describes with particular poignancy the extent to which the politics of theory have become decisive. Whatever the explanation for sociology's spectacular stodginess, its cool refusal of a different theory of theory is index of the many ways in which the move Gouldner made in his theory of intellectuals was but one left option, a limited one at that. Insofar as others have since taken a similar course, they have come, surprisingly, to represent the right wing of the new cultural left, at least with respect to theory. Thus the story brings us back to the relation between the politics of theory and the status of political intellectuals in the academy.

Behind the confusion, epistemological and other, created by postmodern social theories lies one simple idea. Politics, in the last generation, has become increasingly the politics of social identities. One corollary to the looming, possible collapse of the great, dichotomized cold war is the way in which so many, though not all, Third World wars of liberation, and social movements internal to the Europeanized societies, have rejected nationalism in favor of recapturing lost or repressed traditions of social and ethnic identity.

The emergence of identity politics has also played a pivotal role in the recent politics of theory. More than any other factor, the shocking charge of racism against white feminist theorists led to the exploration of postmodernism as an identity politics. In the words of Donna Haraway's ([1985] 1990, p. 199) postmodernist "Manifesto for Cyborgs":[4]

> I do not know of any other time in history when there was greater need for political unity to confront effectively the dominations of race, gender, sexuality, and class. I also do not know of any other time when this kind of unity we might help build could have been possible. None of "us" have any longer the symbolic or material capability of dictating the shape of reality to any of "them." Or at least "we" cannot claim innocence from practicing such dominations. White women, including Euroamerican socialist feminists, discovered (i.e., were forced kicking and screaming to notice) the noninnocence of the category "woman."

The sentence immediately following bears special notice: "That consciousness changes the configuration of all previous categories; it denatures them as heat denatures a fragile protein." Even if the "forced kicking and screaming" line is an exaggeration, the charge of racism, leveled against the most radical of social theorists (many of whose predecessors in the 1960s leveled the charge of sexism against SNCC), demonstrated the social theoretical inadequacy of any single analytic category—gender, sexual orientation, and ethnicity as much as class and race. The only obvious first response, implied in Haraway's remark, was to clear the deck of all categories and begin anew not with a global "we" but with a micropolitics of social identities in local, and occasional, affinity.

This brings my short history of the politics of left social theory both up to the moment and, necessarily, back in an odd way to the beginning. Rethinking the theory of difference with reference to identity politics is high on social theory's list of unfinished business. But this requires a comparable reconsideration of the academic intellectual. The as yet unresolved dispute over political theories of social identity serves powerfully to diagnose the sometimes weird qualities of the ideas that framed this discussion. Bloom's academic intellectual has no social identity, and cannot have one, because he admits no differences. There is and can be, for him, only one truth, one politics, thus only a university. Jacoby, and those who share his understandings, surely recognizes the differences with which most people live. But, in his haste to defend the public intellectual, itself a sort of grand analytic, Jacoby has not reconsidered the more powerful oppositive to public. Those who live in and for their difference do so with keen appreciation of the pain publics can inflict on private life. For them the opposite of public is not university, but private. In this connection, we should remember that Gouldner, like C. Wright Mills and the early New Left, had a definite notion of the personal basis of public politics as well as of social theory. Today this sensibility reenters in the form of theories of fractured social identities.

Possibly, it is the time to refine and rework an old idea of the New Left—that social theory and left politics must account as well for the specific troubles that, Mills taught us, we experience in the most acute reaches of our social identities. What we experience there determines in some good measure what, and how, we know and do about public issues. In 1962, the year of the Port Huron Statement, and the year C. Wright Mills died, few people had any real theoretical language with which to think the social differences among human beings. Now, 30 years later, we do and can. Indeed, we cannot escape differences—not politically, not intellectually, not personally. This, I think, is the contribution, and still the challenge, of left academic intellectuals today.

NOTES

1. This quotation is in fact an amalgam of statements made in print by the National Association of Scholars and in numerous public statements by the head of the National Endowment of the Humanities, Lynne Chenney.

2. This quotation was among the material excluded from the abridged version of the article that appears as Chapter 2 of this volume.

3. For a discussion of Gouldner's politics of social theory, see Charles Lemert and Paul Piccone (1982).

4. The essay originally appeared in the *Socialist Review* in 1985. On identity politics in the context of social movements theory, see Barbara Epstein (1990).

REFERENCES

Bloom, Allan, 1987. *The Closing of the American Mind: How Higher Education Has Failed Democracy and Impoverished the Souls of Today's Students.* New York: Simon & Schuster.

Epstein, Barbara. 1990. "Rethinking Social Movements Theory." *Socialist Review* 90(1):35-66.

Escoffier, Jeffrey. 1988. "Pessimism of the Mind: Intellectuals, Universities, and the Left." *Socialist Review* 88(1):116-35.

Flax, Jane. 1990. "Postmodernism and Gender Relations." Pp. 39-62 in *Feminism/Postmodernism,* edited by Linda Nicholson. New York: Routledge.

Gouldner, Alvin. 1970. *The Coming Crisis in Western Sociology.* New York: Basic Books.

———. 1979. *Future of Intellectuals.* New York: Seabury.

———. 1985. *Against Fragmentation: The Origins of Marxism and the Sociology of Intellectuals.* Oxford: Oxford University Press.

Haraway, Donna. [1985] 1990. "A Manifesto for Cyborgs: Science, Technology, and Socialist Feminism in the 1980s." Pp. 190-233 in *Feminism/Postmodernism,* edited by Linda Nicholson. New York: Routledge.

Jacoby, Russell. 1987. *The Last Intellectuals.* New York: Basic Books.

Lemert, Charles and Paul Piccone. 1982. "Gouldner's Theoretical Method and Reflexive Sociology." *Theory and Society* 11:733-57.

Rorty, Richard. 1979. *Philosophy and the Mirror of Nature.* Princeton, NJ: Princeton University Press.

Ryan, Michael. 1982. *Marxism and Deconstruction.* Baltimore: Johns Hopkins University Press.

Skocpol, Theda. 1979. *States and Social Revolutions: A Comparative Analysis of France, Russia, and China.* Cambridge: Cambridge University Press.

———. 1986. "The Dead End of Metatheory." *Contemporary Sociology* 16:10-12.

———. 1988. "An 'Uppity Generation' and the Revitalization of Macroscopic Sociology: Reflections at Mid-Career by a Woman from the Sixties." *Theory and Society* 17(5):627-43.

Stacey, Judith and Barrie Thorne. 1985. "The Missing Feminist Revolution in Sociology." *Social Problems* 32(4):301-17.

Szelenyi, Ivan and Bill Martin. 1988. "Three Waves of New Class Theory." *Theory and Society* 17:645-67.

Yeatman, Anna. 1990. "A Feminist Theory of Social Differentiation." Pp. 281-99 in *Feminism/Postmodernism,* edited by Linda Nicholson. New York: Routledge.

ABOUT THE CONTRIBUTORS

JEFFREY C. ALEXANDER is Professor of Sociology at the University of California at Los Angeles.

ROSLYN WALLACH BOLOGH is Professor of Sociology at the College of Staten Island and the Graduate Center of the City University of New York.

CRAIG CALHOUN is Professor of Sociology at the University of North Carolina at Chapel Hill.

ALEX DUPUY is Associate Professor of Sociology and Afro-American studies at Wesleyan University.

DICK FLACKS is Professor of Sociology at the University of California at Santa Barbara.

MARTIN JAY is Professor of History at the University of California at Berkeley.

MICHAEL D. KENNEDY is Assistant Professor of Sociology at the University of Michigan.

CHARLES C. LEMERT is Professor of Sociology at Wesleyan University.

BILL MARTIN is Lecturer in Sociology at La Trobe University in Melbourne, Australia.

GEORGE ROSS is Morris Hillquit Professor in Labor and Social Thought at Brandeis University.

IVAN SZELENYI is Professor of Sociology at the University of California at Los Angeles.